Strip Pan Wrinkle

(IN NAMIBIA AND BOTSWANA)

DAVID FLETCHER

(IN NAMIBIA AND BOTSWANA)

Copyright © 2014 David Fletcher

The moral right of the author has been asserted.

Apart from any fair dealing for the purposes of research or private study, or criticism or review, as permitted under the Copyright, Designs and Patents Act 1988, this publication may only be reproduced, stored or transmitted, in any form or by any means, with the prior permission in writing of the publishers, or in the case of reprographic reproduction in accordance with the terms of licences issued by the Copyright Licensing Agency. Enquiries concerning reproduction outside those terms should be sent to the publishers.

Matador
9 Priory Business Park,
Wistow Road, Kibworth Beauchamp,
Leicestershire. LE8 0RX
Tel: (+44) 116 279 2299
Fax: (+44) 116 279 2277
Email: books@troubador.co.uk
Web: www.troubador.co.uk/matador

ISBN 978 1783060 375

British Library Cataloguing in Publication Data.
A catalogue record for this book is available from the British Library.

Printed and bound in the UK by TJ International, Padstow, Cornwall

Typeset in 11pt Bembo by Troubador Publishing Ltd, Leicester, UK

Matador is an imprint of Troubador Publishing Ltd

For Phil and Heather

2011

1.

It was undeniable. Brian was a loopaholic. Whereas some people are addicted to alcohol, or to Dr Who or even to British socialism, Brian was addicted to loops and, it has to be admitted, to a minor extent, to alcohol. But that is by the way. And to return to his looping predilections, it can be stated with absolute certainty that whenever he made a trip anywhere – under his own steam – he would go out of his way (sometimes literally) to return by a different route to that which he'd originally taken, to achieve the craved-for loop in his itinerary and the consequent gratification of his addiction.

Yes, Brian's loops could all be drawn on a map. So, for example, a visit to Waitrose in Droitwich would entail his driving along the Saltway through Hanbury, but then his taking a more circuitous route home through the lanes around Crowle. Similarly, a longer trip to, say, Tenby would be executed by taking the M5 and then the Heads of Valley Road for the outward leg and then a more leisurely amble through the Brecon Beacons and rural Herefordshire for the return leg. And it went beyond this. For he had approached a tour of Scotland by driving up its east coast, then along the length of its north coast and finally down its west coast and back to his starting point – and the end of his loop. Ditto in both islands of New Zealand, on the Atlantic island of Boa Vista in Cape Verde, and around the whole of the nation of Namibia. In fact, his loopaholism was so intense that he could now not really contemplate a visit anywhere in the world that would involve a trip from A to B, other than when A and B were the very same place and the start and the end of a suitably gratifying loop. He was a completely hopeless case.

So, no great surprise then that in planning his latest expedition, Brian had organised another looping itinerary. But this one was different. It was to be the loop of all loops. A loop that outpaced that Tenby expedition by miles, a loop that put the Scotland excursion into the also-rans, and a loop that even exceeded that ambitious drive around the whole of Namibia. For this loop would be through three countries. And not silly little countries either, like Luxembourg or Liechtenstein, but big proper countries, and not in innocuous Europe but in inimical Africa. Well, no, not really inimical at all, because the three African countries to be visited (and through which a loop would be conducted) were the old favourite of Namibia, its neighbour, Botswana, and its rather more remote neighbour, Zambia.

Yes, as anyone who has visited either Namibia or Botswana will confirm, the likelihood of coming to harm in these nations is probably less than it is in Tenby (after closing time). And as for Zambia… well, the loop would just scratch a corner of its territory, and the biggest threat that might be encountered there was the unwanted attention of mosquitoes. That said, there would be roads to find, lodges to find, borders to cross and, no doubt, animals to avoid. So it wouldn't be a walk in the park. Not even a circular walk. No, it would be the biggest loop Brian had ever driven. And, all being well, it would satisfy his loopaholic cravings for weeks, if not months. Even if, to start with, it was difficult to believe that one was on any sort of loop at all. And that, of course, was down to Namibia's roads…

The journey had commenced in Namibia's capital, Windhoek, and Brian and his wife, Sandra, were now driving north up this country's main thoroughfare, the seemingly endless two-lane B1. And this road, like most other roads in Namibia, is just a surfaced straight line. It is a strip of undeviating tarmac, edged with wide cropped verges cut through an infinite spread of thornveld, where there is as much chance of meeting a bend as there is of meeting one's maker, (for as well as being straight, this major road is virtually traffic-free, and collisions with other vehicles would have to be arranged by prior appointment).

But anyway, at the moment, Brian was conscious only of the straightness of this highway, and was intrigued by the thought that his currently curve-less progress was still an integral part of that much discussed loop. For after all, don't most loops have at least a degree of curvature in their design?

He was also intrigued by the thought that this straight-line road – and all the other straight-line roads in Namibia, whether metalled or un-surfaced – were a product of the country's colonial past. This place had once been a German possession. And could it be that these unfussy, not to say strictly disciplined, by-ways were the result of Germanic precision and Germanic resolution? In the face of Teutonic determination and single-mindedness, would a bothersome topography stand any chance at all? 'The road needs to go zat way, and zat is where ve vill build it.' Uhmm, a little unfair possibly, and on the same basis, all the roads in ex-French colonies would be full of contortions, bifurcations and deviations, and in ex-Brit colonies, they'd just be completely higgledy-piggledy and full of dead-ends and dips. So maybe it was something else, like the absence of a discernible population in the country. If you needed to build a road here, there were barely any towns or other settlements to avoid. You simply built it where it needed to go – in a straight line – and no one was inconvenienced.

These sorts of musings got Brian past Otjiwarongo (where there was a discernible turn in the road that now took our two travellers in a north-easterly direction rather than due north) and only ended when Sandra made an observation about the time.

'How long now?' she said. 'We must be almost half way.'

Unusually for Brian, he was prepared for this question and responded without hesitation.

'Two and a half to three hours, I reckon. And yes, we're just over half way. So, all being well, that'll be five hundred kilometres in under six hours.'

'Umm, that's good.'

'You don't mind sitting in a car for almost six hours then – just looking at all the thorn trees?'

'Why would I?'

'Well, think of all the other things you could have been doing instead.'

'Such as?' queried Sandra.

'Well, I don't know… I mean, given six hours, you could have… '

'Yes… ?'

'You could have read two thirds of that Alistair Darling book on the banking crisis… '

'You mean that one that made you despair?'

'Yes, that one. Or you could have wormed your way through BT's automated fault-reporting system and found a human being to speak to… '

'Unlikely.'

'Or you could have watched six episodes of the *X Factor* – if it's actually possible for anyone to watch six in a row. Or you could have had a dozen or so colonoscopies… '

'It's OK, Brian. I did mean it. I do enjoy sitting in a car. And you know I do. Especially when the car's in Namibia. And, of course, when the car is a Land Cruiser… '

Brian turned to face his wife and smiled.

'Just checking,' he said. 'Just checking.'

But he wasn't really. He was just giving his wife and himself an opportunity to relish their situation – which was in Namibia, a country they loved, at the start of a great expedition and, as Sandra had just pointed out, in a wonderful Toyota Land Cruiser.

This one was the new model, a useful-looking beast that was described in the paperwork as "brown", but was actually a rather fetching take on beige. It had a 4.2 litre diesel engine, and this gave it all the torque necessary to pull it through the deepest sand and the deepest mud, if not to propel it up long inclines on long metalled roads with all the umph one would have wished for. But that was the trade off you got in the torque deal: more power for the rough at the expense of speed on the smooth. (Although Brian didn't really know what he was talking about, having peaked in his knowledge of the workings of cars at the age of fifteen, when he'd flunked an evening class in car mechanics attended with some of his friends from school. And no, they never did get their immobile Ford Consul to move even an inch.)

Brian and Sandra's precious 4x4 also had a few extras. There was a big bull-bar thing on its front that made it look like an overgrown offensive weapon; there was an extra spare wheel on its roof rack (if one was feeling in need of a strained back); there was a fridge in the rear (for water and medicinal alcohol); and there was an "inverter" behind the front seat. Brian had no idea what it inverted, but one could plug things into it and recharge batteries, and Brian suspected that even Jeremy Clarkson hadn't got one of these. Oh, and there was also a GPS on the dashboard – which consistently showed just a vertical straight line on its screen: the apparently endless B1, just as disciplined and just as unswerving as it was when it first left Windhoek.

Of course, it wasn't endless. Only government incompetence and mismanagement is endless. So eventually, Brian and Sandra found themselves near Tsumeb, where the B1 doesn't actually end, but where it makes a sharp turn north-west to begin its last act as it skirts the eastern edge of the great Etosha National Park. Brian and Sandra would be with it for just a little while longer (for they too were on their way to the eastern edge of the park), but before then there was a diesel stop to attend to, and that meant a serious pause.

There are no self-service fuel stations in Namibia. Because, if there were, it would threaten the existence of one of the principal Namibian art forms, namely that of the filling of a fuel tank by a forecourt attendant until there is simply not a cubic nanometre of space left in the tank available for any more fuel. Such art work cannot be hurried, and there is therefore always time at these stops to visit the loo, reconcile one's bank account, add a codicil to one's will – or, if one is Brian, to examine a puddle… Because, for the last three hundred kilometres up that B1, the air had been filled with literally millions of white butterflies (and the windscreen splattered with hundreds of their fragile bodies). And now, around a puddle formed by a leaking tap at the back of the forecourt, were hundreds more of them, and Brian wanted to see what he had been killing. They were beautiful. Not plain white, but white with delicate black markings – and Brian felt quite miserable. After all, it was one thing to see a splat, but it was quite another to see, close up, what that splat had once been: an exquisite creature full of life and enchantment. Brian could console himself in the only way he knew how: by reminding himself that his species had, for as long as it had existed, majored in the thoughtless destruction of all other species, and wouldn't it be conceited to consider himself any different from his same-species brethren?

When he then recounted these thoughts to Sandra (who had herself examined the puddle after returning from the loo with her bank reconciliation) she responded by telling him that he obviously needed a drink, and they should push on to their destination where said drink could undoubtedly be secured. And then all would be well.

Brian could find no challenge to this proposal and accordingly pushed on as soon as he had delivered a small fortune to the service-station attendant. (Fuel in Namibia is as outrageously expensive as it is in the UK and, unsurprisingly, 4.2 litre engines demand rather a lot of it.) And lo, within less than half an hour, the pushing on had delivered them to the first of the eleven lodges they would be visiting on this expedition, and this lodge rejoiced in the name of the "Mushara Outpost" – and it probably still does.

Brian approached it up a long gravel track, and when he'd drawn the Land Cruiser to a halt, he immediately decided that it was very similar to the Mushara Bush Camp. This was another of the four lodges in the "Mushara Collection", and where he and Sandra had stayed on their last visit to this Etosha region. The similarity was welcome, because this meant that the

Outpost boasted a beautifully designed open-sided "lodge house" where one could eat and drink whilst enjoying a subtle blend of fawns, blues, greys and whites, and it also offered individual tents that were both private and very comfortable. And by tents, we are here referring to "tent-like structures of wood and canvas", which make tent-type tents look like something from a bygone age. For who in the Boy Scouts would expect his tent to come complete with an elegant loo, a huge shower, a simply gigantic bed, a shaded deck and an air conditioning system!? Oh… and there was a chilled mini-bar as well. And within seconds of arriving in their very own "tent-like structure", Brian and Sandra had concluded that it was now late enough and hot enough (it was roasting) to raid the mini-bar and, by combining some of its contents with the tent's shaded deck, to discover whether the product of this mixing was even better than the sum of its parts. It was. Windhoek was now six hundred kilometres away, but two glasses of Windhoek Lager were just an arm's length away – on the deck's table. And then another two glasses. And this proved exceedingly agreeable; a fitting conclusion to all that driving stuff, and a necessary pause in their itinerary before our two lodgers then prepared themselves for dinner.

There was a mosquito net in the tent-like structure, so although it was highly unlikely that any mosquito could breed in the arid environment around the lodge, Brian decided to deploy his standard mosquito defences. These consisted of a long-sleeved shirt, a pair of long trousers, a pair of standard socks worn over a pair of knee-high flight socks, both doused in DEET, and a pair of tightly-laced desert boots. He wasn't taking any chances. (Unlike Sandra, who could have gone down to dinner naked and would have remained there unbitten and unstung by any insect until the same time next year. She really was that unattractive to bugs with mouthparts and stings and could genuinely claim to be her very own mosquito repellent. Brian envied her something rotten.)

However, as it transpired, she did put on some clothes on this particular evening, so that when Brian accompanied her down to the lodge house, the half a dozen Germans who were gathered just outside it (around the statutory but ludicrous-in-this-climate log fire) didn't become unduly distressed. All they did was nod (in the way that only Germans can nod) and then ignore their new companions. This was a little odd, but could have pointed to their being in that tiny minority of Germans who have no facility with the English language (and which is mirrored in Britain by that tiny minority of British people who do have a facility with German). But in any event, it meant that Brian wouldn't be able to debate with them that possible Teutonic influence on the local roads. He and Sandra would have to amuse themselves – whilst tackling the first of their aperitifs – in splendid English isolation.

However, this isolation was not to last. For as dinner time approached, so too did a Scotsman and his wife. And Ted (for that was his name), despite being Scottish, had been attracted by Brian and Sandra's English voices. Or maybe that was just their English as opposed to German vocabulary. But for whatever reason, Ted and his wife, Dot, joined their English preferences for an extended chat – and another aperitif.

The conversation kicked off in the way it always kicks off in a lodge, with questions exchanged on 'where have you come from?', 'how long have you been here?' and 'where are you going next?' From these questions, Brian and Sandra learnt that their new acquaintances had already spent some time in other parts of Namibia and were soon off to Zambia. But they also learnt that Ted had spent a great deal of time in other parts of the world, and parts that they themselves had visited.

It started by accident. But when it had started it soon gathered pace, as Ted discovered that this English pair had been where he'd been in Guyana, where he'd been in Assam – and in Borneo and in Madagascar and in Costa Rica – and in a whole string of other "unusual destinations". It was as though Brian and Sandra had been stalking him. Or was that Ted stalking them? It really was quite incredible; a man whom they had never met before who, generally with his three brothers, took himself off to foreign parts, which were the very same foreign parts that they themselves had visited. And so incredible – and so intriguing – that Ted suggested that for tomorrow's dinner, Brian and Sandra should join him and his wife to discuss this shadow-travelling further.

Brian and Sandra readily agreed. After all, they hadn't yet discovered whether Ted was a loopaholic.

Then it was food, a soupçon more to drink, and then bed. For tomorrow it was a visit to Etosha!

2.

The Etosha National Park is to Namibia what bacon is to a fry-up; without it, it would be impoverished and not nearly so attractive. And incidentally, the park is even saltier than the saltiest bacon... However, rather more prosaically, the Etosha National Park is Namibia's largest and most wildlife-filled wildlife reserve. And it includes a giant salt pan, which gives it its name, as "Etosha" in the local lingo means "great white place".

Conveniently, its eastern gate is just ten kilometres from Mushara Outpost, which, of course, is why Brian and Sandra had chosen this lodge, and why they were now at that gate just a few minutes after finishing their Outpost breakfast (which, interestingly, was a small fry-up with bacon).

They had been to this park on a number of occasions before and were therefore prepared for what they first encountered – which was a healthy dose of Namibian bureaucracy. For here, at the gate, they were required to complete a register and fill in a form, and then wait until the mobile-phone-distracted attendant in charge of the gate had decided that a sufficient delay to their progress had been imposed (in accordance with park regulations) and that they could now continue on their way. Yes, they could now drive on to the nearest park camp where they would be able to purchase a permit, which required a second register to be completed and a handsome contribution to park funds to be made. Indeed, so handsome that Brian wondered just how much of it was consumed by the less than streamlined entry procedures, which, if they were streamlined, could instead be applied to the upkeep of the park. And had they thought about a ticket machine or its permit equivalent?

Well, Brian hadn't been able to keep these thoughts to himself. So, when he vocalised them back in the safety of the Land Cruiser, he was immediately chastised by his wife who told him in no uncertain terms that access control to the park wasn't just a matter of issuing tickets or permits, but also a matter of recording who had been let in and when. Didn't he know that there were poachers in this country? And he'd be the first to complain if they let in a busload of them.

Brian felt a little foolish. Sandra was spot on, and he had no response. So instead, he immediately changed the subject. He engaged her on their intra-park itinerary and, in particular, where they should go first. It was a good move, and soon Sandra had the park map across her knees and was pointing to the waterhole of "Chodup".

They were off – along a white gravel track and towards this famous waterhole, where in the past they had seen countless different animals and birds. And when they arrived there, it was essentially… well, deserted. So they turned around and drove to the next one they'd chosen, a place called Springbokfontein (which, Brian thought, held a cryptic clue as to what its name might mean in English). It also held a gang of pretty kudus and a couple of elephants. As they watched this pair of pachyderms, more of their type arrived. And then more and more. They had timed their visit perfectly and were now being treated to an elephant convention. Albeit, unlike most other conventions, this one had a purpose and it didn't have any speeches, but just a lot of delightful behemoths, slaking their thirst and providing their observers with a stunning start to their wildlife diversions.

Unfortunately for Brian, they also provided his wife with an opportunity. And this was an opportunity (through the use of an established "word challenge") to chastise him again for his earlier foolishness over the entry arrangements for the park. She took this opportunity when Brian pointed out to her the big lady elephant in the middle of the group of elephants who had beneath her what must have been her very young baby. It was so small it could easily stand directly below her. It was charming, but its description by Brian as being "beneath" its mother was Sandra's signal to launch her assault. She started:

'Are you sure you mean "beneath" there Brian? You don't mean "underneath", do you? Or maybe just "under"?'

'What!'

'Well, it's just that "beneath" suggests directly underneath or even extending underneath. And that young ellie certainly isn't extending underneath and I'm not sure it's quite big enough to be directly under its mother – as in the sense of it being intimately under her.'

Brian turned to face his wife and launched his counter attack.

'Do you mean directly under or directly underneath? Or maybe even directly beneath?'

Sandra regrouped and, after a slight hesitation, responded to her husband.

'Underneath that comment, Brian, is a despicable ploy to sneak below my original observation concerning the appropriate use of "underneath", and accordingly it is beneath contempt.'

'Or directly underneath contempt? If I was sneaking directly below your original observation.'

'That, Brian, is below your normal standards, and I can only conclude that beneath that veneer of bravado is a tacit acceptance that you do not understand the difference between beneath and underneath. And that's not below or under the veneer, because your non-comprehension extends underneath it – extensively.'

'You're right,' admitted Brian, now grinning. 'In respect of the correct use of beneath, underneath, below and under, I occupy a lower status than yourself. I am beneath you. But currently, of course, not underneath you. Or below you or under you for that matter. Or indeed prepared to continue this nonsense any longer. Oh, and I think the park's entry arrangements are not in the least below standard and in no way beneath the standards of others…'

At which point, Sandra broke into a smile and appeared to be satisfied that she'd made her point, amiably, rapidly and effectively – and the two of them could now get back to looking at ellies. This they did – until the ellies finally moved off, which was Brian and Sandra's cue to move off as well.

So Brian started up the Land Cruiser and drove further on, and found further delights.

The first of these were two (very rare) blue cranes at the side of the track. Then there were thousands of Cape teal on a stretch of the salt pan that still held water. And, after these, there were wildebeest, impala, giraffe, zebra and a whole assortment of animals and birds that would have sent Noah into a real flap. But that's Etosha: wildlife made easy, wildlife in abundance, and wildlife that is usually safe – but not always.

Brian and Sandra were now observing what they had been told about before they'd left Windhoek: a huge expanse of burnt-out bush where just days before there had been a bush-fire, big enough and fast enough to have caused a great loss of life. Many many creatures had been consumed by the flames. And whether this had been the result of a man with a butt or a god with a lightning bolt, nobody knew. Although Brian suspected it was an Act of Man. Any god would have had more sense.

However, this disturbing interlude from the recent past was now… well, past, and it was time to move on – literally – and for Brian and Sandra to seek out even more of Etosha's offerings. So that's what they did – for the rest of the day. And, in doing so, they saw more and more of Etosha and more and more of its varied wildlife, so that when, in the evening, they had gathered for dinner back at the Outpost, they both felt satiated and very happy, and more than ready for a meal with Ted.

In fact, it wasn't just Ted (and his wife). For at the same table there was also one of his brothers, John, his wife Linda and their Namibian guide, Orla, who, for the sake of clarity, was a man with no female characteristics whatsoever. Indeed, quite the reverse. He looked like one of those sorts who could flip a spare wheel off the top of a Land Cruiser without even thinking, and Brian was convinced that at one stage of the meal he had bent his fork by simply looking at it. He also had a few tales to tell. And inevitably, they concerned some of his previous charges and their attendant national characteristics. Most memorable amongst these tales were those concerning his Italian clients, and their all too predictable Italian characteristics. These included an inability to be quiet (so they saw less wildlife than any other visitors to the country – and never any leopards), an inability to be ready at an appointed time (so Orla always gave them a departure time that was one hour before their real departure time), and an unsurpassed inability to make up their minds. This, according to Orla, was their most reliable idiosyncrasy, and why he never ever gave them a choice. If he did this, his retinue of Italian travellers would still be debating the options an hour after they'd been presented, and Orla would eventually have to impose a choice on them himself. Brian wondered whether these features of the Italians' make up might just possibly have some connection with the economic woes with which their country is now tussling and, if they do, who in the end will make the necessary choices for them.

Ted, of course, had other matters on his mind and, in particular, the fact that he had at his table two people who had been to almost every place in the world that he'd been. Consequently, the conversation soon resolved itself into an exploration of where he'd been that they hadn't and vice versa. The two lists were not very long, and included places such as Mongolia, Cape Verde and Belize. These last two were on the "Brian and Sandra had/Ted and his brothers hadn't" list, and Belize's inclusion spawned a debate as to where to go in that small country, as it was very near the top of Ted's "next-to-visit" list. It was an odd conversation to be having in a lodge in Namibia, but no odder than the conversation that followed, which centred on where to visit in Arizona and New Mexico (one of the entries on the "Ted and his brothers had/Brian and Sandra hadn't" list) and consequently of interest to the English duo. Indeed, odd conversations – with interesting people – were a consistent feature of lodges in this part of the world, and were as much a part of the holiday experience as the scenery and the wildlife. After all, how often does one get to chat to a bright Scot about rugby football, Scottish independence and the scourge of Health and Safety?

This last topic was the last topic debated at the table, after all the wine had been consumed, and its detail was consequently a little "cloudy" in Brian's recollection. But he did remember, after the event, that part of the debate had required the consideration of some of those heinous dangers on which the Health and Safety police had yet to descend. So, amongst other things, that was those razor-edged peaks on schoolboys' caps, which, in these days of unbounded recreational nutting, were nothing less than potentially lethal. Then there was the inherent dangers in duvets, which, if swallowed, could cause all sorts of breathing problems and worse. And finally, the Fire Brigade, which has now been proven beyond doubt to have been associated with virtually every major conflagration in Britain over the past forty years. And surely it was now time to bring to an end this very dangerous and highly incendiary relationship…

It was shortly after these contributions (mostly if not entirely from Brian) that Sandra suggested that they go to bed. She clearly not only wanted not to abuse the hospitality of their Scottish (and Namibian) hosts, but she also wanted her husband in bed in time to recover his sobriety by the morning. Tomorrow was another day, and a day when he would be required to take their Land Cruiser a further five hundred kilometres into Namibia. Yes, they were off to the Caprivi Strip, a distant stretch of Namibia to which neither they nor indeed Ted had ever been before. (Although, judging from their conversation at the table this evening, Ted wouldn't be too far behind them. And it wasn't beyond the bounds of possibility that he might even appear in Brian's rear-view mirror!)

3.

In the event, virtually nobody appeared in Brian's rear-view mirror. He and his wife had embarked on another long drive, this time along some of the most traffic-starved roads in the whole of Namibia. First there was that B1 again back to Tsumeb, then a forgotten stretch of the C42 that took them to a tiny place called Grootfontein, after which there was a road called the B8 that ran precisely northeast for 250 kilometres (and had been built by someone with access to a giant 250-kilometre-long ruler). And on all of these roads, vehicles were the exception rather than the rule. Brian found it all quite delightful.

There was, however, a particular point of interest on this B8 road, which Brian and Sandra encountered when they'd driven about one hundred kilometres beyond Grootfontein – and this was the "vet fence".

This is a fence that stretches across the entire north of Namibia (and into Botswana) and was originally erected to protect cattle (to the south of the fence) from Foot and Mouth disease infection from buffalo (to its north). Since and despite its erection, the number of diseases that affect cattle and that have to be considered as veterinary control problems has increased exponentially. And therefore the future of this fence is assured, even though its negative impact on the current elephant range is profound.

But this clinical explanation of this barrier tells only half the story. For the vet fence, as Brian and Sandra were about to discover, separates two very different Namibias. To its south and all the way down to Windhoek and beyond, Namibia is an "ordered" place. Away from its deserts in the extreme south and on its coast, it is a land made up of a patchwork of enormous farms. Not farms as we would recognise them in Britain, but parcels of land measured in thousands of hectares, covered in scrub and housing just a scattering of cattle and other animals (some of them wild), and all contained within the bounds of huge wire fences. Therefore, even though it looks empty and beautifully desolate, what we have here is still essentially a "commercial" landscape – operated by big land owners and very much on a business-like basis. To the north of the fence, it is not like this at all.

Here, and starting just yards beyond the B8's heavily manned gate in the fence, is another world, a world of concession lands, roadside mud-and-straw huts, wandering animals (as there are no fences to prevent them wandering), peasants (in the true sense of the word) and, if not acute poverty, then at least a degree of real hardship. It reminded Brian of only one thing: Africa – and the Africa that was normally depicted on the news, an Africa where development was minimal and where most people still just subsisted, growing what they could and rearing whatever animals their overworked land could sustain. Only the arrow-straight metalled B8 belied this impression. Where there should have been a red-sand dirt road winding its way into the distance, there was still this undeviating strip of tarmac, the sort of road that wouldn't have looked out of place in Lower Saxony.

Well, that was not quite accurate, as it would be very surprising to find in Lower Saxony any thoroughfares that were so highly populated with goats and cows. They were everywhere here. And, as our travellers would in due course discover, wandering animals of both the domestic and the wild variety were now to become the established road hazard for the remainder of their expedition.

Indeed, when they had driven through Rundu (the fuel-stop settlement at the head of that 250-kilometre straight line) and then turned due east towards the Caprivi Strip, this animal hazard grew significantly bigger – literally. For on this stretch of the B8 there were (wandering) elephant warnings all along its length. This was a little disconcerting, as Brian was well aware that a collision with an elephant could result in road-kill, but that the road-kill would probably not be the elephant. He therefore drove more cautiously than ever and, as he approached the very beginnings of the Caprivi Strip, he attempted to concentrate on his driving, and not on the peculiar nature and the peculiar origination of this slice of geographical nonsense…

If one looks at a map of Namibia, it looks at first glance as if the mapmaker has made a mistake. He's got the bulk of the thing right: a coastline, a series of more or less straight lines separating the country from Angola to the north, Botswana to the east, and South Africa to the east and south – but then he's cocked it. He's put some sort of pot-handle on it, a thin strip of land that runs east from its extreme north-eastern corner right up to Zambia and nudging even Zimbabwe. It can't be right. It must be a flight of fancy. Or maybe the mapmaker's apprentice finished the job off and he just misread the instructions. Geographical protuberances of this sort and of this size simply do not happen.

Only, of course, they do – if they originated in the colonial past of Africa. Yes, up to 1890, this pot-handle was merely the very top slice of the British Bechuanaland Protectorate (most of which ended up as modern-day Botswana) and German South-West Africa (now Namibia) had no claim on it whatsoever. But then in that year Germany did lay claim to British-administered Zanzibar. Now, Zanzibar has very little connection with anywhere in southern Africa, and its seizure by Germany should have had no impact on this sliver of Bechuanaland. But it did. Because the British were a bit peeved at losing Zanzibar and demanded a conference with Germany to sort matters out. And matters were sorted out. In essence, Britain ended up with Zanzibar again – and a strip of German South-West Africa that was appended to Bechuanaland's western edge – for which, in return, the Germans were granted the North Sea island of Heligoland – and a strip of northern Bechuanaland, now known as the Caprivi Strip. It was an exercise in land swapping on an epic scale that could only ever have been done under the auspices of colonial ignorance and its associated arrogance, and ultimately it went down very badly with the Lozi people. These were the poor saps who happened to be living in the Caprivi and who only discovered they were under German control some twenty years after the swap. (It wasn't until 1908 that the German government dispatched an "Imperial Resident" to oversee the place.)

The Lozi's reaction was to round up all the cattle they could find (including those of rival tribes) and then to drive them out of the area. The cattle were apparently eventually returned to their rightful owners, but the majority of the Lozi chose to remain in Angola or Zambia rather than to submit to German rule. Difficult to believe, but that's quite definitely what happened.

So, not a great outcome for the Germans. They had not only upset the locals, but, of far more importance to them, their plans for the use of the Caprivi Strip had been frustrated by those perfidious Brits. Yes, their entire motivation for acquiring this stretch of real estate was to give them access from their South-West possession to the Zambezi River, and to provide them with a link to (German) Tanganyika and ultimately to the Indian Ocean. Good idea, but unfortunately (for them), Britain's colonisation of Rhodesia stopped them well upstream of Victoria Falls, which proved a not insignificant barrier to navigation on the Zambezi. They were stuffed. And one only hopes that all those Lozi heard about the collapse of their grand scheme and had a jolly good laugh at their expense. Brian knew he would have laughed his socks off.

But this was no good. He was slipping into thoughts of how the Caprivi Strip originated, when all his thoughts should have been on the unexpected appearance of an elephant. And this was a serious consideration. He was now into that part of the Strip that is only thirty-two kilometres wide, hardly wide enough to accommodate an elephant and a Land Cruiser side by side. Although, there again, the current elephant-related dangers in this spindle of land are nothing like they were a few years ago. Because then, due to a spill-over from the conflict in Angola, there were the sorts of threats in this region that demanded the use of obligatory armed convoys along the road, to say nothing of the need to drive around any elephant dung *on* the road – as it was quite likely to have been fortified with explosives by the local guerrillas…

Brian was still musing on this execrable use of excrement when he finally entered the settlement of Divundu, which was very close to the end of their journey. He then switched to a consideration of what he and his partner had achieved. They hadn't hit any elephants (or goats or cows or people), they had avoided any forgotten explosives, and they had safely clocked up a thousand kilometres from their start point in Windhoek. So Brian now thought that they both deserved a drink and, as with their first day on the road, he knew full well that this drink would be forthcoming as soon as they arrived at their next lodge. So, stopping in Divundu only long enough to refuel and to take in the untidiness and generally litter-strewn nature of the place, he was soon off again to drive just a few kilometres south down the road towards Botswana and to lodge number two, a lodge that went by the name of the "Nunda Safari Lodge" and that sat on the banks of the Kavango River.

Frankly, it didn't look too promising. Divundu, which is principally a road junction with a fuel station and some road-works, leaks down this southern side road – along with its attendant litter and rubbish. Brian was finding it difficult to see what sort of lodge could exist in this sort of situation. But there it was, at the side of the road, a sign announcing the entrance to the lodge and a sand-track off the road that led to the lodge itself. Brian turned onto this track and drove slowly down, scanning the track ahead for the appearance of any suspicious-looking poo. But there was none, and he was soon approaching the gates of the lodge – and the lodge's "greeter".

This was a sunny little man who, as soon as he'd opened the gate, came to Brian's side of the Land Cruiser and didn't just welcome his new guests, but thanked them as well. He thanked them for coming, he thanked them for choosing the Nunda Safari Lodge as opposed to any other – and for helping the local community by making this choice – and for colonising Rhodesia and so spoiling the plans of those horrible colonial

Germans. No, on reflection, Brian didn't think he'd thanked him for the Rhodesia bit, but at the time he'd been so overcome by this outpouring of gratitude that he'd become quite confused. After all, in England, you consider yourself lucky if, in any hostelry, the welcome routine runs to a smile, never mind a thank you. And it's very rarely followed by a view of two hippopotamuses…

Brian and his wife had now checked in and were having that much-needed drink. They were doing this on the lodge's deck overlooking that Kavango River, and in this river were a pair of hippos. It was all very charming. So too was the lodge, albeit it was a little old-fashioned and it certainly lacked the "chic-ness" of Mushara. The main building was the usual agglomeration of bar, lounge and dining room, all under a traditional thatched roof, but it was a bit fussy and a bit uninspired. In fact, with its wall-mounted oversized telly near the bar, if one ignored the view of the river, the thatched ceiling and the intense heat, one could just about imagine one was in a Wetherspoon's pub. Or at least Brian could.

The chalet was a little better. It too had a river aspect – and a shaded deck – and it was surrounded by a pretty little garden. It was also spacious, with a generous open-sided bathroom, and it had two single beds around which was one huge and already-deployed mosquito net. Brian was gratified by the presence of this formidable protection, but at the same time concerned by what the need for this protection might mean in terms of the incidence of biting insects. It would definitely be long trousers and multiple socks again this evening…

But that was a couple of hours away, and before then there was another drink to deal with and the coming to terms with the ambient temperature. It was hotter than ever, and so much so that Brian's perspiration was in full flow when all he was doing was lifting a glass to his lips. Maybe it would be cooler later on.

It was. But only a little. So when he and his wife reported back to the bar for a pre-dinner tipple, the bar was being cooled by one of those fans that blows a mist of water into the air, and that he had never in his life seen in a Wetherspoon's pub. This did help, but real relief only arrived when the sun had finally left the sky and Brian's second drink had settled in his stomach. And then it was time for dinner.

This was shared with a handful of other couples (at separate tables) and two groups of travellers. One of these groups was French, and had the appearance of one of those extended French families that are usually featured in French films about what they get up to on French holidays. You know, they are staying at a rambling French mansion somewhere near Nice, and if it's not infidelity on the part of the grown-ups, it's troublesome teenage sex amongst the children... And then the other group was British and comprised what could have been a bevy of overweight retired (female) teachers, a couple of elderly gigolos they'd brought along with them (and who seemed more interested in their food than in their lady clients) and a couple of guides. Indeed, it was one of these guides who had planted that gigolo idea in Brian's head, as his footwear this evening was a pair of black and white patent leather shoes. They looked extremely incongruous when compared with his casual safari attire. But maybe he was making a statement – about the integration of black and white people and how they complemented each other, especially when they were shiny. Or maybe he wasn't.

Anyway, the food was a bit pub-ish as well, and it wasn't long before Brian and Sandra had left the Frenchies to their sexual indiscretions and the Brits to their potential peccadilloes. And, if there were any Germans at those other tables, to their contemplation of what might have been if only the Brits hadn't gone and screwed it all up with Rhodesia…

To secure a safari in the Nunda Safari Lodge, one had to pay for it. This was a little unusual, as at most of the other lodges in which Brian and Sandra had stayed in the past, drives were included along with the food and booze. But those lodges, thought Brian, weren't in the J D Wetherspoon Group and didn't have the misfortune of being within walking distance of Divundu.

Yes, when Jonny, their guide, drove his safari Land Rover out of the lodge and back onto the road, the litter was still there, and there was more of it as he drove further south. It seemed that this road to Botswana had spawned a bit of ribbon development (especially between the road and the Kavango River on the left) and the cast-offs and rubbish from this development were everywhere around. This was a pretty shabby sort of area, and it made Brian wonder what its residents thought of the world beyond Divundu and this world's often rather more salubrious condition. For amongst all the simple mud huts at the side of the road were shiny white satellite dishes. That outside-Divundu world was being beamed in here all the time. Even more intriguing, that beaming in of the outside world will have inevitably included scenes from Windhoek and scenes of the national politicians there in their fine clothes and their fine cars. So what did these local guys think about that? And did any of those politicians make the one thousand kilometre journey here to find out the answer? Brian doubted they did, other than when elections were coming up and they'd dreamt up a new batch of promises…

Brian had done it again. Here he was on the start of a safari drive, and all he could do was censure the local population for being too poor to afford a rubbish service and, possibly worse, impugn the motives and the honesty of the country's hard-working politicians. It just wasn't right. And for all he knew, it was these same politicians who had installed these satellite dishes – as well as surfacing this little-used road to Botswana. Well, for a couple of miles anyway…

Yes, the tarmac had just disappeared, and Jonny's Land Rover was now rattling down a wide gravel road with, in its wake, a gigantic cloud of dust. This wasn't a problem for its three occupants, as the gravel road was very well graded and the ride was relatively smooth. But, of course, that was only the case for as long as the road ahead remained clear. Inevitably, it didn't indefinitely. And, although infrequent, there were soon meetings with other vehicles coming the other way, each with its own gigantic cloud of dust. And in a safari Land Rover, an open vehicle with a canvas roof, there are no windows to wind up. Consequently… Brian decided that safari vehicles are great for safari drives, but not for driving to these drives on gravel roads where one meets fast-moving vehicles. They should have used their Land Cruiser.

Things improved when they finally reached the gates of the Mahango Game Reserve. This is a protected area of Namibia just to the north of its border with Botswana and it was their destination for the morning. This meant that after an obligatory visit to the gate-house to pay an entrance fee, Jonny was now at liberty to turn off the road and drive slowly through the reserve, where instead of approaching vehicles there should now be a collection of all-too-often-receding animals and birds.

Well, maybe it was the care that Jonny was taking with his driving – or the already stunningly high temperature – but many of the animals and birds forgot to recede even a little. So, within a remarkably short time, Brian and Sandra had been treated to some very close views of common impala (as opposed to Etosha's black-faced impala), waterbuck, red lechwe and buffalo. There were also close encounters with southern long-tailed starlings, violet wood hoopoes, spur-winged geese and a selection of other birds. This was proving to be a very rewarding expedition and it soon got even better when Jonny stopped near an ancient baobab from which there was a view of the Kavango River and its surrounding marshes. For here there were hundreds of different water birds together with oodles of hippos, dozens of baboons and many more of those waterbuck and red lechwe (two of Africa's most handsome antelopes).

The baobab wasn't bad either. Reckoned to be over fifteen hundred years old, it was as elegant as it was huge (its mass must have been the timber equivalent of a thousand Eric Pickles). It was also apparently of use to the locals. Jonny said that they took a little of its bark to mix with oil and then they fed the resulting paste to their newborn, not to make them like Eric Pickles, but to make them strong. Brian couldn't find too much fault in this. The tree was so huge and had so much bark that he doubted the locals would ever produce enough new babies to do it serious harm. They also, of course, revered it, and would not wittingly ever do it damage. And not surprising really. Baobabs of any size are impressive. But old chaps like this monster are just awesome – as well as being the stuff of legends…

Yes, baobabs are special, and have a special place in the world of myths and legends, and most of these myths and legends concern the fact that a baobab is often seen as a tree that grows upside down.

The simplest of all these old stories is that the baobab fell from the sky – upside down – and then stayed in this upside-down configuration as it continued to grow. Mildly interesting but not so imaginative as another legend that is based on the idea that when God created the world he gave a tree to each animal, and the hyena ended up with the baobab. He wasn't pleased and immediately threw it down in disgust – with the tree landing upside down. And so its remarkable shape. Then there is another legend that is more imaginative still…

This one says that the first baobab sprouted beside a small lake, and as it grew taller and looked about it, it couldn't help noticing that all the other trees had straight and handsome trunks, beautiful leaves and even more beautiful blossoms. Then one day the wind died down, the surface of the lake became smooth and mirror like, and the baobab finally got to see what it looked like itself. It was grossly fat, its bark was like the wrinkled hide of an old elephant, its leaves were tiny and insignificant and its blossoms lacked colour. Well, to cut a long legend short, there then followed a strongly-worded complaint to the tree's creator and a protracted debate on all its perceived shortcomings – until the creator decided that he'd had enough, and brought matters to a conclusion by grabbing the baobab by the trunk, yanking it out of the ground, turning it over and then replanting it upside down. And from that day on, the baobab has been unable to see its reflection or make a complaint. Instead, for thousands of years, it has worked in silence, paying off its ancient transgression by doing good deeds for people. Which is why, all over Africa, people see the baobab as something very special – and very helpful. It is regarded with great affection.

However… what all these legends fail to recognise, even if they quite rightly confer the tree with a loveable nature, is that, far from being some sort of ugly duckling, the baobab is one of the world's most exquisite trees. It's not just a big tree; it's a truly beautiful tree. How could something with so much ravishingly sculptured woodwork be other than gorgeous? And then there is something else about the baobab that all these legends fail to address, and that is its likely purpose. Because it was quite possible (or so Brian believed) that the baobab wasn't just a tree, but that it was also a sentinel, a literal plant on this planet, put here by aliens to record over the centuries what we are getting up to. Yes, one only had to look at these remarkable trees(?) to see that they appeared to stand apart from all other trees and all other life, just observing and maybe just storing in their massive insides all the information that the aliens will need when they visit us in the future. Like a sort of woody GCHQ, each baobab on the planet was eavesdropping on our lives and storing away all the information gleaned for their alien creators…

As soon as Brian had recounted this latest theory to Sandra, he noticed that she approached Jonny and whispered in his ear. Shortly thereafter, they were returning to the lodge, where Sandra was unusually eager to get him to the bar and get him to drink a beer. Maybe she was concerned about the temperature and its effect on her husband's state of hydration and his general wellbeing. And it was hot. According to the thermometer outside the lodge's entrance, it was actually 43°C. Which is very hot indeed. Anyway, Brian was more than ready for a drink and didn't put up a fight. In fact, he had another drink directly after he'd finished his first.

It had been a good morning. And now it would be a good afternoon, because it was far too hot to do anything other than be as inert as possible back at their chalet. They both managed this quite well, and Brian even managed a little doze for a while. So that by early evening they were ready to engage with the lodge's catering facilities one more time and, to start with, by sampling its gin and tonics on its expansive outside deck.

It had to be expansive because tonight (and presumably on many other nights) it had to accommodate not just the lodge's guests but also a troupe of African dancers. Well, that is to say, dancers who were African – and no more than twelve years old. They were from a local school and they were here to perform some local dance numbers – in suitably African dress. Albeit Brian couldn't get out of his mind that their bead skirts were just smaller versions of the bead curtain he'd left back in Britain and which kept the flies out of the conservatory in summer. But that was just Brian, and any decent-minded guest with an ounce of courtesy in his or her makeup would simply have seen the performance for what it was: a polished and enthusiastic demonstration of the local culture, and a demanding exercise, well deserving of the contributions that were collected at its close.

Then it was dinner. The retired teachers and their gigolos and guides were still there at their table, but the French degenerates had disappeared, probably to somewhere near Nice. And the food hadn't got any better.

So the day ended. But not before Brian and Sandra checked the thermometer outside the lodge entrance on their way to their chalet and, in doing so, noticed a sign there. It read: 'This is Land Rover territory. On a quiet night you can hear the Toyota Land Cruisers rusting away in the dark.' Brian and

Sandra were amused, even though they were driving a Land Cruiser themselves, and even though it was on a Land Rover this morning that they'd each had to ingest five ounces of Namibian dust. They were also fascinated – to discover whether this Land Rover/Land Cruiser rivalry would be encountered anywhere else on their circumnavigation.

And had Brian thought about it, he could probably have learnt the answer to this particular question by asking that baobab up the road…

5.

When one enters the Mahango Game Reserve, just down the road from the Nunda Safari Lodge, one does one of two things. One either pays an entrance fee in an upstairs office of the reserve's gate-house – when one is entering to observe game – or, if one is simply driving through to Botswana (as Brian and Sandra were doing), one simply records one's vehicle details in a book. (And this book is quite well hidden behind a fence of stakes just outside the gate-house.) Now, it appears that these dual procedures, unbeknownst to Brian and Sandra, constitute a package of knowledge that all human beings are born with. And should any of these human beings turn up at the reserve's entrance, they not only already know what to do but, if they are simply driving through, they even know the whereabouts of the concealed book.

Unfortunately, as implied in the above, a glitch in Brian and Sandra's DNA meant that they had been cast into this world without this all-important info. All they knew was that there was a book to sign (because Jonny had told them of this yesterday) and they stupidly assumed that this book would be in the gate-house office, which is why they passed a lady sitting on a chair outside the gate-house and texting with her mobile and climbed a flight of stairs to the said office. There was nobody there. Not until, five minutes later, the lady with the mobile had managed to elevate her burden of obesity all the way up those same stairs (by employing a slovenly shuffle that was so slow it looked like the onset of rigor mortis) to deliver a severe reprimand to her hapless punters. It transpired that she was the officer on duty today, and that she had a firm expectation that everyone should know the rules of this gate-house and, in particular, where her book was. Because that way she wouldn't have to drag her bloated carcass up that steep flight of stairs…

Brian and Sandra returned to ground level and, when Brian found the blasted book, he furnished it with the required details of their vehicle. He then contemplated furnishing the fat surly operative with his opinion on her behaviour and her demeanour. But Sandra counselled against it. So he never got around to pointing out to her that, whilst she was possibly not overpaid, she did have a job – in an area where the percentage of the population that was "economically active" was probably in single figures – and this job was not that demanding (in that it allowed her to sit in the sun and text all day). He was also never able to inform her that she should go and see how the greeter at Nunda Safari Lodge approached his job, and how, by adopting a sunny disposition in the conduct of his work, he was probably a far happier person than she was and a great deal happier than all those shop assistants, bank clerks, immigration officials and even pettier officials who, with only rare exceptions, seem incapable of being other than resentful and offensive in their dealings with the public. And why, in heaven's name, couldn't they all be as good-humoured and agreeable as Brian was himself? Not that he was a complete paragon. But he was never really surly – and he never shuffled his feet…

And he would certainly never let a less than perfect encounter first thing in the morning sour his mood for the rest of the day. Especially when he had a new lodge to visit – and a new country to enter! Well, not new in that he and Sandra had been to Botswana before. But previously they'd always flown in. They'd never before driven in – through one of its border posts, like the one at Mohembo on the southern edge of the Mahango Reserve.

They were nearly there now. They'd left the winner of Caprivi's recent Miss Disagreeable contest, driven through the reserve and were now filling in emigration forms in the Namibian border post, before entering in its vehicle log, every conceivable detail of the Land Cruiser including its VIN number and the number of its engine. This would become something of a habit. And if proof were ever needed of this, it arrived immediately in the Botswana border post, where the same information was required, along with a completed immigration form. But at least the process on both sides of the border had been hassle-free and none of Miss Disagreeable's fellow contenders had been involved. So, all in all, it was an easy crossing (with the only surprise provided by the Land Cruiser's GPS device, which found its [American] voice at the actual border crossing moment to announce that 'You are now entering Botswana' whilst at the same time displaying on its screen a waving Botswanan flag). Isn't technology wonderful?

So yes, Brian and Sandra were now through the border and the Botswanan border post, and were for the first time driving on a Botswanan road. It was similar to a Namibian road. It had essentially no traffic on it and it passed through a landscape of scrub, with, here and there, the odd hut or even a small settlement made up of a number of huts. These were again similar to those in Namibia (or at least to those in the Caprivi Strip), albeit there were two distinct differences. In the first place, the huts were not surrounded by litter and, in the second place, all these little round, thatched-roof huts, whether standing on their own or within a small village, were standing well away from trees. Rather than building their homes under some shade, it seemed that the Botswanans much preferred their accommodation under the full blaze of the searing sun, despite what this must have meant for its interior temperature. (Outside today, it was already at a heatwave level again). Brian knew why they had this preference. It was because they weren't that keen on snakes, and snakes can drop from trees. As he drove past these exposed huts, he thought that their owners should possibly rethink their views on these reptiles, and just go for the shade option. It was only later in the day that he rethought things himself.

The next lodge on the itinerary was called "Nxameseri Lodge", and it was located no more than one hundred kilometres into Botswana, just past the village of the same name. Here, the Kavango River is beginning to broaden out before it fans out into what is the incomparable Okavanga Delta (of which more later). So rather than sitting on the side of the river like the Nunda Lodge upstream, the Nxameseri Lodge sits in the river, or, more precisely, on an island where the river inundates the surrounding flat land. Brian was really looking forward to it, and to the ease of reaching it. Not a five hundred kilometre drive, but one of less than one hundred and fifty. And then just a sign by the side of the road, a quick whiz down a sand-track to a landing stage and, when he'd dumped the car there, an even quicker boat-trip to the island. Perfect.

However... there wasn't a sign by the side of the road. Brian had now driven twenty-five kilometres past a side-road that led to the Nxameseri village and there had been nothing, not even an arrow or a bent stick. So he turned around and then embarked on what were the less than straightforward procedures for locating and finally securing an arrival at the sought-after island-bound lodge. These, he discovered, were as follows.

One first drives into Nxameseri village and, when in its centre, one then asks the lady owner of its singular shop as to the whereabouts of the lodge. She then produces a gentleman who directs one back to the main road and instructs one to drive south 'a couple of kilometres' to where one will see a pole in the ground, and the start of the sand-track to the lodge. One then thanks this gentleman, follows his instructions and then fails to find the pole, after which one drives approximately twenty kilometres north to put the same lodge query to a policeman at a police road-stop there. He recounts the same story about this mythical pole, and one is therefore obliged to drive south again, fail to find the pole again, and instead try an unmarked sand-track that has no pole at its entrance but is, at least, on the correct side of the road. After a few kilometres of difficult sand driving, one then discovers that this track is a dead end and one turns around, tries a side sand-track that is nearly blocked by a fallen tree but that eventually leads one into Nxameseri village again. Here, by approaching it on this sand-track, one passes the house of the gentleman who supplied one with the original guidance who, having seen one driving aimlessly, rushes out of his compound and informs one that he will now provide himself as an escort. He climbs into the car, and directs one south once again, and takes one so far south (about ten kilometres past the village) that he is finally able to point out the pole that is often referred to as 'the pole just a couple of kilometres outside the village'. One then takes him back to his house, tips him generously and then returns to the pole and proceeds down the sand-track. One then discovers, after seven kilometres of increasingly difficult sand, that the track becomes a number of tracks, so that when one finally gets stuck in the sand, one doesn't even know whether one is stuck on the right track. One then panics for a moment until one's spouse draws one's attention to the diff-lock system. One then engages this (with only a modicum of difficulty) and one thanks one's lucky stars when one's vehicle drags itself forward, and ultimately arrives at the water's edge and a little landing stage there, near to which are parked a couple of vehicles. There being no sign and no human in the vicinity, one then backtracks to interrupt the lunch preparations of some local residents one has previously spotted beneath some trees, to check with them that this really is the right place to get to Nxameseri Lodge. Their nodded confirmation is reassuring but also mildly irritating, in that they accompany it with the hand-signalled suggestion that one should now ring the lodge – for a boatman – but one can get no reception on one's friggin' mobile. One therefore returns to the landing stage, checks one's food and water supplies, has a beer, and contemplates how comfortable or otherwise it will be, sleeping in the car overnight. And when one has finished one's beer, a boatman arrives and takes one to the lodge. And one feels mightily relieved…

One also immediately forgets the challenges one has endured in locating the lodge, because the boat-ride to the lodge is a boat-ride through heaven. It is a huge waterscape edged with reed banks and tree-covered islands simply bursting with birds. And these birds are something special: slaty egrets, lesser as well as African jacanas, black crakes, white-faced whistling ducks, African pygmy geese, squacco herons, malachite kingfishers, pied kingfishers and even long-toed lapwings. This is the real thing – and in the middle of nowhere. Brilliant!

Then Brian and Sandra arrived at the lodge and their hearts leapt again. For here, perched on a brick-built quay and framed by giant trees, was a charming lodge building that looked as though it had been there forever. In fact, it had been there for quite some time. Nxameseri Lodge (as with Nxameseri village, named after the bushman word for 'the sound that the wind makes when it blows through the reeds') is one of the oldest lodges in the whole of Botswana, and one of its "cosiest". It can accommodate only a handful of guests and accordingly its open-sided lodge building is both modest and homely – and completely enchanting.

Here, Brian and Sandra had a very welcome beer. "Socks" (their boatman and guide) had handed them over to Tiaan, the lodge manager, and, as they drank, Tiaan explained to them when breakfast was and all that sort of stuff. He was a young, white South African, but a little older than the assistant manager, Bianca, who was also white and South African but, furthermore, also the lodge's resident pilot. (Brian and his wife soon learnt that virtually all the visitors to this slice of paradise were flown in, and that one had to be marginally mental to drive in. Hence the lodge's indifference to the clarity of its signage.)

Bianca had just flown in another guest. Or, as soon became apparent, *the* other guest. There were just three customers of the lodge today – and for most of tomorrow. Great! And it meant more than ample portions as these three visitors and their two hosts sat down for lunch.

Here it was discovered that the third guest was a Zimbabwean by the name of John. He had a tidy beard on his ruddy (white) face, and a tidy number of years under his belt. He also had a sad history. For here was a man who used to be the director of Zimbabwe's Natural History Museum until a monster in that country by the name of Mugabe destroyed it. It no longer exists. Neither does John's principal technician who one day just disappeared… And now John sits in Bulawayo, remembering the past and resenting the present, a present of broken roads, broken water pipes and broken lives. And, of course, as he readily admitted, there was no way that he could now ever afford to leave his blighted country. Hell, if only that awful man could be forced to confront what he's done – and how many lives he's ruined. Or failing that, if only he could have a very unfortunate accident.

Lunch over, it was time for Brian and Sandra to inspect their chalet. This was approached along a winding wooden walkway through the island's giant trees and was positioned near the island's edge where, framed by just a few of these trees, was a view of the water. It was, like the main lodge building, of a modest size and it had, at its front, a modest deck from which one could survey that view of the water. Indeed, one could survey this same scene from within the chalet itself, for the chalet's front elevation consisted of a two-foot high wall where it met the deck with, at its centre and acting as its front door, a two-foot high wooden gate. One could reach in and touch the nearer of the two single beds, and presumably at night, lean out of bed and touch the outside of that very low wall. This was novel, and indeed something of a first for our travelling duo. Brian certainly couldn't bring to mind anywhere in which the mosquito net around his bed had been the only thing between him and the African night.

However, he soon came to terms with this rustic aspect of their accommodation, to say nothing of its resident spiders and bees and the need to keep everything packed away (as he was warned that the island's vervet monkeys tended to visit the open-fronted chalets and make off with anything they could carry). In fact, even when he was sitting on the deck, in just his shorts, observing the river, and saw a long thin snake on a tree stump just a few feet away, he was not in the least bit concerned, and even had the presence of mind to take a photo of it. (And he didn't admit to himself that he had recently read that snake bites are best dealt with if the identity of the snake that has delivered the bite is known – by having a photo of it.) In fact, it wasn't until a medium-sized lizard dropped onto his bare thigh, turned around and looked at him before running off down his leg, that his equilibrium was perturbed. He immediately thought of all those Botswanans who don't build their houses under trees, and the fact that if a lizard could drop onto him (from the tree above the deck) so too could a snake. And the snake had disappeared.

It was clearly time to sit on his bed for a while, and it wasn't until it was nearly time to prepare for dinner that either he or Sandra decided that they could have some more deck time. Even if it meant keeping an eye on those branches above the deck.

Down at the lodge building, they then kept an eye on the branches above the evening's log fire. Not only had the lodge guys created an enormous heat-giving conflagration on this hotter than ever night, but they'd placed it on the edge of the lodge's quay, right below a tree whose low-hanging branches were now being seriously singed. Brian just hoped that it stayed at the singeing level, as he doubted that the island had a resident fire brigade. It did, however, have a very capable resident cook, who presented her five diners for the evening with some fantastic fare.

It was a thoroughly enjoyable evening, as all five around the communal table discussed everything and anything, ranging from ichthyology, through snake identification to the origins of rugby (it being close to the final matches of the Rugby World Cup in New Zealand).

The ichthyology featured because it soon became known that this was John's speciality, and it was also the reason he was staying at the lodge. For at this time of the year, as the Okavango Delta diminishes in size and tens of thousands of prey fish swim upstream into the Kavango River, their predators, fish called "barbels" (or "tiger fish"), congregate in great numbers in order to feast on them, so giving rise to something called the "barbel-run". This was unknown to Brian and Sandra, but is common knowledge amongst most fishermen, who also congregate at this time – to catch the barbels. Indeed, so well known is it that out on that water somewhere was a film crew on a house-boat, here to make a film of the barbel-run for the fishermen viewers of some world-wide syndicated fishing programme. And to provide this film with an authoritative, fish-expert commentary, John had been brought out of retirement. Like some dusty old book, he had been taken off a gloomy library shelf (somewhere in Bulawayo), dusted down, opened up one more time and put to good use – and all at the expense of the film company. He was as happy as could be.

Snake identification centred on the identification of "Brian's snake" – from Brian's photo. Real dusty books were referred to, and the initial consensus was that the snake was a boomslang. This revelation made Brian consider an unscheduled but rapid visit to the loo. But fortunately, the boomslang was quickly downgraded to an olive grass snake. So not death in the night if it slid under the chalet's front gate, but just some serious pain and suffering. And he could easily deal with that.

Indeed, more easily than he could deal with the revelation

by Bianca that she believed rugby originated in ancient Greece! She was serious – as well as being seriously misinformed. Good then that not only did Tiaan break the news to her that she was embarrassingly ignorant – for a citizen of a famous rugby-playing nation – but also that the game was conceived not in ancient Greece (before the days of German funding) but in a town in England – called Rugby. And even better that Brian was able to confirm this correction in her knowledge by informing her that, as a true-born son of that very town, he was absolutely certain that Rugby was where it all started. (Although, like many people around the world with whom Brian had discussed this little piece of sporting trivia, Bianca was at first reluctant to believe that there was really anywhere actually called Rugby. After all, why would anywhere want to name itself after a rough and tumble field game?!)

Ultimately, it was time for bed. It had been a long and tiring day and Brian was looking forward to a sleep. He was also looking forward to the olive grass snake having as much difficulty in locating his bed as he'd had in locating the lodge.

Or, there again, as Brian had eventually made it here, maybe that should be "more difficulty" – and so much difficulty that eventually the snake would give up. (And, of course, not find his way into Sandra's bed instead. And that is obviously "of course"… of course…)

6.

Well, if any snake had visited him during the night, Brian was unaware of it. Furthermore, even though he'd found some mosquitoes in the chalet before retiring – and another of the buggers had been buzzing around his head as he woke – none of them appeared to have left a visiting card. He was mosquito-bite free. Perhaps it was because he was such a wonderful human being…

However, when Brian proposed this hypothesis to Sandra, she was reluctant to agree, and instead suggested that he just get on with his ablutions. They had a date with Socks at 8 o'clock, and before then there was a breakfast to deal with. Brian did have to concede that the early morning was probably not the best time for theorising, especially when the theories in question were undeniably crackpot. So he shut up, got into the shower and prepared himself for the day. And what a day!

To start with, Socks took them out in a little tin boat, the idea being simply to drift around the adjacent waterways, soaking up their ambiance and enjoying their abundance of birdlife. The idea worked. The waterways were enchanting – and humbling. Brian and Sandra may have expended a little time and effort in getting to this place, but they had not lost sight of how privileged they were to be here – and to be here on their own. There was simply nobody else about. It was as though they were in their very own and very exclusive version of the Elysian Fields. And better still, they hadn't been required to pass away before they were allowed to enjoy it (an observation that might just have a certain resonance this coming evening).

Anyway, that's what they were doing now: enjoying it, principally by engaging in some serious bird-observing. Because there were just so many about.

There were darters, who were rubbish at taking off but deadly at diving. There were squacco herons, who tended to hunch and not to squack. There were fish eagles, who looked far too elegant and far too important ever to engage in fishing. There were skimmers, who looked far too delicate ever to exist. And there were white-faced ducks – who just looked confused. Whenever a flock of these gregarious charmers was encountered, all its members would simply be sitting – on a raft of vegetation – looking in the same direction, and doing nothing but looking. They never seemed to feed or to preen, or to have a clue as to what they were supposed to be doing. Brian found them fascinating. And their sheep-like mystification as to their purpose in life – and their complete inactivity – put him in mind of all those people who are housed in the MoD… But it was a passing distraction, and he was soon back to observing birds and to luxuriating in the beauty all around him. For indeed, it would have been terrible to let the nonsense of the outside world intrude on this nirvana for any longer than a few seconds.

Ultimately, however, it was time to draw this voyage through paradise to a close, and to find some shade. It was now approaching the middle of the day – and the onset of sun-stroke. Both Brian and Sandra were beginning to fry. So it was back to the lodge and a lunch with Bianca and then an extended period of barely-clothed bird-watching back on their deck. John was off providing his commentary to the film crew, the staff of the lodge had melted away for a siesta, and Brian and Sandra had Nxamaseri to themselves. So what better way to enjoy this perfect solitude than by engaging in some sedentary ornithology, punctuated as necessary by visits to the help-yourself bar for refreshment – and the interior of the chalet for whatever came to mind... It was a splendid afternoon that now deserved a splendid evening.

This was delivered. John was back from his film work, looking very sun-burnt, Tiaan had returned from a long-distance shopping expedition, and the lodge had a crop of new guests. They were "dads and lads", three fathers and their combined four sons who, with their own pilot, had flown up from Joburg for a weekend of barbel fishing. So there was a full house to provide both interest and entertainment.

The Joburg crowd kicked this off by immediately defending their home city as a place to live – even though nobody had in any way impugned it. But it was clearly what they felt they needed to do. And it has to be admitted, doesn't it? It will be a very long time before Johannesburg ever features on the list of the best-cities-in-the-world-to-live-in. Indeed, it may never. Nor is it likely that fishermen will not at some point in a conversation want to talk about fish. And this is what happened. The discussion soon became one that was centred on baits and barbs, with less than infrequent contributions from the professional ichthyologist within their midst, the sun-baked and now well-lubricated John.

In fact, his knowledge of fish in this gathering of fishy people gave him an authority at the dining table, and he was soon using this authority to take the conversation away from fish. He seemed even keener to talk about his past life than he did about the piscatorial present. So, before long he was recounting stories about his time at Rhodes University in South Africa where he'd trained as a naturalist, and one story about this place stuck in Brian's mind. It concerned one of his professors there who was a notable academic and a very well respected one, but who, at the same time, was just a tiny tad eccentric. And the most overt aspect of his eccentricity was the belief that one always needed to keep in contact with the Earth's electricity, and the way to do this was to conduct every aspect of one's life in bare feet, even if one was otherwise normally attired in a suit and an academic gown and one was delivering lectures.

The university authorities were not impressed by such unconventional behaviour and made it clear to the professor that he had no alternative but to adopt shoes as part of his wardrobe, and limit his bare-feet behaviour to his off-campus life. He reluctantly acceded to their demands, but he was still not prepared to insulate himself from all that vital Earth's electricity with an "unmodified" pair of shoes. No, his would need a special feature. And this special feature was a sandwich of copper. Yes, inside each shoe, he fitted a plate of this metal on its lower surface, and this plate, on which his foot would rest, was wired to a similar copper plate on the shoe's outer sole. And in this way he was still connected to his Earth.

This arrangement apparently worked very well – for all concerned – but came to an abrupt end when the professor killed himself by drinking a glass of prussic acid. It appeared that he held very strong views on the subject of getting old and becoming in any way a burden and a barrier to those who were younger. And in his opinion, seventy was quite old enough for anybody, even if, like himself, they were entirely fit and well. So, when he reached this age, he removed himself from mankind, and one cannot dispute the fact that he never became a burden – on his relatives or the state – and he blocked none of those behind him. One might also conclude that, however eccentric he might have been, he was still a man of supreme resolve, extraordinary courage and, above all, profound insight.

Now this tale – and the manner of its ending – spawned a new debate at the table, and this concerned how many ways one could divide mankind. That is to say that one could probably divide all the people on this planet between those who would see the professor's final deed as the most thoughtful and considerate act that anyone could undertake (albeit they might question the choice of the cut-off point of seventy!), and those who would see it as any combination of cowardly, sinful, selfish and criminal. The diners around the table were reluctant to identify into which group they fell, possibly because of the minors in attendance. But they did then rise to the challenge of how else to divide up mankind.

So, for example, it was suggested that one could do this on the basis of those who believed that during their life they should do only that which they could afford (whether this was having offspring or engaging the services of a high-class hooker on alternate weekends) and those who did not believe this. This latter group was made up of people who believe that they can do exactly what they like and others will pick up the bill. Although, of course, they rarely refer to these others as "others". They much prefer the term "the government", a strange autonomous entity that exists outside the human realm and that is funded not by money taken off other humans but by money showered on it by goblins and fairies, and in such quantities that it always has plenty to spare. And by regarding "the government" (or "the council") as a bottomless pit of resources, completely unconnected with other people, these do-as-they-wanters never consider what they can afford before they do it but only how they can get recompensed for it after they've done it. (And, more commonly, this get-on-and-do-it stuff concerns having offspring and not hiring hookers. Although probably not exclusively.)

Then, moving from morality to mirth, there is that great division between those people in this world who have a sense of humour and those who don't. And it was soon agreed that whilst those with a sense of humour can be drawn from virtually all walks of life and even from virtually all nationalities, those deficient in this essential quality can be more narrowly defined. So the humourless include serious left-wingers, Iranian clerics, most football managers, Chinese politicians, super models, evangelists, public-sector union officials and, of course, all Prime Ministers born in Scotland.

And one final divide: those who give credence to the theories espoused by economists and those who regard the whole "science" of economics as an off-shoot of astrology.

This topic of conversation could have gone on all night, but the fishermen (and boys) at the table planned an early start to their fishing in the morning and John was clearly exhausted by his film work and by the effects of the sun and Windhoek Lager. So the evening drew to a close and Brian and Sandra joined their co-lodgers in retiring to bed. They too were drained by the pleasures of their day and they too had to rise early in the morning. Tomorrow would see them leaving Nxameseri and making their way to another lodge. And with only a few years left before they reached seventy, they wanted to make quite sure they made it…

7.

When Brian awoke in the morning, he remembered a dream. It was a dream in which the European Commission was throwing a party for all the MEPs and all the leaders of Europe to celebrate their solving of the debt crisis. The Eurozone was now locked together, the citizens of all its member states were firmly resolved to work together (and to work as hard as all those Germans), their economies were already rebounding and the outlook was for a new golden age for them and for all the people of the European Union. There was even the likelihood that every European, within just a matter of months, would become a multi-millionaire and therefore deliriously happy.

Of course, it was just a dream. After all, who in their right mind would believe that becoming a multi-millionaire would inevitably make everyone happy? There were bound to be a few amongst all those fortunate Europeans who would view the prospect of unlimited wealth as really quite onerous.

Meanwhile, however, Brian and Sandra had a boat to catch and, when they'd been delivered back to that landing stage, a Land Cruiser to navigate back to the road – without it getting stuck. With the help of Socks – and a permanently engaged diff-lock – they managed both these tasks, and were soon back on the main road with their vehicle pointing north. For now it was time to drive back into Namibia and on to a lodge on the Kwando River. And the Kwando River was about two hundred and fifty kilometres away, further east along the Caprivi Strip – and on the other side of that international border.

Coming through it had been a doddle. Despite the tiresome paperwork, the Namibian side had been very straightforward, and the Botswanan side had been positively pleasant (the immigration staff had been actually jolly). Going back, however, wasn't such a "positive experience". The Botswanan side was again OK, even though it included a vehicle inspection by the Botswanan police. But the Namibian side was a trial. Essentially, there was only one immigration officer on duty (along with a dozen or so other officials who had yet to decide on their roles), and this one immigration guy was dealing both with those leaving his country and those entering it. As three busloads of emigrants had just arrived and were waiting to be processed, any immigrants who happened to be in his border post at this time were just going to have to wait. And so they did – perspiring gently – with Brian wondering whether he dare actually use that suggestion box on the counter…

Sandra advised against it. They had four more Namibian border-post visits to come, and she had no desire to ruffle any feathers at this stage. Brian could see her point, and just stood and suffered in silence, until eventually they were registered and stamped and they were free to go. So it was back up through the Mahango National Park, past the lair of Miss Disagreeable (who, because she was recovering from a bout of work-related stress, was not on her chair today) and then past Nunda to arrive again at Divundu. Then it was a sharp right turn and more of that B8 along the very thinnest section of the Caprivi Strip, with both Angola and Botswana almost within touching distance. Well… if not within touching distance, then certainly close enough to make Brian feel as though he was driving on some sort of causeway with, to either side of it, not water but a sea of endless sand and endless scrub. This was a fairly out-of-the-way part of the world, with even the road-side huts petering out, and all Brian and Sandra had for company on their causeway passage were the ubiquitous elephant-warning signs – and dust devils…

These chaps are fascinating: towering whirlwinds of rushing air defined by their cargo of dust – and seeming to be almost animate, as though they're nothing less than strange spinning life-forms, haring across the landscape and threatening at any moment to turn in your direction. Of course, their genesis and their maintenance as a phenomenon are rather more prosaic. Apparently, they are formed when hot air near the surface of the land rises quickly through a pocket of cooler, low-pressure air above it and, if conditions are right, this rising air may then begin to rotate (along with all that dust). Then, as the air rises, the column of hot air is stretched and this causes the spinning to intensify. This then leads to more hot air being sucked in at the bottom of the vortex, more intensification of the spinning, and the dust devil becomes self-sustaining. It has become a chimney, a chimney for spinning hot air. And now it can spin off to wherever it wants – and not fail to impress all those who see it.

One had once attacked Brian's car – near the Etosha Park – and thrown a fairly substantial branch against its windscreen. Another had attacked his wife when she was inside a little wooden loo – in the same park. And whilst both these assaults had been memorable, each in its own way, neither Brian nor Sandra had experienced one unshielded by either metal or wood. Brian wondered what such a direct assault would feel like. He imagined it might be a little uplifting – in the literal sense of the word – and more than a little uncomfortable. It might even put one in mind of *The Wizard of Oz* or possibly *Gone with the Wind*. But he would probably never know. Just as he would never know why, just like Nxameseri Lodge, Susuwe Lodge hadn't put a signpost on the road.

He had now driven into Kongola (another tiny, litter-strewn settlement) and had turned south along a gravel road to find their next lodge. It wasn't there. No sign and not even a promising unmarked sand-track. So Sandra, having discovered that she had a signal on her phone(!), used it to enquire of the lodge why it had moved from its promised location and to find out to where it had moved. Well, it appeared that it hadn't moved, but one could discover it only if one knew that it was approached via a sand-track signposted to another lodge on the other side of Kongola. Brian didn't quite understand the logic or indeed the sense of this, but he dutifully turned his vehicle around and retraced his tracks – to find the track they required. And so, after only a short delay, they were on this track, being led in by one of the lodge's vehicles, driven by a guy called Stephen, their guide for their stay.

After a tortuous fifteen-kilometre drive, Stephen stopped and indicated to Brian that he should park his vehicle under an awning, for they were now at that Kwando river, and there was now a boat ride to take. Yes, as with Nxameseri Lodge, Susuwe Lodge is built on an island. Although, unlike Nxameseri, this island is no more than a few breast-strokes from the landing stage on the shore, and therefore the boat ride took all of fifty seconds. This was not a bad thing. It was still early and, even after settling into their chalet, there would easily be time for a game drive before dinner.

The lodge was stunning. The main building was like a circular courtyard, framed by huge thatched constructions on one side, a stand of huge river-side trees on the other and a huge open-sided "tree-house" between the two. And as for Brian and Sandra's chalet... well, in addition to it being spacious in the extreme, it came with a generous outside deck – and a plunge pool. This they could manage, just as they could manage the news that they were the only guests in the lodge. Hardship indeed.

Anyway, it was now time for that game drive. Stephen invited them back onto his boat, and they were soon ensconced on his safari Land Rover and ready to roll, just as the sky appeared ready to provide some "weather". For it was no longer the standard-issue blue, but instead a very dark grey, and the grey was getting darker by the second. So, just after Brian had taken a photo of two hadada ibises sitting in a tree, it was no great surprise that a strong wind blew up out of nowhere and, as it continued to strengthen, it was accompanied by rain. And this rain was not normal rain that, however heavy, always has a degree of verticality in its path to the ground, but instead rain that was so horizontal that it risked missing the ground entirely. It didn't, however, miss the occupants of the open Land Rover. And despite Stephen's best efforts in rapidly distributing capes to his hapless passengers, Brian and Sandra (and Stephen himself) got remarkably wet within seconds. The wind was so strong now that cape deployment had become an exercise in the absurd and Brian was still struggling with his when the hailstones arrived!

Then it all disappeared – in an instant – and the only evidence of the storm's passing was the moistened vegetation, a crust of melting hailstones on the ground, and a white man in a Land Rover with, around his body, a dripping hooded cape – with the rear of the hood across his face. Sandra shook her head in disbelief. But Brian didn't see her. Nevertheless, when he'd unwrapped himself from the now redundant cape, he did see a few other things.

First there were elephants, lots and lots of elephants. Then there were antelopes – of all different sorts. And then there were even more elephants. Stephen had driven to a stretch of the Kwando River where it forms an enormous and simply exquisite horseshoe-shaped bend. And here there were dozens of these giant creatures going about their business. Just as there were dozens of baboons going about theirs – which was to see whether any of the nibbles served with Brian and Sandra's sundowner drink might have fallen unnoticed to the ground. Stephen reckoned there were more than two hundred baboons in this particular troop and this was far too many. Fights were now breaking out between its more senior members, and at some point in the near future the troop would fracture. Baboon society, he said, simply cannot function properly when the community has become too large. This piece of information stirred some thoughts in Brian's mind, first concerning the population of Britain, then that of the European Union, and then that of the whole world. But he kept these thoughts to himself. He had no desire to spoil such a wonderful sundowner in such a wonderful setting.

When he and Sandra were then returned to the lodge, any residual concerns about population growth were soon displaced in Brian's mind by the singular concern of extracting himself from his wet clothes. After this he was further distracted by the need to get from their chalet to the lodge's main building, for which purpose one needed an escort. This was to guard against the possibility of an unscheduled meeting with an elephant, in the same way that obligatory closed shoes were to guard against the attentions of scorpions and snakes. And it all worked. Soon, he and Sandra had made the transition to that part of the lodge with a bar, and were sitting with a drink in their hand and a host at their side. This was Eddy, the (Botswanan) lodge manager, who lost no time at all in informing them that he was new at this lodge, having just returned from a year in Florida working for Disneyland! He told them that he had been the only (black – or even white) Botswanan on the staff, and he'd met no visitors who needed his facility with Setswana, his native language. He also told them that he found it rather quieter back here in this Namibian lodge. And, of course, how could he not? Several hundred thousand punters versus two people waiting for their candlelit dinner, and with not a parade or a fireworks show within miles. However… for his two guests, it wasn't quite as clear cut as that. Because, unbeknownst to him, his Disneyland revelation had unleashed a thought process in Brian's mind that would, this evening, successfully disrupt the serenity and the other-worldliness of this Susuwe Lodge – by its casting a shadow over the forthcoming dinner. And this shadow would be in the form of (another) verbal assault by Brian on his wife, sparked by the revelation and involving, this time, the long-suffering Church of England…

His essential point was that with so much pulling power – and probably more "pilgrims" each year than even Mecca gets – Disneyland quite clearly represented a possible source of salvation for the Church of England. And this source could be tapped if only the Church of England authorities were able to engineer a tie-up with this popular institution, possibly through a reverse takeover, and thereby harness all that popularity for the revival of their own fortunes. Of course, it wouldn't be just a matter of joint branding and cross-over promotions, but real integration, and real integration through the inclusion of a few tempting C of E attractions within the amusement parks themselves. This is where that shadow over dinner was at its most intense – when Brian regaled his wife with his ideas for these new attractions…

'Yes, there'd have to be a "Hell and Heaven Experience", of course, and this would be modelled on one of those 3D shows they have. You know, in a specially kitted-out theatre, where all the punters sit in rows wearing 3D goggles, and then get subjected to all sorts of sensations as well as the 3D show itself… '

'Really,' discouraged a despondent Sandra.

'Yes. So in the hell half, you'd have scenes of hell in all its forms – with imps and trolls and things, all in 3D – and with lots of flames appearing to shoot out towards you, while, at the same time, your seat would get uncomfortably hot and your bum and legs would get pricked by miniature mechanical tridents – hidden within the seat's upholstery. And when you'd got through all that, it would be a 3D heaven, with dazzling angels and maybe some Disney cherubs – all delivered while the atmosphere of the theatre was being infused with a big dose of Prozac… '

'Really… ' continued Sandra.

'Yes,' responded a smiling Brian, 'although it wouldn't be a patch on "Schism Wars"… '

'Pardon!'

'Well, there'd have to be two actually. One for the traditionalists and one for the liberals.'

'I'm all ears.'

'Yes, well, for the traditionalists, you'd have these little individual car things – maybe for two traditionalists at a time –

and in the shape of an oversized dog collar... And the cars would be whisked off through a maze of theological obfuscation and religious pedantry – in which, at random intervals, would appear the images of scary women bishops. As these spectres revealed themselves, the cars' occupants would be challenged to use on-board (virtual) "shafts of biblical justification" to knock off their mitres – and thereby earn points... Whilst at the same time the church liberals would be being whisked off through another maze – of equivocal thinking and more equivocal thinking – in cars with no shape to them at all... And in this maze there would be, at random intervals, the images of scary un-reconstructed African bishops whose own mitres would have to be removed with a well-aimed virtual stream of reasoned enlightenment. And that's the way they'd earn points... '

'And what does one do with all one's points?' asked a now horrified-looking Sandra.

'Easy. Those participants with the top five scores each year would all be awarded a seat on the Church of England Synod. I mean, it would really give it an edge, wouldn't it? It would make it a real contest between the trads and the reformers – as well as it being bloody good fun... '

'Is that it?' enquired Sandra nervously. 'There aren't any more, are there?'

'Well, yes. There is another one. And it'd be called the "Mad Archbishop's Ride".'

'The Mad Archbishop's Ride?' echoed Sandra. And then she closed her eyes as though she barely wanted to know what this ride would entail. But it was to no avail. She got to discover what the ride would entail within seconds.

'Yes. Well, you see, you'd have a conventional rollercoaster ride where you get strapped into one of those rollercoaster carriages – but when it moved off, it would first of all move very slowly, to take you past a long billboard, full of a particular Archbishop's proclamations, together with extracts from his sermons and newspaper columns. And then, to fuddle your brain and disorientate you even further, the carriage would speed up to take you through a series of loops and rolls – only to slow to a virtual walking pace for the remaining 80% of the ride, to reinforce that sense of confusion beyond any doubt and to ensure that you went away from the ride with an enduring sense of disappointment…'

'You're mad,' pronounced Sandra. 'Completely mad. You need help. I mean some real therapy. And soon. As soon as we can arrange it.'

'What do you suggest?' asked her now grinning husband.

'Easy. A boat-ride in the morning. And then, later on, another game-drive. Albeit preferably one without hailstones…'

'Definitely one without hailstones,' agreed Brian. 'Although that does give me an idea for a new attraction, one involving all the plagues of Egypt. And just imagine what we could do with a plague of frogs and a plague of boils. And what about some animatronic locusts as well… ?'

8.

The boat-ride didn't happen. Neither did the game-drive. This was because of what had happened instead in the night – in the loo. In the morning, Brian was comprehensively indisposed and was obliged to spend the remainder of the day in bed.

Well, what a waste. And what a test of Brian's ability to occupy his mind between bouts of comatose drifting. It was just as well that he had his religious musings of the previous evening to feed off, because he was already feeling guilty about being quite so mean to the Church of England. Because, in his early innocent life, he'd been raised a Catholic…

Yes, it was time to apply his semi-conscious mind to this other Christian institution, and he did this by first imagining a discussion with the Pope, a discussion in which he asked the Holy Father about the role of the Devil. More specifically, he tried to conceive how this head honcho of the Catholic Church might explain how his Catholic god would respond to an honest request by the Devil that he be forgiven and be allowed permanently to mend his ways. In short, how would God react to a request by Satan to forsake his evil role entirely and to return to his earlier job as the heavenly Lucifer?

Well, Brian could easily surmise that this sort of question would be met at least initially with the response that such a request by the Devil would be highly improbable and, as such, it barely deserved an answer. Even if he pushed his demand for an answer, he would probably get no further than something completely anodyne along the lines that 'only God would know what to do'. But that would be wrong, because, although his recollection of Catholic doctrine was now rather vague, he did remember that redemption was one of its principal features, and that as God would have the power to look into the soul of Satan – and thereby discover his sincerity – he would have no other choice but to give him back his original job. For what greater redemption can there be than that of welcoming back into heaven the Devil himself?

Now, this would definitely have consequences, and these consequences were what Brian now considered. And the first of these, he believed, would be the Catholic Church's need to revise some of its iconography and probably its need to issue an addendum to the bible – as well as preparing itself for the inevitable collapse in the market for exorcisms. But it would go far beyond this. Because no longer would there be anybody there to lead its adherents into temptation and no need to deliver them from evil – as well as there being no eternal damnation to scare the pants off them. (After all, with its sole proprietor gone, hell would be out of business within hours.) And frankly, who, in his or her right mind, buys insurance to cover a risk that no longer exists? It would soon become apparent to the Vatican that the whole of Catholicism was facing nothing less than an overwhelming and unavoidable existential threat. Put simply, overnight, it would have become irrelevant and essentially redundant.

Brian could imagine it: a desperate attempt to redefine its role – by offering its parishioners a new service – or at least a newly emphasised existing service. And this would be to intercede on their behalf for the protection by a merciful god against the worst excesses of a wrathful god. But it wouldn't work, would it? One can't base a successful religion on the spiritual equivalent of Jekyll and Hyde, even if one can base it on some very questionable myths from the past. And that would be it. The Catholic Church would be on the scrap heap (along, it has to be admitted, with the Church of England as well).

There again… it might soon be discovered that many human beings still had that much advertised freedom of choice, and that with this freedom they didn't necessarily need Satan to lead them into temptation. They could do it very well on their own, and that by taking this path they could soon uncover the fact that the Devil hadn't got around to patenting evil. It was there for the taking by anyone who desired it. That is to say, that a whole host of the Catholic brethren might prove quite adept as self-starters; they could get up to all sorts of mischief even without the help of the Dark One. And then another problem for the Church (if it still existed at all). Like how would it dissuade these sinners from their reprehensible behaviour, now that it didn't have fear to control them and the ultimate fear of an eternity in hell? The best they could do would be to introduce a league system into heaven. This, they might claim, would see the pious and the most sickeningly good admitted into its Premier League, whereas the ordinarily good would rate a place in one of the lower leagues – right down to the rapists and murderers who would be obliged to occupy the paradisical equivalent of the Football Conference. And Mugabe, serial poachers and most terrorists would end up in a Football Conference team that was permanently teetering on the edge of administration…

No. It wouldn't work, would it? In fact, the more that Brian examined all the consequences of his theoretical conundrum posed to the Pope, the more he realised that they were all as completely terminal to the Church as they were fanciful. And he also realised just how important to Catholicism was the continued existence of the Devil… Indeed, he was more than important; he was vital. Take away Satan and the whole edifice of a "great religion" crumbles to the ground within no time at all. And what does that say about this religion or, for that matter, all other religions in this world? Like rotten dictatorships, they can often only survive by identifying some external (and entirely imaginary) threat. Remove that threat and they fall over, and their patrons begin to realise just how much they've been hoodwinked. Not that Brian was bracketing the Pope with people like Assad and all those frightful people in Iran – but there were similarities in their modus operandi. Indeed, in Iran, don't they actually refer to the USA as the "Great Satan"?

Anyway, by conducting such a mean-minded hatchet job on all those well-meaning Catholics, Brian at least felt he'd reinstated some sort of balance between the C of E and their more dedicated Roman counterparts – as well as partially distracting himself from his stomach-centred suffering. So that was some sort of success, even if, much later in the day, the acute discomfort in his abdomen was still there.

And as much as all the splendid guys at the lodge did to alleviate this suffering – and his wife's confinement in the chalet with him – they could do nothing to banish the gastric invasion by agents unknown. Brian just had to hope that these agents had withdrawn by the morrow, for then there was another drive to undertake – and another border to make their way through.

Yes, the next day was to be their first day in Zambia, and Brian desperately hoped that it wouldn't be his second day in purgatory (assuming, of course, that, along with hell, purgatory hadn't been shut down as well…).

9.

It was gone. Overnight, a battle had been fought between his body and those invading agents, and the agents had been vanquished – completely. Brian felt like a new man – and a decent breakfast. And, after he'd consumed this breakfast, he was ready for the road – and for Zambia.

Of course, before the road there was a river to cross and a sand-track to tackle. But soon these hurdles had been overcome and Brian and Sandra were once again back on the B8 and on their way to "Katima Mulilo". This is the last town in the Caprivi Strip before Namibia runs out and one finds oneself in Zambia. It is therefore very much a settlement "at the end of the road", a road, incidentally, which was now effectively without traffic and had for company only a few impoverished villages, a few bags of charcoal for sale at its side and a few wandering goats.

Brian thought this a bit odd. After all, there was an international border up ahead and, at this border, Namibia's only access point into Zambia, its north-eastern neighbour. So where was all that cross-border traffic, all those hordes of visitors to Zambia? Brian and Sandra couldn't be the only ones – could they?

The mystery continued in Katimo Mulilo itself, a really sleepy sort of place – with no indication that it was next to a major(?) border crossing and with little more traffic in it than they'd seen on the road. Nevertheless, there was a clear sign to the "Sesheke" border post at the only junction in the town, and having fuelled up with another load of diesel bullion, Brian headed off in the indicated direction, and within only a kilometre or so he arrived at the Namibian-side border post. Inside it the emigration procedures were tiresome but familiar, and the whole process took very little time. This was because the post was almost deserted. There were no other vehicles passing through and the only other customers were a handful of "foot passengers", who had come from and were going to God knows where. So after just a few minutes, Brian and his wife were crossing the border into Zambia and steeling themselves for the entry procedures on the other side (as they had been warned that these procedures could take a little time).

What they had not been warned about, however, was that at this crossing point, the Zambian border post is a little unconventional. And that really is the kindest possible term that can be applied to its character. Indeed, others might choose to describe it as a complete fucking disgrace. And in all honesty, this latter terminology is probably a great deal nearer the mark.

Brian was looking at the crossing now: a T-junction within fifty yards of the border, littered with ancient, overloaded lorries, abandoned cars, dilapidated shacks – and actual litter. And in this mêlée of dereliction and waste there was only one thing missing: a Zambian border post! It had to be here – somewhere. They wouldn't just have forgotten to build one. But where had they built it?

Brian drove forward and peered around. There was really nothing that looked anything like an official construction. And as there appeared to be just a line of more of those overloaded trucks to the right of the T-junction, he turned left here, and peered once again. And there it was – possibly. It was a battered chain-link fence overgrown with creeper, and just visible behind it was a small building. Brian decided to drive in through the gate. Or rather he decided to drive in through an opening in the chain-link fence where there was a sign covered in fading and now illegible writing – because he was convinced that this just had to be the place.

He was right. As soon as he stepped from the Land Cruiser, he was assailed (eagerly but politely) by three youths clutching bundles of Zambian "kwacha" and offering him a market-beating rate of exchange. This currency is effectively unavailable outside Zambia, and hence these "kwacha touts". But more significantly for Brian, their presence confirmed that this really was the border post, because border procedures within it called for a number of payments to be made. And these chaps were here to provide the currency for these payments, notwithstanding the fact that the authorities accepted foreign currency directly, and consequently the tens of thousands of kwacha being proffered to Brian could safely be ignored. He therefore declined their proposed deals as politely as he could and, with Sandra, made his way into what he was now confident was Zambia's Sesheke border post.

Inside, it was like a film set, where the set has been built to represent the interior of some run-down, third-world border post – complete with a framed faded photo of the president taken the day after he'd become president more than twenty years before, and a trio of slightly sweaty border officials sitting beneath it – behind a counter. It even had a cast of extras, a row of locals sitting against a facing wall and not apparently involved in any border-type activities, and four more of them not queuing at the counter where it appeared that all the real business of the post was conducted.

Brian and Sandra approached the counter and, before they had an opportunity to queue or not to queue, they were directed to complete a couple of immigration forms and Brian was instructed to fill in a book. This was quite encouraging – and relatively straightforward – as the book was just the normal vehicle details register and the immigration forms were fairly standard – and quite legible. However, this was just the start of a process that would now take rather a long time…

The opening minutes of this marathon were spent explaining to one of the officials, who was the passport supremo, that his two new customers had already purchased their Zambian visas back in England, and if he inspected the two passports now in his possession he would find them. (And he might even discover their exorbitant cost.) When this issue had been resolved, there was then a debate as to when they might get their passports back, as Brian and Sandra were now being beckoned to a back room – to purchase their "carbon tax voucher". They were assured (more or less) that their passports would be returned to them when their other business was done. And they therefore made their way down a dark corridor to the office as directed – and just kept their fingers crossed as tightly as they could.

On the way to the office, it became apparent that they were in a building that would have heaved a sigh of relief to have been described as just ramshackle and not as "disgustingly shambolic". Inside the office itself, this less-than-salubrious ambiance was maintained – if not reinforced. For here, as well as a patched ceiling and a worn floor, there was a little gang of desks arranged in such a way that the single occupant of the office who sat behind them had about 90% of the floor space, leaving only 10% for his guests, or approximately one square yard (when the door was closed). From here, his guests could marvel at the disorder on display on each of his desks and at a shelf on the wall behind him, full of lever-arch files and leaning inwards at such an angle that it was only a matter of time before the files were no longer on it.

Brian was given a form to fill in. It required all the information he had already written in that book on the counter – and then some more. Fortunately, when he had been provided with the Land Cruiser, he had also been provided with all the information concerning the vehicle that he would ever need, except, as he now discovered, its insurance details and, in particular, the name of the insurance company and the policy number. Well, he wasn't going to admit to that, and instead he found the name of a Namibian roadside assistance company and recorded this as the insurance company – and its telephone number as the policy number. The official was already distracted with some other paperwork, and Brian was filling in the form on the top of his printer (there was no other space). He therefore could not be observed even if the official became un-distracted. And anyway, Brian reckoned that his form would soon be in one of those lever-arch files on that shelf, in which case, it would soon become untraceable as it joined the avalanche of all the other forms when gravity finally won out over optimism and the shelf parted company with its files. So business done – at a cost of two-hundred and fifty Namibian dollars (which is equivalent to as many Zambian kwacha as you might like to imagine).

Brian now took his wife back to the counter, where they were immediately escorted out of the building, past a midden of discarded bottles and cans – towards a caravan… .

Now, these days, the term "caravan" can far too easily convey the image of some huge, sleek, finely-finished and fully-equipped "carriage of the road", in which one can spend not just a weekend but, if one so wished, the remainder of one's life. But this caravan did not accord with that image. Not one little bit. Instead, it was small, if not tiny; it was not sleek but more the rather humpy shape of a traditional 1950s caravan (because that's probably what it was); it was not finely-finished but just plain "finished", and it was fully-equipped only with the twin features of irreversible dilapidation and serious decay.

Brian and Sandra stepped inside this novel office and the first thing Brian noticed was the ground beneath it (through the gaps in its floor), and then he noticed that in its former life it had slept just one person (that was half a person on one bunk and the other half on the other). Either that or it had been made for hobbits… It certainly hadn't been made for a perspiring, six-foot two Englishman, who now had to hunch over as he filled in another bloody form (for road insurance?) whilst, at the same time, trying not to peer down the cleavage of a lady who was wearing a very revealing dress, not normally found within the confines of a border post. She was the dispenser of the road insurance (?) document, for which Brian, still hunching, had to pay over rather more South African rand than he thought reasonable – for what was, after all, no more than a scrappy bit of paper that would only be of any use to him for the mere three days he would spend in the country. In fact, the five-hundred and forty rand he paid for this (say £50) made the fifty rand he then had to pay for another piece of paper seem like a really good deal. This one was issued by the lady's diminutive male assistant and was three inches square, yellow and, as to its purpose, something of a mystery. And there was now only one more piece of paper to secure.

This was obtained from a gentleman in a freight container on the other side of the midden. Someone had taken a metal-cutter to one of the sides of this container and had carved out a long "window". This window was also a counter, for at its bottom was a rough wooden shelf, on which there were more forms. By completing one of these, filling in another book with one's vehicle details – and handing over US$40 to the gentleman within – one could acquire, this time, a transport tax (?) document (another scrappy bit of paper), and then one was able finally (and thankfully) to redeem one's passport and the passport of one's wife – and sod off. Yes, the passports were still there, in the conventionally built part of the border post, and Brian and Sandra were now free to depart.

However, it had not only taken them an hour to win this freedom, but they had also had to pay a heavy price for it. For with a carbon tax charge, a road insurance levy(?), a transport tax(?) and a fee for a square of yellow paper, they had parted with the equivalent of over £110. And who knew what exchange rates had been "chosen" in arriving at all these multi-denominational charges – and where that money went. For sure as hell, it didn't go on maintaining the border post or, almost certainly, on overpaying its cast of officials. Nor did it go into streamlining the border procedures applied to all those overloaded lorries around the place (which could apparently spend up to three weeks getting across the border). But on the plus side, Brian and Sandra both now understood why there had been so little traffic on the way to the border in Namibia and why they had been the only motorists being processed in the border post for the whole of their time there. Yes, one had to be mad to take a vehicle into Zambia, especially for just a few days. And one had to be a raving lunatic to take it in through this Sesheke border post where, despite the amiable nature of its staff, it was a shambles and a rip-off and, one could legitimately say, a complete fucking disgrace.

The road to Livingstone wasn't quite so bad. But it wasn't perfect. For, to start with, after a mile or so, it passes through the town of Sesheke, which might best be described as looking better the further from it one is when one's looking. And then there was the road itself, and here the problem was that the tarmac from which it was made had rather too many edges. Yes, as well as the edges to the tarmac at its sides, there were quite a few edges to the tarmac around the holes within it. And there really were more holes in the road's surface than there were in an Ed Balls economic argument – albeit, unlike any of those that he's ever made, this Zambian road did at least lead somewhere… Anyway, it was probably the frequency and depth of these potholes that explained the leisurely progress of all other road users. That is to say, the ten kilometres per hour that was being managed by the handful of taxis that were encountered on the way, all of which looked capable of at least twenty kilometres per hour if not slightly more, and all of which were painted in a hideous shade of blue. Brian had never before seen the "bright pale" tone of this colour, other than on seaside buckets and spades and on toddlers' building bricks. But now it was on all of these official taxis, and could only have been chosen as a deterrent against theft; for who in their right mind would have wanted to steal one of these – other than the colour blind and possibly the odd children's entertainer?

Well, other than these slow-moving eyesores – and a couple of bullock carts and the potholes – Brian and Sandra could still have been in Namibia. The two hundred kilometres of road to their destination passed through a similar landscape to that of

Caprivi. But then Livingstone appeared before them and all was about to change…

Quite clearly, Livingstone was a sizable town. It was easily the biggest conurbation they had encountered since leaving Windhoek, and it even had road junctions with traffic lights. It also had its own ambiance, a special blend of obvious prosperity and rampant neglect, so typical of many other African settlements that have, within their bailiwick, a world-famous destination. And destinations don't come much more world-famous than the Victoria Falls. On the subject of which… Brian and Sandra now had to seek out their accommodation at the Falls, for which purpose they employed a hand-held GPS (the Land Cruiser's own having abandoned them at the border).

It was useless. In fact, it was worse than useless. It instructed them to turn left – repeatedly. It directed them around a roundabout – and then back around it. And it informed them with increasing frequency that it was 'recomputing, recomputing'. Brian would have done better with a magnetised dildo. And in the end, he did quite well enough with his own sense of direction. Having switched off the stupid damn machine, he just drove out of town to where he thought the Falls might be, and therefore to where their hotel might be. And there it was: a smart set of gates and a sign to the "Zambezi Sun Hotel". They had found their accommodation.

It wasn't a lodge – obviously. It was an enormous "resort hotel", complete with faux African architecture and a group of faux African dancers outside reception. But that is to be more than a little jaundiced. For this was also a hostelry that offered air-conditioned comfort, a manicured setting, complete security, entertainment in the shape of its other guests (or should that be "in the shape of the shape of its other guests"?), and a situation that was within walking distance of the Victoria Falls.

Well, the Falls would have to wait. There was a lunchtime visit to the bar to attend to first. After all, it had been a very long and very demanding morning, and liquid refreshment was now a priority. So very soon, Brian and his wife were ensconced in the pool-side restaurant-cum-bar, with drinks in their hands – and bemusement in their minds. This bemusement was as a result of those other guests – already. Yes, first in their capacity to make a loaded plate of comestibles disappear faster than even David Blaine could have done, and then in their unwillingness to conceal the long-term results of their dietary habits. And there was one chap in particular, wading around in the shallow zone of the pool, who could clearly not see the absurdity of combining a posing pouch with an imposing paunch. Or there again, maybe it was Brian and Sandra who were being absurd. He wasn't harming anyone, and in a way he was being very courageous. After all, Brian would never have dared to entrust such an important part of his anatomy to such an insubstantial piece of fabric, no matter how big his stomach. So you had to give the bloke credit for that. Just as you had to give credit to Sandra for agreeing to Brian's suggestion…

It was now early afternoon and hotter than hell at its hottest. So Brian's proposal that they take a stroll to the Falls was not only foolhardy but also unlikely to be met with Sandra's agreement. But she did agree. Not least because Brian had assumed that the stroll in question would be a short one and had presented this assumption as fact. They would not be out for long, and, after their quick visit, they could soon be back in their air-conditioned haven of a room. It would take no more than minutes.

In the event, it didn't. Albeit that the number of minutes actually taken was a shade above that anticipated – by a factor of about ten. The Zambezi Sun Hotel is adjacent to the Victoria Falls, but not intimately adjacent – more geographically adjacent. As such, there is a long walk to the Falls – if one wishes to observe them from the prime lookout. And this walk is not without its ups and downs, not just in Brian and Sandra's relationship as they undertook it, but also in its physical nature. And a flight of steps, where the top of the flight is not visible from its bottom, is really not what one wants to encounter on such a roasting afternoon.

So… the Victoria Falls would be a memorable experience for both our travellers, even though foremost in their memories might not be the torrent of water at the Falls themselves, but instead the torrent of perspiration that accompanied their visit there. The Falls are a spectacle, but at the same time, a spectacle-challenge, as, every few yards, Brian had been obliged to wipe his eyepieces before stumbling on. And if this description of a privileged witnessing of one of the marvels of nature betrays a certain sense of churlishness if not downright joylessness on the part of the witnesses, then it must be borne in mind that these particular witnesses were both aspiring to becoming full-blown curmudgeons as their twilight years approached. Such an ambition would, of course, hardly make them unique, and in no way would it prevent them still finding enjoyment and entertainment in a genuinely fulfilling experience. Like, for example, when they learnt later that same afternoon that somebody had shot Colonel Gaddafi…

It was on the telly in their room, an account of how some Libyan patriots, on finding their national monster, had decided immediately that meting out prompt natural justice was far more important than creating jobs-for-life for a gang of overpaid lawyers in some overseas international court. Especially when that same court would provide a platform for the rantings of said monster for many years to come, to say nothing of a comfortable no-cost-to-him lifestyle for the rest of his life. So… well done, the patriots.

Well done also to whoever had prepared the evening's buffet in the restaurant. It was quite a spread. Even if it didn't include that classic Zambian dish known as "Sesheke Pudding". This is a dessert that has a base made of layers of paper, a filling of interminable and irritating bureaucracy, a crust of time-consuming procedures – and is normally served up in a crumbling and ramshackle container. And despite its total lack of appeal, it is an extremely costly concoction for all those who are obliged to taste it, and it should be avoided if at all possible. Especially by those who are travelling with a vehicle and who might just be harbouring some curmudgeonly aspirations…

10.

Brian thought it might be a little cooler in the morning. It wasn't particularly, but he and Sandra had come to Livingstone to see the Victoria Falls, and they couldn't let their exhausting excursion of the previous day put them off entirely. So, directly after breakfast, they set off again, this time with more resolve and now a clearer understanding of what was in store.

Well, perhaps it was this clearer understanding that caused the resolve to shrivel so rapidly… However, they still managed another inspection of this great marvel of nature before the resolve disappeared entirely, and they even managed to accommodate an extended stay at a lookout. Because, from this shaded observation point, they could see the Victoria Falls Bridge, and so confirm their long-held belief that bungee-jumping made about as much sense as granite-chewing or carrot-spinning. Only, of course, with granite-chewing and carrot-spinning, one didn't risk one's life in the process.

Nevertheless, there was no shortage of punters for the more dangerous and clearly demented diversion on offer here. And, as they peered at the bridge, one after another of these ill-advised idiots launched themselves off it, relying, for their continued integrity, on a length of what they normally used just to hold up their drawers. And OK, it was probably a darn sight thicker and a darn sight stronger than most knicker-elastic, but these leapers were a whole lot heavier and a great deal more susceptible to multiple fractures than most knickers. And who hasn't experienced that alarming phenomenon known as "the elastic's gone"? Easy to deal with when it's only a pair of drawers in peril, but not so easy – or indeed in any way feasible – when it's one's life in the balance.

However, thought Brian, if there really were so many people prepared to jump off bridges and indeed to pay for the "privilege" of doing so, why hasn't someone made a serious attempt to find some rather more worthwhile outlets for their madcap inclinations? Hell, we're still using crash dummies, for example. And if these guys are prepared to lay out good cash for a short-lived (largely) predictable vault into space, think what they'd pay for a high-speed collision with a wall, and a collision where they'd keep their no-claims… Or how about mine clearance? Not in the conventional way – obviously. But through some sort of competitive challenge – involving horseshoe throwing, say, with, of course, the compulsory retrieval by hand of all those horseshoes that failed to hit a mine. And if that didn't provide the necessary degree of "buzz", these irrepressible danger-seekers could always be encouraged to become cartoonists, and then to be very careless in what they chose to lampoon. And then the thrill wouldn't last for just a few seconds but probably for a whole bloody lifetime.

But maybe not. Maybe, thought Brian, one cannot equate dread with excitement. And at least with bungee-jumping, nobody can take offence. In fact, quite the reverse. Because those observing it rather than participating in it can find it very entertaining indeed. So much so that there was now a group of visitors sharing Brian and Sandra's lookout spot and enjoying the antics on display. Some of them were also enjoying the spectacle of the bridge itself, a formidable arch of metal that has now spanned the gorge here for over a hundred years. And amongst those focusing on the engineering rather than the insanity were a handful of Americans and their guide. Brian couldn't help overhearing them – and their guide's lecture on the bridge's construction, which included a snippet on its celebrated designer, George Andrew Hobson, who had conceived this remarkable feat of engineering whilst working for a British firm of consulting engineers known as Sir Douglas Fox and Partners. The snippet contained not only the name of the designer and the identity of his employer, but also the fact that this clever Mr Hobson had been assisted by another chap by the name of Mr Ralph Freeman, who, twenty-five years later, went on to design, all on his own, the world-famous Sydney Harbour Bridge.

All very interesting, thought Brian. But possibly not quite as interesting as learning that the Sydney bridge wasn't quite as world-famous as he'd previously thought. For when the guide had mentioned this Antipodean connection, the question from one of his American clients that followed was: 'Where is the Sydney Harbour Bridge?' As the guide then replied in a deadpan voice with the single word 'Australia', Brian wondered whether he wouldn't have done better to have chosen instead the single word 'Sydney'. But he also wondered what was going on here. For the questioner was a normal-looking guy, probably in his forties, who was sufficiently acquainted with the world to find his way to Zambia, but who had not heard of the Sydney Harbour Bridge. And come to think of it, the fact that he was standing here looking at the Zambezi River didn't necessarily prove he knew where Zambia was. Perhaps he thought he was in South America – or in Australia – but just not in Sydney.

It reminded Brian of a guide he and Sandra had met in Costa Rica who had lost count of the number of Americans who had asked him what it was like to live on an island – under the mistaken impression that they were in Puerto Rica, or in the belief that all places in the world ending in the word "Rica" had to be islands. And then there was that Californian woman in Brazil who had been shocked to discover that parrots fly, because 'Back in America, all ours just sit on a perch. Or if they're feeling really adventurous, then maybe on a pirate's shoulder'.

Now, Brian believed that the United States of America, for all its many failings, was one of the truly great countries in this world. In its relatively short life, it has produced, through its citizens, some of the best music that has ever been heard on this planet, some of the most outstanding literature in the history of mankind and a wealth of movie-masterpieces that will probably never be equalled. Others in this nation have assembled between them a huge stock of Nobel Prizes, others have been responsible for countless discoveries in every field of science, and yet more have moulded these discoveries into world-beating technologies in every discipline imaginable. Whether it's space exploration, information technology, communication technology in all its forms – or sophisticated weaponry – the United States now leads the world, and has done for many years. Yes, on any measure one adopts in the field of human endeavour and human achievement, America leads the pack. It is nothing less than a goldmine, a rich store of ability and ingenuity that will never be exhausted. However… within this goldmine, there are some serious geological faults. For running through it there are seams of adamantine-hard ignorance, intrusions of acute dumbness that are virtually impermeable to knowledge in all its forms and, in particular, to any knowledge about the world.

Yes, Brian knew there was no denying it. Within that infinite wealth of American talent, there are a significant number of that country's population who know as much about the planet outside their country as he knew about the practicalities of gynaecology. And in a way this is hardly surprising. For if one lives in an enormous country and one is saddled with a work ethic that makes it difficult to travel beyond its borders, one may easily begin to settle for just what's within those borders and pretty well give up on anything else. And this isn't just sophistry. How, for example, could you explore Papua New Guinea if you lived in Iowa and had, as a boss, someone who thought anything more than a seven-day vacation was a sign of latent communism? Hell, by the time you'd got yourself there it would be time to come back.

Now, whether this was the full story, Brian had to concede, was open to question. After all, many Americans were still able to develop an interest in world geography – and world events – despite their being stranded on a huge landmass and being saddled with some rather odd attitudes to holidays. So, for those who made up those resistant seams of rock in the goldmine, perhaps it was something more, something to do with an inbuilt indifference to the wider world – rooted in a simple lack of confidence. Stick with what you know. Embrace the familiar. Embrace America. And not only don't travel outside it, but don't even give what's outside it any thought at all, let alone learn about it. And if you do have the misfortune to find yourself beyond its boundaries – in let's say a place like Zambia – don't, under any circumstances, step outside that American bubble. Pretend you're still there. Take pride in your patriotic isolationism as you do at home – and in your patriotic ignorance – even if it means that some supercilious Brit overhearing you will steam into superior mode, and (despite being in a bubble of his own) get all philosophical within seconds. It's just his hard luck. 'And don't these Brits know that they're all washed up? Shit… who the hell cares what they think anyway?'

Oh dear. Brian's own lack of confidence was now surfacing. Possibly it was time to moderate his opinions. Yes, maybe he was being a little hard on America. After all, it was indisputable that every country in the world has its own share of dummies and drongos, people for whom enquiry and curiosity are anathema, but not in every country was this "battalion of the ignorant" so blatantly obvious. And it is so blatantly obvious in America because this is a country that is endowed with so many capabilities and achievements as already revealed. So it's the contrast. Like white against a black background, the unenlightened minority stand out against a sea of the erudite and the informed – in precisely the same way as they don't in many other countries, because in these countries the erudite and the informed are nowhere to be seen…

Oh god, here he was still looking at bungee-jumpers, and Brian had managed to let a casual remark by an American tourist lead him into another mope about all those countries in the world where ignorance is a way of life, where medieval values are sewn into the fabric of their culture, where enlightenment is a word that can't be translated into their native tongue, and where you would be bloody surprised if you met anyone who *did* know the whereabouts of the Sydney Harbour Bridge. But he couldn't help himself. It was just the way he was, especially when he was becoming concerned about the onset of dehydration and the consequent urgency of administering to his person a couple of glasses of hydrating Windhoek Lager. Sandra, it transpired, had the same concerns, and it wasn't until she vocalised them that Brian abandoned his reflection on the intellectually moribund of the world and instead considered further his rather too severe judgement of the American psyche. And he did this on the way to the bar.

Well, today there was a gratifying absence of posing pouches, but still rather too much pneumatic flesh on display to encourage Brian and Sandra to linger very long. Instead, they would make use of the hotel's other facilities and, in particular, its air-conditioned rooms and its satellite TV. Yes, they would retreat from the furnace heat of the exterior to the cooled comfort of their bedroom interior, and first of all take advantage of the coolness… and after that they would switch on the telly.

Initially, this switching-on decision proved inspired, as they just managed to catch the end of the final of the Rugby World Cup, which resulted in an almost deserved victory for New Zealand – and a lot of very dejected French guys (none of whom, apparently, had participated in dwarf-throwing contests on their way to the final). However, after this fragment of sporting spectacle, Brian could find only news channels to fill the screen. And after two weeks away from any news, it was all as predictable and as depressing as usual. Serbia was still being obnoxious to the Kosovans, public workers were still on strike in Spain, everybody was still on strike in Greece – and the latest octogenarian successor to the Saudi throne had renounced his claim to the throne, on account of his being indisposed as a result of his not being alive. He had apparently keeled over within grabbing distance of kingship, even though he was still in the prime of his twilight…

This got Brian thinking again. And this time he didn't keep his thoughts to himself. Instead he assailed Sandra.

'They're all mad,' he started. 'And even if they weren't mad to start with, they very soon become mad.'

'Who's that?' responded Sandra. 'Lighthouse-keepers?'

'Lighthouse-keepers!' shrieked Brian. 'Lighthouse-keepers? No... of course not lighthouse-keepers. I mean, they don't even have them anymore. No. I'm talking about the people who run the world...'

'I think you mean that you are *about* to talk about the people who run the world. Or am I mistaken?'

Sandra followed this question with a pointed squint of one eye – and Brian followed this with a resolve not to be deterred. He *was* going to talk about the people who ran the world and his wife would listen. She had to. It was part of their unwritten pact. He did the heavy gardening, the bins, the money stuff and the tax returns; Sandra did the cooking, the cleaning, the light gardening, ordering the fuel – and listening. And anyway, what he had to say was worth listening to. It always was.

So Brian barely hesitated before carrying on. And he carried on first with an answer to Sandra's question.

'No, you are not mistaken. I am indeed going to make just a few observations...'

'Promise?' interrupted Sandra. 'Just a few?'

But now she was smiling, and Brian could see that she was really quite interested in what he had to say. So he carried on again...

'Well...' he said, in a Robert Peston sort of way, 'you see, you only have to look at some of their weirdo behaviour...'

'Such as?' encouraged a still-smiling Sandra.

'Such as dyeing their hair. It's what all those Chinese geezers do. And what sort of behaviour is that – for people running a third of the world's population? It's bonkers. It's like having a politburo full of Silvio Berlusconis – only without the grins and the whores… And then there's all these Saudi princes who, apart from all looking identical, all have the same appalling taste in armchairs. All that gilt and carving and all those terrible fabrics. I mean, it's not normal, is it? And they all have those trimmed beards as well. Not the chairs, the princes. It's as though they've not got minds of their own… '

'It doesn't mean they're bonkers,' suggested Sandra. 'I mean, have you ever looked at all the young women in Britain. They've all got straight hair. And they're not mad. Well, not all of them… '

'OK, how about bad haircuts and boiler suits… ?'

'You mean that guy in North Korea?'

'Yes.'

'Well, he is mad, isn't he? Everybody knows that.'

'And forgetting how to shave?'

'Well. He's mad as well. Anybody who claims that there are no gays in Iran has got to be completely round the bend.'

'And thinking you're Napoleon?'

'You mean Sarkozy?'

'Yes.'

'Well, he is very small.'

'OK. But how about believing that people will mistake a KGB mafia for a government if its head-honcho is filmed bare-chested on a horse – or sitting at the end of a long table berating some of his stooges for the latest mafia cock-up… ?'

'Ummm… '

'Yes, they mount up,' announced Brian triumphantly. 'And then add to these real weirdoes all those bleedin' idiots who have run Europe into the ground, all those despots in Africa and Central Asia, and all those feudal lords and villains in the

Indian sub-continent – most of whom probably think they're doing an absolutely sterling job – and you can easily see why I think that they're all completely loony. All completely bonkers. Or if not out and out bonkers, then so bloody deluded, it really doesn't make any difference. And it's the whole world. No wonder we're in such a mess…'

At this point, Brian hesitated in his polemic. He was looking for a response from his wife. But when it didn't come, he continued. But what he said was a bit half-hearted. He now knew that Sandra remained unconvinced.

'Well, I just think it's a reflection of the human condition. As a species, we are just incapable of running ourselves as a society on any scale. And when you've scaled things up to the size of a country, it's completely hopeless, and you end up with a load of nutters in charge – who, when they're not erecting bloody great posters of themselves all over the place, are buggering up people's lives – and buying oversized baroque furniture…'

Sandra smiled and her smile turned into a grin. Then she spoke.

'You forgot Gordon Brown.'

This had the clearly desired effect. Brian laughed out loud, he abandoned his appraisal of the sanity or otherwise of international leaders, and he suggested that instead they prepare themselves for an early drink and an early dinner. After all, they faced another bout of driving in the morning.

So, soon they were back in the bar, and soon after this they were partaking of another buffet dinner. It was very enjoyable, but not quite as enjoyable as the Asian fiddler who appeared on this eve. And no, this wasn't a new breed of giant crab, hell-bent on displacing Britain's own domestic varieties, but a Chinese-looking lady who, with her violin, had been hired to entertain the hotel's guests from its pool-side stage. She was brilliant – and Brian thought it unlikely that she dyed her hair.

When back in his room, he then had another thought, not about hair-dyeing but about bungee-jumping and a madness index. For he reckoned that if one constructed an "insanity gauge", calibrated from one to ten – where ten was "as mad as was conceivable" and one was… well, somebody like himself – then one could soon arrive at an inescapable conclusion. And the first element of this conclusion was that, with characters like Mugabe, Kim Jong-un, Ahmadinejad and Chavez around, all of whom merited a ten – and with seven-plus scores for most of the other guys in power – the mean madness for all the world's leaders must be well over eight. And the second element of the conclusion was that, no matter how hard one tried, it would be difficult to argue that the mean for all bungee-jumpers was much over seven. Which meant… that the final element of the conclusion was that the world would be a measurably better place if it were run by a cadre of thrill-seekers, if every country had, as its leading elite, a bunch of people who threw themselves off bridges. Hell, this was worthy of an academic paper. One could discuss one's reasoning at length, one could construct some elaborate models to underpin one's case, and one could even explore some of the self-evident advantages of this new breed of rulers. Like, for example, their obvious ability to bring a new perspective to politics – by hanging upside down. Or how about the ease of dispensing with their services when they were getting things wrong? (One would need only a large pair of scissors.)

Yes, Brian was sure he was on to something here. And had it not been for a sudden onset of sleep and a tendency to forget immediately any project that might involve more than a token effort, he might well have pursued his idea. And he might even have found a way to include in his work his concerns about American parochialism – and his views on how its stubborn durability might finally be overcome – by installing in that famous Oval Office, a world-savvy bungee-jumper...

11.

Shortly after breakfast, Brian had in his pocket more than a third of a million kwacha. He had not won the Zambian National Lottery, but instead had bought this small fortune at the hotel's on-site bank – for the express purpose of topping up the Land Cruiser's fuel tank for the forthcoming journey. He reckoned that the 350,000 kwacha he had acquired would be more than enough for the half-tank's worth he needed, as this considerable quantity of the local lucre had cost him all of forty pounds.

All these noughts in his pocket made him think. Because he had now calculated that one kwacha was equivalent to no more than about one hundredth of a British penny. And why would any country want to operate with a national currency, one unit of which was effectively worthless? For, after all, there was no way that a single kwacha would buy you anything whatsoever in Zambia – other than possibly a couple of Frankie Boyle DVDs. And not only was there this "worthless" taint to the local currency, but there was also its potential impact on Zambian society. How would it manifest itself in everyday life here? So, for example, was there a chain of cheapo shops in Zambia known as "Ten-thousand-kwacha-land" or, when you went to the loo here, did you announce that you were off 'to spend a hundred'? And if you had to get by on just a million a year, were you classed as being below the poverty line – and as one of the country's near-destitute millionaires? Well, Brian had no answers to these questions, but he did believe that the Zambians would be a whole lot happier if they had a currency that bore at least some relation to those of their neighbours in Botswana and Namibia and that didn't put all their visitors in mind of the Weimar Republic. And, apart from anything else, it would make primary school maths lessons a great deal more relevant. For what must all those young Zambians think when they were obliged to learn their two to ten times tables, when within them the biggest figure that they'd ever encounter had just a trifling two noughts. It could hardly prepare them for the multiplicity of noughts that they'd soon have to deal with.

Nevertheless, the not-quite-so-young Zambian at the service station appeared to deal with them pretty well, and soon Brian was fiddling with his remaining bank notes, trying not to give the guy a tip that would double his pay for the day. And soon after this, he was ready for the off, ready to leave Livingstone and ready to commence the next leg of his loop. Albeit not entirely ready to engage with the Zambian authorities – and twice in fairly rapid succession.

The first of these engagements was within a few hundred metres of the service station. Here, on some football pitches to the side of the road, was some sort of mass gathering of the local Livingstonians. And whilst Brian had no idea as to the purpose of this gathering, he had a very good idea of the problem it posed for his progress. Because on the road itself there was now a very lengthy ad hoc linear car-park, and this was completely blocking his out-of-Livingstone lane of the road. No traffic could pass it, and the only traffic that was moving anywhere was that which was streaming towards him in the other lane in an unbroken procession. He was stuck, along with all the other traffic heading out of Livingstone, and there looked to be no end in sight to their predicament. Even the presence of a chap up ahead who looked like a car-park attendant didn't hold out much hope. He seemed to have some responsibility for traffic control. But, whilst he may have been discharging this responsibility with both diligence and energy, its actual controlling-of-the-traffic component wasn't working well at all. He seemed to have no understanding of the necessity of attending to the needs of traffic in both directions, or, alternatively, he was completely oblivious to the existence of Brian and his co-non-movers. The result was inevitable. The driver of the first vehicle in the obstructed queue (a taxi) pushed the nose of his vehicle into the centre of the road, and then just kept on pushing it. This had the desired effect. The oncoming vehicles didn't stop, but they pulled over, just far enough to allow the taxi driver to squeeze forward between them and the line of parked vehicles. And this was the signal. Almost immediately, the driver of the second car in the stationary queue followed him, and behind him came all the other frustrated drivers.

Now, the driver of this second vehicle was Brian. And as his vehicle was noticeably larger than the taxi in front, its navigation between parked and moving vehicles was something of a challenge, especially as Brian was intent on keeping up with the taxi and following its every move. However, he rose to the challenge and was even able to lurch through a gap in the oncoming traffic – just like the taxi had done – when the opportunity arose. And he would then have followed the taxi down a dirt-track on the opposite side of the road, had not the car-park attendant – who had now metamorphosed into a Zambian police officer – commanded him to stop and then pull off the road.

What followed led Brian to believe that the officer in question was suffering from a lot of stress. He had within him a tangle of angst, brought on, no doubt, by his honest intellectual appraisal of his own shortcomings. Quite simply, he knew that when it came to effective traffic control, he was absolute shit. And now he simply had to externalise this trauma – in the only way he knew how. Yes, by picking on some foreign sap with too big a car and giving him a severe verbal battering, he would secure some much-needed relief. And the fact that the idiot being battered would also be aware that the leading taxi had gone through unhindered by police intervention, and that all the other cars which had recently been behind him were now being similarly ignored, would make the tongue lashing that much sweeter – and accelerate the process of anxiety mitigation really quite significantly.

It was done. The policeman had been predictably aggressive and Brian had been suitably supine, and he was now able to proceed. Not down the road – as this was still blocked – but down that dirt-track which had been used by all the other vehicles and which ran past a cemetery. It was now completely clear, save for the odd overhanging branch and the odd perambulating pedestrian. But Brian managed to avoid all these impediments to his progress and finally rejoined the metalled road on the outskirts of Livingstone. Here he made two resolutions. One was not to return to this town and the other was not to be quite so embarrassingly supine in a similar confrontation with a representative of authority in the future. Little did he know that he would be putting this second resolution to the test within only a very few minutes…

It was a road block a mile or so out of Livingstone on the road to Sesheke, and it was manned not by a policeman but by a man with a clip-board. Brian's heart sank. This might not be a guy with the power of arrest, but when, if ever, do men with clip-boards provide an experience that is even marginally edifying and not instead just downright depressing?

He pulled the car to a halt and wound down his window. The man approached and looked at the vehicle. He was clearly taking in not just its foreign registration but also its size and, on his salary, its infinite un-affordability. Brian feared the worst. The man then spoke, not to identify himself or the ministry for which he worked, but to demand a document. Brian had no idea which of his collection he should proffer, so he proffered the lot. And from this bundle, Mr Clip-board selected the small one, the four-inch square of yellow paper that had cost next to nothing. Good. He could inspect it and Brian and Sandra could then be on their way. But no. There was a problem. Brian could see it in the man's face. And then the man spoke.

'This is not from Kasane. You need it from Kasane.'

Now, Kasane is the site of another border post, just down the road, where one can exit Zambia directly into Botswana across the Chobe River. This exit point, according to popular and reliable myth, is actually worse than the one at Sesheke, as not only does it have Sesheke-standard facilities, but it also has an unavoidable ferry. This is a vessel that is designed to float on water, but for which there is no absolute guarantee that this primary design objective will always be achieved, and that instead it might not sink, overturn, split in two or be swept downstream. Understandably, therefore, Sesheke, despite all its dismal credentials, had been chosen in preference, and Kasane avoided. But here was this clip-board idiot demanding one of its own squares of yellow paper…

'We came through Sesheke,' started Brian. 'And that's where we're going to now.'

'You need a Kasane voucher,' parried his antagonist. 'From Kasane.'

Brian was building up pressure.

'How could we have got a Kasane voucher when we came through Sesheke? That's nonsense.'

'No. Kasane,' insisted the official. 'It must be Kasane.'

The pressure was now into the red…

'We came through Sesheke. Get it? And that's where we got that voucher from – and paid for it. So how in hell could we have got one from Kasane as well? And I'll tell you something. I am not going to pay for another bloody voucher – as, apart from anything else, I think I've already paid a bloody fortune to come into this country – and I won't be doing so again. It's a bloody rip off and I'm not having any more of it. Understand?!'

The man's clip-board seemed to droop, and Brian immediately felt a heel. He had won. But not only had he won, he had also completely annihilated his opponent – and so easily. All it had taken was a reddening face and an explosive address. So when the nice man with the clip-board immediately abandoned his interest in yellow vouchers and instead asked Brian how he had enjoyed his stay in Zambia, Brian could only respond with an almost sick-making and incontestably over-effusive reply – along the lines that this country had been one of the most wonderful places he had ever visited and, despite what he'd said earlier, he would soon be back. But at least he hadn't been supine…

One hundred and ninety kilometres and a similar number of potholes later, Brian and Sandra were at the Sesheke border post again – and fearing the worst. But it wasn't too bad. There were no more documents to purchase and, having completed the vehicle registration log one more time and having had their passports stamped, they were soon heading back into Namibia. Here the border formalities would have been equally uncomplicated, had not those Zambians had one last stab at Brian's equilibrium. For when he and Sandra presented their passports to the Namibian immigration official, it was soon pointed out to them that their documents contained no exit stamps, and that they therefore needed to attend in his office!

This was unbelievable, especially as Brian had observed the stamps being impressed into their passports just minutes before. So they examined every page of the passports in minute detail – until they found them. Only they weren't so much "stamps", but more feint watermarks that would have foxed even a forensic expert. Yes, the Zambian border post had stamped their passports using an ink pad that had no ink in it! Or maybe you had to pay extra to get them to use a pad that did.

Brian grumped on about this final insult all the way through Namibia. Which wasn't quite as bad as it sounds, as his transit through this country was only through the width of the Caprivi Strip at its eastern extremity, and within twenty minutes of entering Namibia, he was about to leave it again – and pass into Botswana!

Three countries in less than half an hour. It must, he thought, be some sort of record. But, inevitably, before he was properly into Botswana, he had to negotiate another Namibian border post and a Botswanan border post and, between the two of them, a "dip". Not a depression in the road, but a vet-dip, where, by driving through a shallow bath of some sort of disinfectant (after stepping onto a mat soaked in the same liquid), one could leave any unwanted animal diseases back in

Namibia. This process also entailed an inspection of the on-board fridge to establish it was free of meat products – and the attendant opportunity for the responsible official to invite Brian to inspect her knickknacks. Yes, they were on a homemade stall by the side of the dip, a modest demonstration of local entrepreneurship that was designed to take advantage of the passing traffic and no doubt to supplement her official income. Well, Brian was impressed, but not impressed enough to make a purchase. All he was in the market for was a cool Windhoek Lager, and the stall contained none of these.

So, when through the dip and then the border post (with minimal hassle), Brian pressed on quickly to locate their next lodge, a place called the Muchenje Safari Lodge, and rumoured to be within minutes of the border. It was and, with only a minimal amount of guidance from a local inn-keeper, Brian found it – although not quite within minutes. It was lovely. It consisted of a huge vaulted lapa, housing the lodge's restaurant, lounge and bar, and just ten imposing thatched chalets. And the lapa and all the chalets were set on the very edge of a huge escarpment overlooking the floodplain of the Chobe River, which was simply teeming with water-birds, waterbuck, zebra – and cattle(!). It really was an idyllic place in an idyllic setting, and it had an unending supply of cool Windhoek Lager.

It also had a small swimming pool in which one could stand and take in that view of the river. And, as it was now mid-afternoon and frighteningly hot again, this is what both Brian and Sandra did, before they then retired to the deck of their chalet to take in the same view while sitting down. And then it was time for an aperitif and a much-needed dinner.

The lodge, it transpired, had just ten guests. Brian endeavoured to introduce himself and his wife to all of them during the aperitif stage of the proceedings, and then engineered seats next to those most promising as companions at the communal dining table. He could be a bit of a sneak when he wanted to – and he knew it. But he consoled himself in the knowledge that those he chose would then have the benefit of his and Sandra's company. This might not be perfect, but both of them knew how to use their cutlery properly, ate with their mouths closed and didn't use their elbows as offensive weapons. And these commendable behavioural credentials constituted, on their own, a set of highly desirable qualities that would be welcome at any dinner table anywhere in the world. There was no question about it.

So, undeterred by such preposterous reasoning, Brian got stuck into his dinner – and, with Sandra, into his selected co-diners. He and his wife had sat opposite each other across the table, and had to one side of them, a very pleasant German lady and her family (who, of course, spoke exquisite English), and on the other side, a couple from Houston who rejoiced in the most American of names, for he was Rick and she was Cindy. To start with, they were harder work than the Germans, and Brian soon found himself listening to German reports about the beauty of Liverpool (the German family had been there recently to watch an international football match). But then the Americans warmed up, and disclosed that as well as being rather staid, they were also rather bright, interesting, interested (in lots of things), and they knew about the world beyond America's borders. Their only real drawback was that they both worked in IT, which meant that from Brian's perspective they might as well have worked in palmistry or phrenology. He understood nothing about any of these disciplines, had no interest in them, and certainly no desire to discuss them or even acknowledge their existence. He was therefore obliged to steer the conversation away from IT and into, for example, American society and, in particular, its attitudes to taking vacations.

Well actually, Rick and Cindy had almost invited him to steer the conversation towards this subject – because they were thoroughly sick of being "stranded". As they explained, living in Houston was a little like living on an island. You were so far away from anywhere that, if you didn't get on a plane, you could find yourself preparing to return from wherever you'd gone almost before you'd got there. And even if you did get on a plane – and maybe came to a place like Botswana – there was still an expectation that you would soon be coming home. Because if you were in any form of employment, that was the established expectation, and it was an expectation that wasn't ignored because it was rooted in a climate of fear!

Rick was quite adamant on this point – how job insecurity, as well as the work ethos in America, meant that employees were genuinely fearful of taking extended vacations. Not only would this be seen as "un-American", but it could also mark you out as being a prime candidate for redundancy if a business had to "downsize" and "let people go". Indeed, this fear factor was why he and Cindy were doing their current African adventure at something of a gallop. South Africa, Botswana, Zambia and Houston all within a couple of weeks, and therefore just about acceptable to their respective employers. Although maybe not for next year as well.

How strange, thought Brian, that such a powerhouse of a nation still imposes these sorts of constraints on its citizens, especially as a proper, relaxed break from work can only improve a person's performance. It had always worked with him (or so he liked to believe), and it was just as likely to work for

Rick and Cindy and millions of other Americans. If only they'd see the light. And if only everybody saw the world through Brian's eyes and with Brian's perceptive mind. It would be such a wonderful place…

Yes, it was that time of the evening, a time when Brian's cognitive compass begins to veer from true north, a time when the full impact of fighting dehydration with alcoholic beverages finally catches up with him – and then plays havoc with his magnetic flux. So, with the encouragement of his wife, Brian decided to call it a day and return to their chalet. There they could enjoy a good night's rest in readiness for a "full-day safari" in the morning. It sounded really attractive, and apparently it entailed no policemen masquerading as car-park attendants, no men with clip-boards, only a few potholes and, for tips, only a few pula (the local currency) and not a few million kwacha. And no border posts either. Hell, what more could one want… ?

12.

Well, that promised good night's rest to start with – and not a night that was an exercise in endurance…

It was the chalet. It was beautiful, it was well-appointed, it was spacious – and it even had a seat in the shower. But it also had two very significant drawbacks. One of these drawbacks was known as papio ursinus and the other had the title of mellivora capensis. These guys are more commonly known, respectively, as chacma baboons and ratels (or honey badgers), and they had earned their drawback status from their persistent desire to invade Muchenje's chalets and cause havoc within. There were a great number of both species around the lodge, with the baboons constituting the threat to the chalet interiors during the day and with the ratels taking over for the night shift. Consequently… it was a lodge rule that as far as possible the chalets were sealed against intrusion (for a full twenty-four hours a day) either by keeping all the windows closed or by deploying heavy screens when the windows were left ajar. This regime may have worked in cooler weather, but in "normal" weather (when it was bloody hot), it didn't. It simply reduced the interior of the chalets to an airless, steamy hell, in which it was just about impossible to sleep.

However, it wasn't normal weather at the moment. No, it was considerably hotter than normal. And this was certain.

Because, according to the lodge staff, the whole of northern Botswana (together with Caprivi and southern Zambia) was experiencing an official heat-wave. Daytime temperatures were consistently in the forties, and they weren't much lower than this during the night. So the sealed feature of Brian and Sandra's chalet was reducing its interior not just to an airless, steamy hell, but to something even worse – where sleep was completely impossible...

Brian had lain in bed for what seemed like hours (and it was hours). He was naked save for a film of perspiration that covered the whole of his body, and he was debating in his mind whether this all-embracing slick was the worst feature of his present condition, or whether the real pits was the sense that he could hardly breathe. The atmosphere in the room wasn't just steamy; it was also deeply oppressive, something like a suffocating theocracy blended with a blanket of smothering pillows... Anyway, in the end he settled on the atmosphere. He just had to get out of the chalet.

Well, it was a little bit cooler out on the deck (at two in the morning) – and a great deal less stifling. Sandra agreed with this conclusion, even though when she'd joined Brian outside, she'd arrived with some clothes on. Brian had been less modest – as he wanted to air his entire person. And he thought it rather more likely that they'd have the company of a ratel on their deck than that of any of their fellow guests. And ratels didn't give a fig. As far as they were concerned, you could wear nothing, a tutu, a sandwich-board, a suit of armour or an ostrich on your head, and they wouldn't give a damn. And, in any event, not one of them arrived, and Brian and Sandra were left in peace to enjoy a reviving interval in their truly sweltering night. Eventually, of course, they did return inside – when it seemed exhaustion held out the promise of some further respite. And whilst they might not be able to sleep very well, they could at least lie on their bed (with, beneath them, bath towels soaked in water) and drop into the sort of semi-conscious state that would enable them to pretend that they'd slept.

And it worked. In the morning they felt amazingly rested and, despite such a dreadful night, ready for a safari!

The only guests remaining in the lodge were the German family and Rick and Cindy. (Maybe Brian's failure to select the others as table companions on the previous evening had caused them to leave.) But no matter. It meant that the safari could now proceed with the Germans on one vehicle and Brian and Sandra together with Rick and Cindy on the other. And with room for nine people in the back of each of these open safari Land Rovers, that meant plenty of room for all. And plenty of room for the water. (The temperature was still ludicrously high, and to avoid dehydration, the occupants of the Land Rovers were required to swig from a water bottle about every ten minutes.)

Muchenje Safari Lodge is situated just a couple of kilometres from the north-western gate of the Chobe National Park. So, very soon the convoy of two was in the park, and its multi-national occupants were in observing mode. They didn't have to wait too long to find something to observe.

It was a group of ground hornbills. The title of these endangered birds didn't signify that they were a result of any grinding action, but instead that they spent virtually all their time not in the air. They were very much ground-living creatures, possibly as a result of their being the size of overfed turkeys and their having a huge (horn) bill, which, when taken together, must have reduced their aerodynamics to somewhere around the level of pure aerostatics. Brian rather liked them, although he doubted this affection was in any way reciprocated. In fact, they never even looked in his direction.

The elephants did. But there again, elephants always take an interest in their observers. They are always wary – and always enchanting. And here in Chobe they were everywhere. Brian had never seen so many before, especially down near the river… For both Land Rovers had now left the main route through the park and had driven down a testing sand-track to the Chobe flood plain. It was elephant city. They were all over the place. As were water buffalo. Hundreds of them, lying in the shade of bushes and probably contemplating why they had been dealt such a crap hand. Big bodies needing copious amounts of fodder (and leaving very little time for any more appealing diversions), bodies that were far too attractive to passing lions (with whom one could never come to any sort of accommodation), and then, towards the end of their life, the prospect of a solitary existence and terminal suffering. No wonder when they got to this point of their existence they were so angry and so dangerous, and so dangerous that they accounted for more human deaths in Africa than any other creature. And then they had to carry around those ruddy great horns as well. They really did have a rough deal.

There again, it wasn't a picnic for many of their neighbours. The warthogs were on the lions' set-menu as well. The giraffes spent their life worrying about the next time they'd need a drink, and the consequent obligation to bend over in the most ultra-vulnerable pose imaginable. And the impala were constantly being pecked at by oxpeckers, one of the few birds that Brian found really creepy and that put him in mind of a "bird out of hell". They would never, he was convinced, make good pet birds, although they might just find a home with one of those shaven-headed dumbos who think that owning a pit-bull terrier makes up for their having halitosis and an undersized or misshapen penis.

Fortunately, there were none of those sorts here today, but just the ever-pleasant Rick and Cindy and then, when the convoy stopped for lunch, the similarly pleasant Germans, and, of course, a pair of great guides. These chaps had driven all morning and had found all sorts of stuff for their respective guests. But now they were about to have a rest, because, directly after their lunch-in-the-bush, all eight guests were to be delivered to another guide. This one had a tiny tin boat, and this boat was moored on a small jetty on the outskirts of Kasane (the very same Kasane where one could purchase small squares of yellow paper and risk one's life on a ferry). For during the morning, both Land Rovers had been travelling more or less east and, in doing so, had followed the course of the Chobe River to where it passes Kasane. And apparently, as well as being the home of small yellow vouchers and scary ferries, this place was also renowned as a wildlife hotspot, where the wildlife in question spent its life in or around the river. Hence the new guide, his tiny tin boat and the imminent prospect of a cruise on the river.

It was fantastic. The new guide, who wore a cowboy hat and looked more like a Country and Western singer than he did a boatman and guide, soon found for his passengers a whole treasure trove of creatures. There were permanently obese hippos, both in the river and on an island within it. There were enormous crocodiles, either grinning on the shore or being ominously disconcerting in the water. And there were more elephants than ever – along with herds of red lechwe, groups of waterbuck, and even a few of a very uncommon antelope in

Botswana called a puku, which Brian and Sandra had never before seen. Then there were the birds…

There were jacanas, which are known as Jesus birds from their apparent ability to walk on water. There were open-billed storks, which are known as… open-billed storks – from their possession of bills that are never quite closed. And there were goliath herons, which are known as… well, as the biggest herons in the world, and which are a great deal bigger than giant African kingfishers – which were also about, and, although tiny when compared to the goliath herons, are still pretty big for a kingfisher. And whilst on the subject of comparative zoology, there were also very big fish eagles, medium-sized sacred ibises, relatively small pratincoles and very small bee-eaters, to name but a few. And many of these charmers were happy to sit within just yards of the boat. It was all really quite thrilling.

And there was more. Because their cruise had taken the Muchenje party all the way around a small island in the river (where the hippos had been grazing and where there were crocodiles and water monitors) and, according to their guide, this island had been the subject of a case in the International Court of Justice in The Hague! Yes, as improbable as it sounds, this tiny scrap of land had led to a serious dispute between Botswana, on the south bank of the Chobe River, and Namibia, on its north bank. For here the river forms the border between the two countries, and Namibia to the north hasn't quite disappeared into Zambia. Anyway, both countries claimed the island, and only after the court case, when it had been ordered that the depth of the south and north channels around the island be measured, was custody awarded to the Botswanans. And just in case the Namibians ever forget that they were the losers, Botswana has now erected a pole on the island from which flies its blue, white and black flag, to which the hippos and crocodiles appear entirely indifferent. What a world – and what a load of nonsense. Two countries with absolutely huge land areas and the thinnest populations in Africa, squabbling over a miniscule patch of land that has no economic or strategic value and of which the overwhelming bulk of their populations will only ever be aware through a silly court case. What hope for the rest of the world? It even makes what's going on in the Middle East seem mildly rational. At least there, there are genuine economic and strategic considerations… as well as all that out and out lunacy.

Brian had all these thoughts while afloat. But as soon as he regained dry land he also regained his senses, and remembered that he was on a safari and not on an away-day on international relations. So he soon forgot about disputes and got back to observing. The party was on its way back to the lodge now, but that didn't mean that there wouldn't be anything more to see. And, as if on cue, after only a few kilometres of driving, a small herd of sable hove into view. These antelopes deserve a word to describe them that hasn't yet been invented. So, for now, it is necessary to get by with "exquisite". And if that fails to convey their true beauty, then one might want to add the word "stunning".

The lions by the side of the road were pretty handsome as well. Although, of course, they don't have a sable's long horns…

It had been a great day. Brian and Sandra both felt enriched – and very privileged. But even so, they now wanted more – in a glass and at the right temperature. Yes, it was drinking and feeding time again, and time for another unavoidable encounter with Richard…

Richard was the husband of Kim. And Richard and Kim were the joint managers of the Muchenje Lodge. Kim was fine. She was personable and extremely amiable. Richard, however, was rather hard work. He was very well-meaning and as amiable as his wife, but he had done so much in his fifty years on this Earth and he was so keen to tell all his guests exactly what it was that he'd done, that he was simply exhausting.

After just twenty minutes of his company the previous day, Brian had been fully acquainted with the circumstances of the accident through which he had shattered his feet. He also knew the full details of how his knee had been damaged in a judo attack and, if challenged, he could have repeated with ease all the main elements of Richard's CV, which included lodge management (of virtually every lodge in southern Africa), lodge design and construction, a management role with Coca Cola, running a medical communications outfit, rebuilding and maintaining Land Rovers (on a professional basis) and delivering cars in the United States – as a sort of holiday entertainment. And Richard had met everybody and had an opinion on every subject. Oh… and he didn't seem to need sleep. He was apparently up every night – doing things – and presumably fretting about not having anybody to talk to. Or maybe he talked to Kim – whether she was awake or not.

However, despite this demolition description of this chap, Brian still liked him. It was impossible to do otherwise. He was therefore prepared for another session with him, and another few chapters of *The Life of Richard* in ten chunky volumes. Maybe tonight he would learn about his stint with MI5. But he didn't. Instead he learnt a little gem, another insight into national characteristics, a subset of the more general topic of human behaviour that never failed to arouse Brian's interest.

It stemmed from Richard's long association with safari lodges, and learning along the way how to deal with a problem chalet. Because there is often at least one chalet in a lodge where the cistern has a leak or the fan won't work or there is some other minor glitch... and if the lodge is full, it is the lodge manager's job to decide whom to put in it. Well, one apparently never chooses Americans. Americans will immediately demand that the problem be fixed and keep on demanding until it is. Germans are out as well. They will want to move to another chalet – immediately. That, as often as not, leaves the Brits. And it is the Brits who are, without fail, chosen to be the occupants of the duff chalet. As Richard explained, they rationalise things – along the lines of: 'Well, we're only here for two nights, dear. We can manage it for that. And they're such nice people. It seems a shame to make a fuss...'

It rang so true. Brian was quite sure that Richard was being deadly serious, and that it really was the Brits who got this special form of special treatment. And hell, it even reflected how the whole of Britain now deals with the rest of the world. Yes, our confidence is now so shot to pieces, that we don't just tolerate dodgy rooms but, as a nation, we also tolerate a whole raft of dodgy behaviour. Whether it's rolling over in the face of an onslaught on our indigenous culture, bending over backwards so as not to offend a whole slew of people who richly deserve to be offended, or caving in to the egregious demands of a load of tossers in Brussels, we're more than up for it. And the quicker we can roll over, bend over or cave in, the better. It's so dispiriting – and so obvious to the rest of the world. No wonder they put us in dodgy chalets...

Nevertheless, there was a crumb of good news in Richard's insight into national traits, and this was that, if at all possible, you don't put Argentinians into any of your chalets! He was adamant. Whether a chalet is dodgy or perfect, the Argentinians will regard any of its contents that are not fixed to the chalet itself as part of the all-inclusive deal, and they will remove these contents when they leave. This all sounded rather jingoistic to Brian, but Richard assured his audience that he had seen it with his own eyes. And not just towels and bathrobes disappearing, but also bedside lights and pictures, indeed anything that could be squeezed into their overlarge cases. He even instituted a case-search at one lodge. The chalets were being stripped of everything but the beds.

Well, Brian was quite prepared to believe this, and was confident that Mrs Thatcher would have as well. And the Falklands aren't even really portable…

And so, with this further revelation on the nuances of human behaviour tucked firmly in his memory, Brian moved on to dinner with his wife and with a crop of new guests. None of them was from South America, and accordingly no cutlery or crockery was removed from the table. In fact, the only thing to disappear was Brian's energy and alertness. As well as being a splendid day of wildlife observing, it had also been a very tiring day, especially after last night's intermittent dozing – and he was ready for bed. He just hoped that this night wouldn't be quite as enervating, and that tomorrow he would have some energy back – so that he could properly enjoy his sixty-something birthday…

13.

It was a remarkably better night. It was still sticky and oppressive, but maybe exhaustion, alcohol and Richard had together done the trick, and both Brian and Sandra slept very well indeed – despite the ambient conditions. And Brian dreamt. In the morning he was even able to recall the main feature. It had been a new *Carry On* film – where the original characters had been usurped by a new crop of comedians. So Sid James had been replaced by Lord(!) Sugar, Hattie Jaques by Sarah Ferguson, Kenneth Williams by Alan Carr and Barbara Windsor by Anne Robinson – whose body had undergone a further bout of medical rearrangement especially for the role. And Brian could also remember the title of the film; it was *Carry on being Really Embarrassing*. He also remembered it had nothing in the way of a plot. It was just the new cast of characters acting as themselves, and clearly not realising how they were regarded by the public. Inevitably, it was not very good.

Well, thank god, thought Brian, that he was here in Botswana and not in that world of lunacy back home, where talent has been overtaken by self-promotion and where merit now takes a back seat to money, connections, hype and profound mediocrity. And thank god, thought Brian, that today was his sixty-something birthday and not his forty-something birthday. It was all going downhill so quickly that he didn't think he could cope with the idea of being only halfway through his life. Much better to have the end not so much in sight but at least perceptible through the haze. (Albeit he had no plans whatsoever to follow the lead of that redoubtable South African professor, either in the choice of his footwear or, more pertinently, in the choice of his lifespan.) And anyway, he had a birthday to enjoy, and what better way to enjoy a birthday than by writing a few postcards?

Sandra and Brian had acquired some in the lodge's curio shop, which contained not just postcards but the usual assembly of tee-shirts, safari shirts, books and "artefacts" – where "artefacts" is a generic term for hand-made wooden animals, hand-made bead jewellery and miscellaneous hand-made handicrafts, much of which is unsuitable for both hand luggage and hold luggage and transportable back home only as an untidy package in an overhead locker. (And never really worth the trouble when you've done it.) But anyway, they had decided to have a relaxing morning on their chalet deck, taking in the local birds and all those animals down on the flood plain below whilst writing said postcards. And what a strange, not to say completely bizarre, convention…

It's not just that postcards are somewhat prehistoric in their nature and have now been overtaken by a whole string of newer and faster communication technologies, but it's also the whole idea of informing people – who know more or less where you are – of where you are, and who, if you're somewhere in the depths of Africa, will only receive this information shortly before or even after you've returned home. Indeed, Brian and Sandra had been the recipients on a number of occasions of holiday postcards posted by their senders in England only after they'd returned from a "difficult" overseas destination 'to ensure you received it'. Hell, that's the sort of behaviour you'd expect from a government department, not from advanced sentient beings. But, there again, was it very much different from what Brian and Sandra were planning to do themselves? Because not only did they believe that they might be home before their postcards were, but they were also far from certain that their postcards would ever get home at all. (They had never seen a post-van in Botswana in their ten years of coming here. Or, for that matter, a post-box.)

Still, tradition always trumps suspicion, and before very long Brian and Sandra were scribbling minor variations of the "wish you were here" theme on the back of each card, and Brian was lapsing into futile ruminations. For he'd begun to wonder how the postal service worked on an international basis and, in particular, if he'd bought a Botswanan stamp issued by the Botswanan Post Office, how the Royal Mail got remunerated for their part of the job, all that sorting and delivering of the card they'd have to do back in England. Because it didn't seem they got remunerated at all. And surely it couldn't just be on the basis of "swings and roundabouts", where the Botswanan Post Office provided a similar free service for items mailed in Britain and sent over here. Apart from anything else, the volumes in each direction would be completely out of balance. (How many Botswanans send postcards from Brighton? And, for that matter, how many Spaniards, Greeks and Tenerifians send postcards from Bognor?)

Brian tussled with this conundrum for some time and eventually came to the conclusion that it was very likely that there was indeed some sort of international agreement that meant that every country retained all the money it had collected for international postage, and that in the case of Brian and Sandra's postcards, Botswana would be quids in and the Royal Mail would have to do its bit for nothing – just like it does for all those millions of postcards from the Med and from a host of other popular holiday destinations. That is to say, Britain has signed up to an agreement where we permanently get the rough end of the deal. No way can we send enough stuff out of Britain to foreign parts to make up for all these damn postcards coming our way. And wasn't that typical! Not content with giving us dodgy chalets and damaging directives from Brussels, the rest of the world is screwing us on postage as well. No wonder the Royal Mail is in such a bloody mess. It's subsidising every other mail service in the world!

Well, this was all too much. Brian now didn't want to send the postcards, even though they were all written. But when he made the appropriate submissions to his spouse, she reminded him that they had already bought the stamps and that therefore there was nothing they could do to prevent the Botswanan Post Office from having their money, and little point in trying to save the Royal Mail a few pennies, for which in any event they would receive no thanks. And furthermore, just because it was his birthday, he didn't have the right to puncture the idyll of Muchenje with another load of his nonsense, and wouldn't it be better if he focused on their rather fortunate physical situation – and on the abundance of wildlife hereabouts – which, if he gave it more than a moment's thought, he might recall was the primary purpose of their having come to Botswana…?

Well, put in those terms, Sandra's observations were difficult to challenge, and Brian promptly abandoned his concerns as to the invidious nature of the international postal system and its deleterious impact on Blighty – and picked up his binoculars. And Sandra was right again. There was wildlife everywhere. And many of its avian representatives were around in the close-by trees and eminently observable with his binocs. There were carmine bee-eaters, arrow-marked babblers, boubous, firefinches and, overhead, some yellow-billed kites. Then the four-footed stuff on the flood plain below: waterbuck, zebra, more sable – and still some cattle. (They really did look incongruous.) Oh, and there were more birds down there as well: all sorts of storks and egrets and even some white-backed vultures. Wildlife around Muchenje was… well, around it. And by just sitting on the deck of a chalet, perched on top of a giant escarpment, one could see it all.

One could also see that the remainder of the day was going to be a somewhat leisurely affair. The benefits of the immediate situation, the heat and the need to have a private celebration of Brian's birthday would make sure of that. And that's more or less what happened. There was a little activity around lunchtime when lunch was taken with a new crop of guests – and their rather ill-mannered children. And a little while after those private celebrations in the afternoon, there was then dinner to attend to as well. But even then, the pace remained leisurely, right up to the near-conclusion of the meal.

This evening session had kicked off with a conversation with the English co-owner of the lodge who had just arrived from Britain – with a case-full of whinges about what he'd left there. These not only put Brian's own whinges in the shade but also spoke volumes about what this chap thought about Britain's liberal elite and what havoc he believed it was wreaking. This led on to some less contentious topics over the meal itself, including the impact of quantitative easing and the correct way to eat bananas, until, just after the main course had been cleared away, the lights were extinguished…

The lodge was full this evening. So there was now a dining room filled with almost two dozen people, all clearly wondering what was going on. Then one person guessed. He did this just a nano-second after he'd heard some traditional African chanting from the kitchen. Yes, Brian knew immediately that a gentleman back in Windhoek, by the name of Robin Marsh-Taylor, who had organised Brian and Sandra's expedition, had also organised something else. And this something else was a rather less private celebration of Brian's birthday than had taken place earlier. He'd no doubt done this by contacting the lodge, and there was no doubt about what was to happen next…

Four of them emerged from the kitchen. Four very traditionally-built Botswanan ladies, still singing, and three of them waving sparklers. And the fourth lady, in her kitchen whites and her chef's hat, was carrying before her not just an ample bosom but also a more than ample chocolate birthday cake. It would feed all the diners with chocolate to spare.

Brian felt hotter than he'd felt all day. And when the African rhythms were abandoned in favour of a tuneful rendition of "Happy Birthday", accompanied by a less than tuneful contribution from the complement of diners, Brian felt hotter than ever. This was an experience which, whatever it was, was certainly not "leisurely". No, it was much nearer to disconcerting, with the disconcerting soon being overtaken by the memorable and then by the quite delightful. How could it not be? Even sour sixty-somethings aren't impervious to generous gestures, and when the gestures involve a slice of communal silliness as well as a slice of chocolate cake, they can be completely pervious not to say slightly overcome.

So despite the initial surprise – and the attendant shock – this ending to the meal had been a fitting end to the day, a day when Brian was clocking up another milestone on the odometer of life and a day when he was just about coming to terms with the world's discrimination against Britain. Although, maybe if Lord(!) Sugar were asked… well, maybe he could come up with a plan, something that would mean that the Royal Mail could come out even and not continue to act as a paymaster to all the other postal services in the world. Something like telling these foreign mail organisations that they were all completely useless and that therefore they were all fired!!

There again, possibly not.

Oh, and the weather had changed. As Brian and Sandra had retired for the night, a wind had blown up and there was thunder and lightning in the distance. All good for the airflow through the chalet – and a comprehensive distraction. Brian gave not a further thought to postal inequities and so-called lords of the realm but instead relished his good fortune. He was now sixty-something plus, but he was still batting, still driving around Botswana in a Land Cruiser – and still celebrating with his wife.

So who would want to be a lord anyway?

By six the next morning, the wind had disappeared. So too had the chance for any more head-on-pillow time for Brian and Sandra. For today they had another journey to undertake, and this journey would need an early start. Not only was it nearly five hundred kilometres to their next hostelry, but part of the way there involved a road from Kasane to a place called Nata, and they had been warned (by everyone) that this road was not in tip-top condition and might take some time. So… by seven-thirty, having said their goodbyes to Richard and Kim, they were on their way, and just a few minutes later they were approaching the entrance to Chobe National Park.

They were on the same route that their guided convoy had taken just two days before. But this time there would be no off-road driving and instead Brian and Sandra would be staying on the main tarmac road, a road that sliced through the park in a straight line and that would take them directly to Kasane at the park's eastern edge. It was a good road but, as it passed through a wildlife haven and there were elephants and other potential road hazards about, it was only sensible to abide by the fifty kilometres per hour speed limit – which inevitably made their passage a rather slow one. However, past Kasane, the limit rose to one hundred and twenty kilometres per hour, and Brian would now be able to make up some time, despite advice to the contrary.

He did. Having refuelled in Kasane and having made his way through just a mile or so of road-works, he and Sandra were on a straight, well-surfaced open road with no side-roads off it and barely any traffic on it, and there was every prospect of their being able to reach Nata, which was three hundred kilometres away, in under three hours. Clearly there was nothing to stop them, and those warnings they'd received about the road were either misguided (and based on some local digging-up around Kasane) or they were completely out of date. Hell, had Brian known then what he knew now, he could probably have spent at least another hour in bed.

However… after fifty or so kilometres, he wasn't so sure.

First there were temporary speed-limit signs for road-works. Albeit these road-works never materialised. All that was ever observed was the evidence of some small-scale road-works in the past, with a few empty tar-barrels at the side of the road and maybe an abandoned digger. But never more than this Marie Celeste encounter and never a road-work-type person in sight. This was all a little unnerving, and it certainly reduced Brian's average speed – quite significantly. Although not by quite as much as the road surface soon did.

It was still tarmac and it was still essentially coherent tarmac, in that little if any of it had started to separate. But that said, it wasn't "encouraging" tarmac. It had a finish to it that wasn't… well, particularly well finished, and in certain stretches even the less than perfect finish seemed to be wearing away. It tended to make driving in a straight line something of a challenge and occasionally (and unpredictably) it was so bad that it threatened to subvert the action of the steering wheel completely. Brian began to feel that he might have an unscheduled meeting with the flat (and un-surfaced) Botswanan landscape to either side of the road at any moment and without any warning. He therefore slowed some more, and the chances of a three-hour journey time to Nata were now looking slim.

More time was then lost at another "vet check", another chemical dip blocking the road, and a dip that required not just the emersion of the Land Cruiser's tyres and a stamp of footwear on a sodden mat, but also a stamp of all one's footwear on a sodden mat, whether said footwear was on one's feet or in one's luggage! Needless to say, a token selection of the packed footwear was made (a pair of Sandra's sandals), and this seemed to satisfy the requirements of the observing officials. But it still consumed time. So much so that Brian was keen to press on and to find "a bit of better road". In the event he found "the detour".

It wasn't a conventional detour. It was nothing less than a one hundred and thirty kilometre stretch of the Kasane-Nata road, where the road itself was pristine, but not in use – and running along its side was the aforementioned "detour". It was a tarmac track, bumpy, narrow, full of holes and eminently scary. And to understand why it was so scary (and increasingly slow) it is necessary to describe its bumpiness and its narrowness – and its collection of holes – in rather more detail.

Sandra likened its surface to the uneven topping one finds on a fruit cake – scaled up to road proportions. Brian considered it more like the surface one finds in a lava field. To him, this detour track was like a long, linear strip of some long-cooled volcanic flow that had been pressed into service as a highway and that certainly hadn't been built by any road builders. Or if it had been, then they hadn't used any steamrollers, but just a giant pallet knife to smear the lava into a series of uneven waves. And then there was its narrowness… which alternated between very narrow and, where the tarmac had frayed at its edges, stupidly narrow. Indeed, in places it was not much more than the axle width of the Land Cruiser, which was something of a problem when the pot holes appeared…

To begin with, they were regular pot holes. But the closer to Nata Brian drove, these "depressions" in the road surface had to relinquish their pot hole handle in favour of "crater holes". Because that's what they'd become: holes which were so big and so deep that they were properly craters. It was as though somebody had grown tired of that giant pallet knife and had taken up instead a giant ice-cream scoop, and had used this to gouge great chunks of tarmac-lava from the so-called surface of the so-called road. Indeed, later on in their holiday, Brian and Sandra would learn one of the standard jokes about this stretch of purgatorial highway, and this concerned rabbits. For it was said that if one was driving down this "detour" and one saw the ears of a rabbit in one of its many craters, one would realise, as one neared it, that they weren't the ears of a rabbit but instead the ears of a giraffe! The Kasane-Nata "pot holes" may be amongst the deepest in all Africa, and those that spanned almost the width of the road must also have been some of the biggest. Thank god, thought Brian, that they had this Land Cruiser and that they were able to drive through these monsters. Or should that be 'drive into them and then out of them'?

His average speed was now about twenty kilometres per hour, falling all the time. Near the end of the tribulation it was barely walking pace, and he was beginning to concede that all those doom merchants who had warned him of this route over the past couple of weeks hadn't warned him sufficiently. Even taking account of the sand-tracks he'd tussled with already on this and on previous holidays in Africa, this really was the worst road he'd ever driven on – by miles.

However, it was coming to an end. On the detour, there was an arrow-sign ahead, and this arrow was directing him back onto a regular stretch of road – with a regular pot-hole-free surface of regular tarmac – and he could finally apply some pressure to that right-hand pedal. He speeded up and kept up this speeded-up speed for more than a kilometre – until he encountered the next barrier in his quest to reach Nata. And this was a fire!

Unbelievable. But he had to believe it. There, at the side of the road, was an enormous conflagration. Not the first that he and Sandra had seen, as in this part of the world, wild fires are common, as is the practice of burning near a highway to keep it clear of encroaching vegetation. But this one was a whopper, and it came with the added features of a blanket of smoke and an intimate proximity to the road. And, with the way that the wind was blowing, that meant that the smoke and the flames were actually across the road. Cue use of footbrake as well as accelerator, some erratic turning of the steering wheel and some growing activity in Brian's sweat glands. So that when he'd finally reached an expanse of Botswana that wasn't alight, his armpits were flowing over only slightly less than was his relief. And now he had only the donkeys, cows and goats to contend with…

Yes, he and his wife had reached the outskirts of Nata – and the outriders of its complement of roaming domestic animals. They were all over the place – including the road. And whilst a few of these four-legged hazards had been encountered earlier on in Botswana (on the way to Nxameseri), they hadn't before been encountered in such copious numbers. Still, once the travelling duo were through Nata, all would be fine. Brian was sure of it. And that meant that although they had taken over four hours to reach this place and not the three that Brian had anticipated, they could make up some time. They had reached the extremity of their southern progress and would now be turning west towards a place called Maun, and the Nata-Maun road had nothing like the notoriety of the way they had come. It would be a doddle.

So too was Nata. Not so much a town, more a junction with a couple of service stations. And having used one of these to fill up again, Brian was soon out of it and on the easier route. And it really was. It was (inevitably) straight, it had a good road surface, it had essentially no traffic – and it had just a few of those mobile hazards, especially donkeys. But soon these occasional hazards had disappeared – to be replaced by continuous hazards! Yes, Brian could barely come to terms with it, but this road, leading into the heartland of Botswana, appeared also to be leading into the heartland of its donkey population. And it wasn't as though the cows and the goats had disappeared either…

Jesus! The odd four-footer he could deal with, but this was like driving through an unending herd of them. And according to the road-safety section of his *Guide to Botswana*, legally they had the right of way. Hit one and not only do you damage an animal and your vehicle, but you also damage your prospects of leaving the country without a fine or even a prison term. Again, Brian found himself driving at a rather sedate pace – and studying the habits of the different species in the ubiquitous throng.

The donkeys were keen on whatever grazing was available at the very edge of the road (which was negligible and looked more like a green spray-can job than anything that was substantial enough to eat). But they were careful – and predictable. Brian quickly learnt that they very infrequently made sudden movements and, in fact, they were pretty disinclined to move a great deal at all – and never at speed. A bit like Brian himself really. But not like the cattle. These chaps tended to move as a group, and if the leader of the group (and there was always a leader) decided to lead his followers across the road, they would all trail behind him and show disdain for any vehicles. They were almost sheepish in their behaviour and indifferent to its consequences. So a little like committed socialists. And talking of sheep, there were then the goats. They were the most unsettling of all, essentially because they were very irrational in their behaviour and they would panic, and if one panicked they would all panic – with unpredictable and potentially disastrous consequences. So they were a bit like bankers…

Almost one hundred kilometres out of Nata, Brian was still musing on these animal/human likenesses – and still avoiding the animals – when he spotted a giant aardvark. It was by the side of the road, a house-size sculpture of this secretive animal, designed by a talented artist and also designed to tell all those who were seeking it that they had now arrived at the turn-off to "Planet Baobab".

Now, it is worth pointing out at this stage that Brian and Sandra had spent almost six hours driving through a country in which features of any sort, including people and constructions, are virtually non-existent. But here they were, in the middle of all this nothing, and there was this surreal object marking their arrival at what was to prove an even more surreal undertaking. For Planet Baobab isn't what one would describe as a standard destination.

Indeed, it wasn't Brian and Sandra's final destination. They had come here simply to pick up an escort. But what a place!

It was a kilometre or so off the road, hidden in the middle of some half-hearted bush and, as its name suggested, accessorised with a number of fine-looking baobabs. Between these remarkable trees had been built an eccentric lodge-cum-camping-site, where the ethos was über-relaxed and the architecture was a mix of colourful African and the downright peculiar.

Brian had parked the Land Cruiser in its small gravel car park, and he and Sandra were now entering its reception. It was amazing. Almost conventional looking from the outside, but within, it echoed the interior of a flying saucer. A smooth-surfaced, porthole-equipped corridor swept in a semi-circle around a similarly-shaped reception desk, which must have given every visitor to this place the idea that they were indeed about to step onto another planet. None of the flying saucer's crew was about at the moment, so the accompanied Brian passed through the ship and into Planet Baobab itself – and found himself smiling. It was such a smile inducing sight.

All around there were low concrete walls, shaped and painted to resemble the local vernacular style of building, albeit a version of it that was more than a little slanted towards the psychedelic. And between these walls were little thatched roundels, an enormous (empty) swimming pool, a large outdoor lounge (with gaudy upholstered furniture) and a large thatched building, which was clearly the bar.

Brian and Sandra were soon within this edifice, not only drinking lager, but also marvelling at its eclectic decoration. For as well as the expected African embellishments, there was a whole gallery of ancient prints and posters (from Africa's colonial past), hide-covered 1960s-style chairs, and a gigantic chandelier dominating the drinking space and fashioned from empty green beer bottles. When illuminated, it must have looked a sight, even more of a sight than it did now in the early afternoon. Brian was impressed. And no less so by the story of its sister chandelier…

He and Sandra had been approached by the captain of the flying saucer – otherwise known as the lodge manager. He, having observed the new visitors to his domain admiring the lighting arrangements, clearly thought they would be interested to hear about its bigger sibling. For the one here, although enormous, wasn't the size of a similarly beer-bottle-adorned monster that, a year ago, had been hung from the ceiling of the lodge's dining room. This, apparently, had taken ten men to lift it to its supports below the thatched roof of this building. And there it had stayed, until just a few days ago when it had pulled the roof to the ground… There had been a shaking, then a creaking, and then the laws of physics had eventually decided that the force it was exerting on the roof of the dining room was a force too far – and gravity took over. Inevitably, the manager told this tale not as an anguished account of a disaster but merely as an amusing end to a preposterous endeavour. And who, in this climate, needs a roof to a dining room anyway?

Well, Brian, at this stage of the proceedings, was beginning to regret that he and Sandra hadn't chosen to stay at this hostelry, if only for one night. It was so odd, but also so inviting and so laid-back, that it was a pity that they had to move on. But they did have to move on. Because, as Sandra was quick to point out, they had an appointment with one of the most expensive lodges they were ever likely to stay in, and their escort to this lodge had now arrived in the bar. So it was time to go, and time to drive further south for another fifty kilometres in order to secure their final destination for the day, which just happened to be located in the dead centre of absolutely nowhere.

Brian and Sandra were currently situated on the northern edge of an area of Botswana which is home to the "Makgadikgadi Pans". These pans were once part of a "superlake" of over 60,000 sq km, which 10,000 years ago, because of climatic changes and geological fidgetings, evaporated completely to leave the largest saltpan complex in the world – and really nothing else at all. And this means that the Makgadikgadi Pans now constitute one of the most desolate places on this planet and represent an area of Botswana where, if one is foolish enough to venture without proper equipment and guidance, one will almost certainly become lost – and shortly thereafter, one will also become dead.

Well, Brian and Sandra were now into venture mode, but fortunately for them they had an escort and the proper equipment in the form of a Land Cruiser. They would need both – immediately. To start with there was gravel. Then there was salt (and a choice of salt-tracks). Then there was rougher salt. And then there was salt that was rutted and split. And then, in the distance, were a few palm trees and the hint of some structures near the palms. And they were there. Their escort had successfully led them to "Jack's Camp".

Jack's Camp is an institution. It may not be quite as world-famous as the Sydney Harbour Bridge, but it is renowned, especially amongst those who are fortunate enough to be able to include southern Africa in their itineraries. And for good reason. For "Jack's" is unique and, of course, it is situated in a unique environment: the void known as the Makgadikgadi Pans.

Its own uniqueness stems from its history, because it owes its existence to a guy called Jack Bousfield, a safari specialist (and supposedly a crocodile hunter) who embarked on a long love affair with the Makgadikgadi Pans in the early '70s. After his untimely death in an air crash, his son, together with a woman friend, established Jack's Camp in his memory, and later on they decided to style it to reflect his safari past. That is to say, they refurbished it to echo the style of East African safaris of the 1940s. Accordingly, ten green canvas tents have been set within a palm grove to create an oasis of comfort in the harshest of environments – and, as Brian and Sandra were about to discover, a standard of comfort that bordered on the absurd.

Their first introduction to the sumptuous nature of the camp was not in one of the ten accommodation tents but in its "dining tent", a construction of extravagant proportions that housed their afternoon tea. But there wasn't just a selection of home-made pies and delicate sandwiches in this emporium, but a whole host of fittings and artefacts that not only belied the remoteness of the camp's situation but also reinforced the fact that Jack's was truly unique. There was an enormous dining table that wouldn't have looked out of place in a country pile. There was a small billiard table and a selection of comfy chairs (which could have been taken straight out of Sherlock Holmes' study), there were shelves of books – and there were countless glass cabinets full of all sorts of specimens. There were rocks, ostrich eggs, stuffed animals, insect remains, examples of bushmen utensils and weapons, butterflies and bones. And all this, under an internal swathe of a Victorian-patterned, purple damask, draped to accentuate its richness, made one feel that one had stepped back in time, but not in any way in standards of comfort. Indeed, it was all so opulent that if one was still dusty and unkempt from a seven-hour journey, one felt not quite in keeping with one's surroundings, and more than eager to repair to one's own rather more modest billet where one could tart oneself up.

This was not a problem. When a little of the afternoon tea had been consumed (there were piles of it and only Brian and Sandra to eat it), Peter, who was one half of the "front of house" team of Peter and Kirsty, led the newcomers to their abode. It was almost as daunting as the dining tent — albeit on a more human scale. It had an internal lining of the same rich damask and it housed, at its centre, an enormous four-poster bed that was equipped with a set of steps with which one could mount it. Around this bed were Persian rugs, Victorian/Edwardian cabinets, more chairs filched from Sherlock's study and even a few more "specimens" — including an unidentified animal skull in a glass case. And behind the bed chamber of the tent was a bathroom that was not only wood-panelled, but that also came with a gentleman's washstand (complete with copper basin) and a leather-upholstered wooden armchair — which was actually a loo. This device was a real period piece, overhung by a wood-encased cistern, complete with the sort of metal-chain pull that Brian hadn't seen since his childhood. Oh, and of course there was also a suitably copper-embellished shower in this bathroom — with another similar shower outside — to ensure that one kept one's body adequately sluiced at all times so as not to offend the ladies. It was all completely bonkers, but all completely wonderful.

So too was dinner. Brian and Sandra had polished themselves up and had returned to the canvas Natural History Museum, and there to greet them were Peter and Kirsty together with the two other guests who were resident in the camp this evening, and Super and Bones. Now, such a miscellany of characters needs a little introduction, so starting with Peter:

Well, Peter was in his mid twenties, had graduated with a degree in the history of art and architecture from Edinburgh University – and sounded as though he had. From somewhere near Thetford, he was now doing his bit on the edge of the world's largest saltpan and putting into use that part of his degree course that had entailed his socialising with strangers. And this he did very well. He was genuinely amiable and entertaining, and had that aura of confidence that signalled that he could deal with just about anybody. Even with visiting Russian oligarchs, one of whom had visited the camp only the previous week (somebody called Alexander Lebedev, who apparently owned, amongst other things, the Evening Standard, which is supposedly some un-tuned organ of our great free press back in Britain). Kirsty had the same aura and similar antecedents and, like Peter, was still enjoying her twenties. Her job was to partner Peter and to look attractive but entirely unattainable.

The "other guests" were a couple by the name of Jonathan and Debbie, who appeared to be representatives of that breed which once had a country of origination (in their case, South Africa and England respectively), but which is now divorced from anything as mundane as a national identity, and inhabits instead some sort of first-class, international super-world, where one flits between one's properties in New York, London and Rome and where one never admits to the patronage of any particular tax regime. That said, they were both quite pleasant, although Brian thought that Debbie deferred to her husband rather too readily – in a way that Sandra had never quite grasped how to do.

That leaves Super and Bones. These black guys were the two resident senior guides in the place, with Super clearly the more senior of the two. Bones was quietly-spoken and obviously very bright, but Super… well Super was super. He was in his early thirties, he was tall and, having been a protégé of the original Jack, he had spent his life at the camp, which meant that he now had even more confidence than Peter and Kirsty, more authority than this pair put together, and a capacity to talk and generally to entertain his guests that was simply unique. In due course, Brian and Sandra would discover that his "super-ness" also extended to his guiding. He was quite a cool guy.

So, anyway, with this complement of disparate but unavoidably interesting fellow diners, the meal was an experience and a joy. The conversation ranged between scary animal encounters, the habits of Botswana's bushmen (the San people), rugby football and Land Rovers versus Land Cruisers. What was also discussed was the rarity of visits to this camp by people in vehicles. Virtually everybody who came here came in a light aeroplane (the camp had its own airstrip) and people who used Land Cruisers were very few and far between – and clearly slightly out of their minds. Didn't they know how far away from anywhere this place was? This cheered Brian immensely. He loved to find a strand of the unconventional in this increasingly conventional world, even if it meant seven hours in a driving seat and tackling potholes the size of cars. He also loved the atmosphere of the meal.

The eight diners sat either side of the enormous table, decked with fine china and fine cutlery – and with cut-glass wine glasses that were each equipped with their own hand-made moth-guard, a weighted round of fabric which discouraged one especially large and colourful variety of moth from supping from the wine within. (And they did try – continuously – no matter whether the wine was white or red. And, according to Super, the vintage and the grape variety made no difference either. They were all just helpless wine-aholics.) Anyway, the table was overhung with those rich purple drapes, and these drapes, along with everything else in the tent, were bathed in the light of old-fashioned oil lamps. There was no electricity in the structure whatsoever. The result was a near-magical ambience made even more magical by the knowledge that this fine dining was taking place not in some city-centre gentleman's club but in the middle of nowhere. Outside, there was only inky darkness, distant animal noises, salt – and a queue of monster moths waiting their turn for a chance at the wine… If only such bewitching experiences could be created more easily and more conveniently, more "closer to home". But, of course, they couldn't. Even if one had access to talented chefs and the benefit of good company, only by transporting oneself into the middle of a virtual void could one savour such a stupendous experience. Brian felt very fortunate – again. And he made a promise to himself. This promise was that as long as he could he would, and this was shorthand for 'No one knows when his or her clock-spring will wind down, and for as long as you're able (both physically and financially) you should go for it, relish the difficulties of attaining it and bloody well enjoy it when you've got it. Experiences are what define your life and you should pack in as many of them as you can, especially if they are anything like the experience of dinner at Jack's Camp. And who wouldn't enjoy competing with a moth for a mouthful of wine?'

Well, maybe it was exhaustion through driving that was getting to him or the number of units of alcohol was now overtaking him, but Brian really did feel well with the world.

So too did Sandra. She said so. Although the next day, with what they would both encounter in the morning, they would soon come to the conclusion that it was quite possible to feel even weller…

15.

It was 5.45 in the morning and Brian and Sandra were sipping coffee. Fifteen minutes earlier, a lady had arrived at their tent with the stimulant in question and a plate of home-made biccies. Much better than an alarm clock and infinitely more enjoyable, especially as the sipping could be conducted on the tent's deck and therefore with a grandstand view of the rising sun. As it rose above the horizon (from our travellers' perspective, between two palm trees) it looked sensational – and very red. Not like some item of exotic underwear, of course, but more like what it really was: a manifestation of the impossible, a daily event that is truly fantastic – and one that gives life to the Earth. All too often this literally every-day miracle is taken for granted – until one sees it like this: as a crimson orb being reborn yet again. Yes, there was no getting away from it. The coffee was really strong. Brian hadn't been stimulated into these sorts of thoughts for years.

But now it was time to move. Super had appeared – at a respectable early-morning distance – with a battlefield-green safari vehicle and the prospect of a ride into nowhere. For, when one left the palm oasis of Jack's, that's all there was: a treeless expanse of Botswana with only salt-hardy grass and essentially nothing else, except, of course, a few skulking birds. These guys were all small and veered towards the little-brown-jobs end of the bird spectrum. But Super knew them all, and found most of them with his ears before he'd found them with his eyes. He was as gifted a guide as Brian and Sandra had ever encountered, and soon he would be providing them with an experience they were never likely to encounter again.

Super had driven them a few bumpy miles away from the camp, had stopped and was now inviting them to ease their buttocks by taking a walk into the emptiness all around. Only, of course, it wasn't quite empty. About fifty yards away there was an almost indiscernible mound, and this was their destination. On arriving there, Super demanded Brian's camera and then suggested that he and his wife sit on the ground – just next to the mound and quite close to a burrow that led directly beneath it. Brian and Sandra knew what would now happen, but this pre-knowledge did nothing at all to diminish its impact when it did happen – which was no more than two minutes after they'd sat down.

There was just one to start with, a wary, almost bleary-eyed little fellow who came to the lip of the burrow and then went back in. Then another emerged and took a few steps outside, followed closely by what could have been the first guy and then by another after him. Initially, they stayed at the burrow's entrance, until more of their number appeared behind them – including a couple of babies – at which point one of them trotted across to Brian, jumped onto his lap, ran up his right arm and sat on his head. Then another of the leading squad did the same with Sandra – albeit he (or she) eschewed a head perch in favour of a shoulder. So Sandra now sported on this part of her anatomy, not a traditional parrot, but a rather more unorthodox resident, and one that is only infrequently found on human heads. Yes, both Brian and Sandra were now wearing, about their persons, a meerkat, and both of them, quite clearly, were coping with the ordeal very well. One might even say that they were not just coping with the experience but relishing it – to the extent that they were savouring the unalloyed delight of having the closest possible contact with one of their very favourite animals. And this was real. This was nothing to do with a comparison of the insurance market on the telly, but just an innocent sort of ecstasy, the sort of ecstasy that comes from the knowledge that a certain desert-living creature has decided to use you for a look-out.

For that was what was happening here. The early rising mini-mongooses were conducting their early-morning survey for potential dangers – principally the presence of circling raptors in the sky above. And when one conducts such a survey, one inevitably chooses the highest point available from which to conduct it, even if this is a cotton-covered human shoulder or a barely hair-covered human head. And even a human bum will do, if the human in question has been instructed to now lie down on its front – to enable more of the meerkats to enjoy an elevated position for their survey. Yes, both Brian and Sandra were now laid out on a bit of the Makgadikgadi Pans and their backs, bums and legs were populated with a gang of upright meerkats, scanning their surroundings for the slightest hint of danger, whilst at the same time recognising no danger whatsoever in their more than willing hosts. And then they were off…

No raptors had been spotted, the direction of travel from the burrow had been decided, the meerkat responsible for crèche duties today had been chosen – and left with the youngsters down in the burrow – and all the other meerkats were off in search of food, and with no further interest in their "humans-for-platforms". It was remarkable, and no less so for the fact that these creatures were in no way tame but just habituated to peaceful, non-threatening "things" that seemed to arrive at their front door each morning, and were distinctly higher than the surrounding land. And who would not be thrilled, even if it was a bit circus and not very authentic as a wildlife experience? Especially if those fortunate enough to encounter this meerkat liaison were meerkat nuts who only once before had seen them in the wild, and had never expected ever to feel them in the wild – on any part of their bodies. This was going to be a difficult act to follow, and needed an immediate intermission in the shape of a posh middle-of-the-pan breakfast served from the back of Super's safari Land Cruiser – accompanied by a first viewing of the scores of photos Super had taken of his charges and their meerkat companions. From these it became clearer than ever; it was going to be an almost impossibly difficult act to follow…

Nevertheless, Super tried his best. When the remains of breakfast had been packed away, he took his party of two further into the wilderness to discover more birds (of the lark and cisticola varieties) and quite a few four-legged types. So, onto the list went slender mongooses, ground squirrels, black-backed jackals and a few wildebeest and zebra. But this wasn't the Serengeti, and in Brian's mind it was astonishing that there was anything here at all. For soon even the grass had disappeared, and the Land Cruiser was crunching its way over a bare crust of salt that must have offered about as much nourishment to wildlife as the pernicious *X Factor* back home offers to genuine talent.

Yes, they were now riding across a genuine pan, and maybe this and not the miscellaneous wildlife spotting was Super's way of following that meerkat act. Because who could not be seized and then transfixed by such an experience? By finding oneself on a solid sea-of-salt with around one none of the normal markers of a natural or manmade world? No grass, no shrubs, no trees, no fences, no anything, but just a glistening sheet of crystals running off into the distance and smothering one's sense of perspective and depth and even one's sense of oneself with its vastness and its blankness – with its unremitting refusal to be anything other than a bare stretch of zilch. Hell, even the blue sky above was a little more "textured" – and certainly more familiar.

Although probably not so for Super. He was as well acquainted with this unending saline crust as he was with his mother, and he also knew how to navigate it and to find for his charges not only more animals and birds but also the evidence of where they'd been. So, here, at the side of the sea of salt, was a hole surrounded by white poo, springbok and wildebeest horns, aardvark and jackal bones and zebra hooves. It was, of course, a hyena den – with, fortuitously, no hyena currently in residence. And over there was a hole below a stand of taller-than-normal grass, where the water table was closer to the surface. And this had been recognised by the jackals, ratels, porcupine and hyena, who all now used the hole as an underground drinking pool – albeit not all at the same time.

Well, this was all very fascinating, but it was now approaching midday and Brian was becoming convinced that there was every likelihood that the temperature recorded at Jack's two days previously might soon be recorded again. And, as that temperature had been 49°C, he was keen to retire from the rather exposed environment of the pan and to return to the comfort of the camp. Super was there before him, and soon Brian and Sandra were back in their tent and preparing themselves for lunch with the aid of a shower. This meal was

'Torque to me, baby.'

Anthropoides paradisea (Blue crane). Pulcher (beautiful).

Nxameseri Lodge – eventually

Surprisingly dainty

Spellbinding

The Botswanan Giant Aardvark

A camp-bed at Jack's

A stripey landscape

Latent mischief

Roller chorister

A reasonably handsome animal

'I've got sixteen wives. It's exhausting.'

A Delta airstrip departure lounge

A sable: beauty within the beast

'Are you sure you know the way?'

A pelicannery

with their companions of the previous evening and was simply exceedingly good. The conversation accompanying it wasn't too bad either, and included an explanation by Super of the ability of the San hunters eventually to outrun a male kudu (because of the enervating effect of its heavy horns) – and a proposal by Brian that anyone admitting to the use of Twitter should be disbarred from holding public office or any job involving even a smidgeon of responsibility. If these people, he contended, wanted to live a kindergarten existence, telling all their kindergarten classmates what they'd had for breakfast or who they'd seen on telly, then they should be kept in their kindergarten world and well away from anything that involves grown-up thinking and grown-up behaviour.

Brian wasn't convinced that his proposal had received universal approval around the table, but nobody actually spoke out against him. Probably because nobody now had the strength. It was just so bloody hot. In fact, it was so roasting that directly after lunch, Brian, contrary to the advice he had received from his mother not to swim on a full stomach – an act that risked death or something equally inconvenient – swam.

Eighty yards from the dining tent at Jack's is its "pool tent". This is, if anything, bigger than the dining tent, and has to be to accommodate a generously-sized swimming pool and another assembly of antique chests and elegant loungers, set around the pool and offering to its users the ultimate in comfort on a hot afternoon. For here they can lie, in between dips and with a drink in their hand, and take in the view of the surrounding void – through the tent's open sides. And, should they be that way inclined, they can also imagine that the afternoon shift from the harem will soon be arriving with trays of Turkish delights and whatever other delights their masters require. Yes, it was the extravagance and the opulence of the tent – and the heat – and having it all to himself… For Sandra had now retired to their own tent, leaving Brian as the sole occupant of this preposterous bath-house – and with a growing acceptance that the afternoon shift was not about to turn up. And accordingly, he had a last dip, finished his drink, dried himself and then rejoined his wife. (And it was now so hot that soon after greeting her he was drying himself again, albeit this time the liquid wasn't pool water but the couple of pints of perspiration he'd generated in returning from the pool.)

Immobility and nudity became the order of the day. Even if it wasn't 49°C, it wasn't far off and, in Brian's opinion, the only way to cope with that sort of nonsense was to lie naked on a bed – with your wife and a wet towel to hand – and to engage in the only waking activity that didn't involve movement (or somebody else moving), which was thinking. And what he thought about was that meerkat encounter, and what this encounter told him about meerkats, about other animals and about the animal called "man".

Now, his thinking was initially no more than luxuriating, revelling in the delight of a close contact with an animal he so loved. But then he began to consider how these animals organised themselves and how each member of the extended family participated in the tasks they undertook, whether these tasks concerned surveying, hunting or even baby-minding. Then he considered what the apparent equality in this participation meant in terms of the meerkats' intellect. And he soon decided that it meant that they were all equipped with more or less the same amount of grey stuff, that there were no genius meerkats – and no real dummies. That their evolution had brought them to a state where there was real meerkat egalitarianism. No meerkat was greater or lesser than any other meerkat.

Furthermore, this uniformity of ability, concluded Brian, was not confined to just meerkats, but it was what one observed in all other animals. Differences in their performance and behaviour were apparent, but these differences were generally a function of their gender or their size – and not of their cleverness or their dimness. One must therefore arrive at the ultimate conclusion that, in the natural world, intellect is handed out in equal measures to all creatures and that this equality in their brainpower serves them very well. Just as the disparity in intellect in our own species causes us all sorts of problems.

For we are different – from meerkats and from all other creatures. There are those of us, for example, who can manage the counter-intuitive conceptualisation of quantum mechanics, or who can, through mathematics, predict the laws of the universe before they've been found in the lab – or who can create great works of art and great expositions on the human soul. Whereas… at the other end of the spectrum, there is that rather more numerous band of individuals who… well, who are interested in the branding of their footwear, fascinated by the goings-on of somebody like Cheryl Cole (who is presumably related to Old King…), delighted by "reality shows" (which are entirely deficient in anything real at all) and hooked on computer games, where the biggest challenge is to remember that "going to the lavatory" is not something you can do in the virtual world and that you really do need to break off from your moronic pastime and go there rather than just carrying on and making a mess in your pants…

And anyway, with such a gulf between human intellects, things were just bound to go wrong. So some clever-dick invented a wheel and it's been downhill for the world ever since – not least because clever-dicks are in something of a minority and all the numpties they've dragged along with them – into our modern world – have no idea of how to treat this world. Instead they seem intent on trashing it or, at best, they're entirely indifferent to its fate. As long as they can get their hands on that new Nike trainer, discover where Cheryl is spending her next holiday and get up to level twenty on *Grand Theft Assassin's Call of Duty – Lynch the Dead Man before you Nuke him*, they couldn't give a fig. And many of them couldn't even give you an answer – to any question you posed them. And certainly not to the one that asks why meerkats and other animals are so "balanced" in their intelligence, whereas they, the poor sods, have barely one tenth of the brain power that was handed out to Einstein. Although, there again, Brian suspected that even the good professor wouldn't know the answer to that one, no more than Brian did himself. At which point in his mental deliberations, his very own intellect was overtaken by unconsciousness, no doubt brought on by the ambient temperature. It was only when the sun had adopted a distinctly downward trajectory – and coincidentally when he had received a nudge in the ribs from Sandra followed immediately by the suggestion that he prepare himself for a drive – that he roused himself from his slumbers.

Yes, it was now late afternoon, and after more delicacies forced upon them in the dining tent, it was time for Sandra and Brian to join Super again for another excursion in his Land Cruiser – and a rendezvous with some weather…

Brian should have guessed it. Near furnace-heat temperatures have to presage something, and that something is generally a storm. And so it was this day. For as the evening approached, so too did a change in the colour of the sky, and then a wind blew up. So that, early into the drive, Brian was recalling his and Sandra's experience at Susuwe, and the ineffectiveness of an open safari vehicle against the drenching power of rain. However, it wasn't raining yet, and Super was still able to deploy his considerable guiding skills to find for his clients, first a cape hare, then a hatch of seventeen-year cicadas and some impala – and then a pair of secretary birds. These chaps are extraordinary on any measure one cares to choose, not least because they are unique as long-legged, almost ludicrous-looking hunters of snakes and other reptiles. Furthermore, according to Super, they are also extremely affectionate, because not only do they pair for life, but the pair-bond is reinforced every day by the two of them swapping their last meal of the day with their partner. And just imagine that happening with humans, especially if she's on a diet and he's into pizzas...

Meanwhile, the wind had not abated. On the contrary, it was now blowing fiercely and, unfortunately, in the same direction as the Land Cruiser's travel. This meant that unless Super pushed his vehicle to quite unseemly speeds, the dust cloud it was creating in its wake would overtake it. And not overtake it as in pass by its side and disappear into the distance, but overtake it as in envelope it in a shroud of thick, choking grit. So now it was like a scene from *Speed*, where if Super slowed below 50 kph, he and his passengers would all be doomed. Only, unlike in that rather engrossing film, Super was not driving on tarmac but on a series of rutted and bumpy tracks, or not to say very rutted and very bumpy tracks, which meant that the possibility of a sudden traumatic injury or the onset of undetected internal bleeding now joined the risk of imminent asphyxiation.

But this was Super at the wheel. And Super had clearly been here before. He could outrun anything the pan could throw at him, and he could stay on the track, and he probably even knew the tolerance of individual internal organs to the forces of external shaking. Accordingly, he soon delivered his precious cargo, both unharmed and undead, to the site of a wonder of nature.

It was a tree. But not any old tree. No, this was a monster of a tree, visible from miles around (and easily visible from Jack's, even though Jack's was nowhere near it). Of course, it was a baobab, and such a huge baobab that it had its own name – taken from a Nineteenth Century explorer who used it as a navigation beacon. And this "Chapman's Baobab" is such a large natural feature in a country with very few natural features of any sort, that it even appeared on some of the early maps of the whole continent of Africa. It really is prodigious – with a 25-metre-circumference trunk, a canopy of a size to match, and an age that can only be measured in thousands of years.

Brian was suitably impressed. So was Sandra. She told him so – just as the first "shards" of rain arrived. Then she appeared to be more interested in donning her waterproof cape than she was in the tree, and Brian became similarly distracted. As feared, it was Susuwe all over again, and not only did the horizontal torrent bring their inspection of Chapman's Baobab to a premature end, but it also, apparently, put paid to an evening meal under the stars. Super told his charges that out there on the pan there was currently a contingent of Jack's best, busy preparing a meal that, for the delight of their guests, would be served on a table in the middle of nowhere – but that, as all these heroes would inevitably be soaked to the skin within the next few minutes, dinner would no doubt be relocated to that dreary tent back in camp. Brian accepted this grave disappointment with fortitude, but felt genuinely sorry that so much effort had been expended for no result. And these guys weren't even building a National Health computer system...

The rain was persistent – and penetrating. Aided by the wind, it even managed to penetrate the defences of the capes. So there was relief all round when Super, by embarking on another bout of boy-racer driving, had outrun the storm. It was now dry, the capes could be dispensed with and, as the sun was about to set (in a clearing sky), glasses could be distributed in their place. Yes, it was sundowner time again. And for this all-important part of the day, Super had found a rare grove of straggly trees, which housed, amongst other things, fiery-necked and rufous-cheeked nightjars. Their songs, together with the sound of jackals in the distance, made this a very special time. With the colours of the setting sun, a fascinating account of Super's life and his travels – and more gin in the sundowners than was sensible – it would prove to be a very memorable time as well.

But there was still dinner to attend to back at camp. This was taken with the normal suspects and, despite the grandeur of the surroundings, in whatever one was wearing (and in whatever state of kemptness one was in) when one returned from ones "activities". And as Jonathan and Debbie's activity had involved quad bikes that came without canvas roofs or readily deployable capes, their kemptness level was below even that of Brian's. However, nobody seemed to care and the meal proceeded as it had the previous evening – with superb fare and agreeable banter – despite a reference to a "celebrity omnivore". For it appeared that this particular celeb had spent a holiday here and had befriended Super. Although, from what Brian gathered, he had not been allowed to indulge his omnivorous habits by tasting meerkat. He may, however, have chased elephants…

It was during coffee: the unmistakeable sound of nearby lumbering giants. And clearly so nearby that an external inspection was called for – to be conducted by all the diners. And there they were: half a dozen furtive pachyderms loitering outwith the tent – with intent – and their intent was the depredation of Jack's stock of palm trees. They had done it before. They had sneaked in under the cover of darkness (as much as any elephant can sneak) and they had pushed over palm trees in order to consume their fronds. All very natural really, but when one is operating a camp in the middle of a desolate place and one's only external shelter is a finite number of palm trees, one is understandably proprietary in one's attitude to these trees, and one doesn't want them felled by passing giants – who can and who do find sufficient, nourishing food elsewhere. So they had to be chased off – or shooed off. For Brian soon discovered that encouraging elephants to go elsewhere is much the same as encouraging rabbits or woodpigeons to go elsewhere. One just makes a bit of a racket in their direction and they leave. Albeit elephants take a little longer to take flight, show more resentment and hurt when they finally do, and then leave one feeling like a real celebrity: completely callous and indifferent to their fate.

But it had to be done. Just as it was unavoidable that Brian and Sandra now had to return to their tent. They had been up since early morning, they had been drained by the heat of the day, and tomorrow they had another journey to undertake. So they needed some sleep. And Brian needed to place that celebrity omnivore on that spectrum of clever-dicks to numpties – and to decide, in particular, how far down the spectrum acute insufferability and even acuter insouciance should drag him…

16.

Breakfast was Marmite and maths, Marmite as an antidote to the foodie over-indulgence of the previous two days and maths in the vain attempt to estimate the ant population of Botswana. And this latter element of the meal had arisen from Brian and Sandra's encounter with this insect on their way to the dining tent. There had been a lot of them, as in countless numbers of them everywhere – to the point that the walk to breakfast had been reduced to a process of skipping across a virtual carpet of the little blighters, and a carpet that seemed to go on forever. It must have been the rain of the previous evening, thought Brian. The ants either favoured a stroll in the anti-antediluvian ground conditions, or the downpour had created an underground flood that had forced them out of their chambers. But for whatever reason, they were now obvious in prodigious numbers, and if there were so many here, within the bounds of Jack's Camp, how many must there be in the whole of the country, which appeared, superficially at least, to be just as unpromising for large-scale life-forms, and therefore probably ideal for small-scale life-forms like ants? Brian applied himself to the problem as best he could. But the absence of a few essentials, like information (on the relative size of Jack's to the whole of the country and a proper estimate of the number of ants outside the tent), a computing ability (which could, in any way, have dealt with an excess of zeros) and something to write with, saw his efforts quickly nosedive into failure. After all, no way could the answer 'effing gazillions' be considered a successful outcome. Furthermore, there were more pressing queries to attend to – concerning the size of tips to be left, what to wear for the forthcoming journey, and how to find Planet Baobab again and not perish in the process by getting hopelessly lost.

Well, all these queries were soon resolved, although the first escort identified to lead Brian and his wife out of the pan could well have landed them in the fire. Because she was a Jack's Camp cook returning home for some holiday, who was very nice but did not, it transpired, know her way to the Planet. She was therefore supplemented by the camp mechanic who did know the way. So, after a series of surprisingly earnest goodbyes, followed by an hour or so of demanding driving, Brian and Sandra were back at Planet Baobab, had deposited there both their escorts, and were now ready for a further jaunt west – and whatever might await them.

What awaited them, directly after another fuel stop, was the metalled road towards Maun where it was sandwiched between two national parks. To its south there was the Makgadikgadi National Park and to its north the Nxai Pan National Park, and it was this surfeit of national parks which accounted for a new animal at the edge of the road to add to the normal goat/cow/donkey hazard. And this animal was the ostrich. There were scores of them all along the road, and all of them with the appearance of a bird-strike about to happen. It was that look on their face, that sort of deranged, staring look, and below that face, that one hundred kilograms of body – supported by a pair of legs that could propel it at a Land Cruiser shattering speed of over forty miles per hour. And they did all stare at the Land Cruiser – with those big starey eyes, as though weighing up whether they should put those legs into action and test whether they really did have the right of way.

Fortunately, none of them did, and Brian and his wife eventually found themselves beyond this (o)stretch of road and back with just the usual four-legged perils. Then they found their turn-off to the south. For now they were about to skirt the western boundary of the Makgadikgadi National Park in an attempt to locate their next lodge, a hostelry that rejoiced in the name of Leroo La Tau. This is Setswana for "Lion's Paw", although Brian would soon be of the opinion that it could also be Setswana for "Entirely Hidden".

It was Nxamaseri all over again, but with a few novel twists. The first (after establishing beyond doubt that there was no signpost to the place) was a drive down a sand-track that did have a signpost, albeit not to the lodge but instead to the entrance to the national park. This led into a small village in which there was a river, and a further signpost by the river indicating a ferry crossing to the park gate on its far bank. However, the ferry crossing was a little short on ferries. In fact, there were no boats of any sort anywhere, and no one around to provide advice on the likelihood of any appearing. The village appeared to be in shut down. Which all meant that this wasn't a legitimate ferry crossing at all, but just a river – and a dead end for Brian and Sandra. So Brian turned around the Land Cruiser and drove back to the main road. He would have to find another route.

He did. It was another sand-track, which brought him back into the village from another direction (now it really was Nxamaseri all over again), and he was forced to accept that he would have to find someone to ask. There had to be somebody about.

There was. She was a local inn-keeper, and she directed Brian to another sand-track out of the village. This looked promising, until, after about seven kilometres, the sand was threatening to strand the Land Cruiser, and the number of turns in the track was threatening to make any retracing of their steps completely impossible. It wasn't looking good. It seemed to be a choice between going on and getting stuck in increasingly deep sand or turning back and getting impossibly lost. But then, just as Brian was about to break his resolution not to panic, a gate appeared in the distance. They had at least arrived somewhere.

Well, they had. But not at the lodge. Instead, they were in front of a massive metal gate in a ten-foot high chain-link fence with, just beyond it, a similar gate in a similarly tall and official-looking fence. And these fences were tall and they were official-looking because they were the impressive parallel boundary fences of the national park, and they were very clearly conveying the message to all unauthorised persons that they should "keep out!"

'Splendid,' observed Brian. 'I think next year we'll go to Cornwall.'

'If we're still alive then,' responded Sandra. 'Aren't you rather assuming we can get out of here – before the water runs out?'

'We've got enough water for a week. And well you know it.'

'Precisely,' observed Sandra – and she wasn't smiling.

Well, Brian didn't get them stuck and he didn't lose his way back to the village, but only his will to live, when an old man at the side of the track, from whom he'd asked some further directions, informed him that those gates in the park fence were never locked – and yes, that was the way to the lodge.

Having recovered his composure after only a very short time, Brian turned his vehicle around once more and drove carefully back down the track. And the old man was right. The gates could be opened, and no more than two hundred yards past the gates was Leroo La Tau – which Brian now decided was Setswana for "They must be having a joke".

Nevertheless, he and his long-suffering companion were now at their destination. And what a destination it was!

A guy called Nelson had met them at the entrance to the lodge, and having been less than receptive to Brian's observations concerning the establishment's effective concealment from the rest of the world, took them through its main "lapa" building to a seat by its pool. And from this seat, Brian and Sandra could start to appreciate just how wonderful Leroo La Tau really was.

The lodge overlooked a river (the same Boteti River that didn't have a ferry in the nearby village). But, as the lodge was set on a high ridge on one side of this river, it didn't so much overlook it as offer a panoramic view of it – and of the far bank beyond. And this far bank was riddled with elephants, zebra, giraffe and kudu. It was incredible: an opportunity to game watch from a poolside vantage point. And, as then became apparent, the same stunning prospect was also available from the deck of their chalet, and even from the loo in their chalet. For it too (the chalet, not the loo) was perched, as were all the lodge's chalets, on the same high ridge – with a view of paradise as a permanent fixture.

Well, what to do for the remainder of the afternoon was now settled. After a little sustenance and a little alcohol, it would be a determined effort to move as little as possible from the two loungers on the chalet's deck and soak up that view. It worked very well, with only minimal movement, but with more animals seen (including some monkeys on the deck itself) and with even a few new birds seen as well. This was quite a place – once you'd found it. And it was quite surprising it wasn't more popular. For apparently there were only two other guests here, and they were the regional manager of the firm that ran the lodge and his wife! And soon Brian and Sandra would be "enjoying" their company.

Yes, dinner would be taken with this pair and with three of the lodge's staff: Ollie, a manageress, Peter, a guide, and Fred, the "over-manager". And the first point to make is that all these people were charming and friendly (and the food provided at the meal was no less than excellent). Unfortunately, however, the meal would prove to be exceptionally memorable – for all the wrong reasons. This was because, despite the abundance of charm and amiability, in order of appearance: Moss, the regional manager, was quiet (as in uncommunicative), his wife, Moleba, was even quieter (as in silent), Ollie was subdued (possibly because of the presence of Moss at the table), Peter was sporadically verbose but almost incomprehensible when he was, and Fred was taciturn and more interested in his food than in conversation. The result was a near monologue from Brian as he tried to goad his table companions into some sort of banter – but without much success. And the overpowering mood of the meal was like that which must have pertained at the Last Supper (assuming, that is, that the disciples didn't tell jokes and Jesus himself wasn't a bit of a wag). And that was the essence of the problem. All these guys around the table in the lodge were Botswanans, and whilst they have a whole raft of admirable qualities, they've found very little room on this raft for humour or even for a bit of lively verbal sparring. They tend to the dull. And Brian knew what he was talking about here; he used to work in a profession that was known for its dullness. He also remembered what Richard had told him back at Muchenje Lodge: that some of their Botswanan staff had to be taught how to smile. Well, Brian had discounted that remark at the time as stupid and mildly offensive. But what he'd witnessed over dinner made him revise his judgement. These guys were bloody hard work. Or put another way, they were nice but not in the least bit naughty.

They also hadn't cracked the moth problem. For here, unlike at Jack's, there were no covers for the glasses – but the same alco-phile moths about the place. As a result, much moth extraction was required, until Peter improvised with some coasters. These worked well enough, but Brian thought he might suggest that they deploy some real covers to cure the problem. And while they were at it, they could put up a sign on the road – so people could find the place and make their own judgements about its less than hilarious staff. But he didn't. It was their lodge, their country, and their prerogative to behave just as they wanted, and not to adopt a demeanour or a conduct that might just suit some bigoted foreigner. And there was probably sod all binge-drinking in Botswana either. So, suitably self-chastised, Brian quitted the dining table together with his wife and returned (under escort) to their chalet.

As he lay in bed this night, waiting to drop off to sleep, he gave some further thought to his tendency to judge people, and to judge them against his own very rigid rules and without making allowances for their different backgrounds and their different cultures. And he decided that he was a lost cause in this respect. Yes, he was quite sure that he was no more likely to adopt a different perspective or to make any sort of allowances in coming to a judgement about other people than he was to arrive at an accurate figure for the number of ants in Botswana.

No, Brian knew himself. He was a believer in absolutism – in the sense that his point of view was always absolutely right. The idea of accepting relativism was anathema to him (particularly as he misunderstood its meaning and thought it meant being relatively undecided about what one thought). So when, tomorrow evening, he was at the dinner table – and again observing the rather stodgy, humourless behaviour of his table companions and forming judgements on them – he would not beat himself up about it. Although he might introduce a debate about absolutism and relativism into the proceedings. After all, who could tell? That sort of stuff might just amuse them…

17.

Jack's Camp had been heavenly. (And it should have been. Brian and Sandra had paid a fortune to stay there.) But this Leroo La Tau place wasn't too bad either.

Indeed, it was fair to say that in the paradise stakes it was challenging Jack's all the way, and it might yet overtake it. And Brian came to this opinion as he sat up in bed at five thirty in the morning and took in the view through the plate-glass windows of the chalet. The panorama outside was truly splendid. And yes, it really was possible to enjoy this same sublime vista as one sat on the loo. Because, thanks to the chalet's position on the edge of a high ridge – and its situation in a people-free national park – the river-side wall of the bathroom was just a sheet of clear glass. Nevertheless, even in this latest episode of heaven, there were, as always, a few minor faults, a few minor defects in its otherwise pristine perfection – and the first one of these concerned that loo…

There was a door-stop bolted to the floor of the bathroom no more than two feet from the loo, and directly in the path of all its barefoot patrons as they hastened to its bowl. Brian had stubbed his toe on it three times already. Then there was the shower. It used water that, just like the water in the bathroom taps, stank of hydrogen sulphide. From wherever the lodge drew its water, the bad-egg smell was down there as well. And if that wasn't enough of a problem with the shower, there was another one: whenever one touched its control knob, one received a shock. The bloody thing wasn't earthed.

Well, Brian considered all these blemishes on the pearly-white skin of Leroo La Tau as he shaved over a smelly wash basin, and concluded that he was probably the biggest fault-finding curmudgeon for hundreds of miles around. That in this empty area of this sparsely-populated country, one would have to travel for hours if not days to find anyone who would focus quite so intently on what were merely trifling imperfections in what was otherwise a true paradise (and even further than that to find someone who would also be such a bastard in the evaluation of his dining companions). Yes, it was time to focus on the paradise credentials of the place – and to forget the imperfections. And that meant it was time to get the day under way and, in due course, to discover that the lodge had a far bigger imperfection than its door-stops and smells…

To start with, everything was fine; an enthusiastic greeting from Ollie and Peter and good coffee and good toast, and then a leisurely walk with Peter to an awaiting boat. He would be Brian and Sandra's guide for the whole of their stay at the lodge, and to conduct this guiding, he first had to get them across the river. Hence the boat. Still all was fine. The boat was comfortable and its aluminium hull was sound, which unfortunately was more than could be said for Peter's mind.

The first indicator that all was not well was when he killed a wasp. It was just minding its own business on the floor of the boat – when Peter decided to stamp on it. Now, such an act does not mark a man out as deranged and many might regard it as a minor indiscretion (although not the wasp). But Peter was a trained guide, and the rigorous training provided to all guides imbues them not just with a detailed knowledge of wildlife and the practicalities of their intended trade but also with a fundamental ethic. And this ethic is that one never interferes with any of the wildlife one encounters, either by making it do what it wouldn't otherwise do or by causing it harm (or death). And here was somebody who had somehow mislaid this ethic. Because, not content with despatching an innocent insect, he was now driving his boat along the river at such a speed that he put a whole host of birds to flight and he then panicked a couple of drinking elephants. The man was a loony.

Then, after completing the river crossing and having transferred his discomfited guests to a safari Land Cruiser, he compounded his idiocy by failing to protect them, or at least by failing to protect Brian. Because, within just a few minutes, Brian had collected three very painful horsefly bites on his exposed left leg. When he then remarked on these and his injudicious choice of shorts rather than a pair of long trousers (or at least the left half of a pair of long trousers), Peter informed him that the horseflies always bit at this time of the morning – and then handed him an insect repellent spray. It was a case of closing the stable door after the horsefly had bolted.

It got worse. Peter had asked Brian and Sandra what their particular wildlife interests were, and had been informed that that they were catholic; anything was of interest – and especially birds. So when, for the next two hours, he drove his vehicle this way and that – with his eyes glued to the ground in search of lion tracks and oblivious of all birds and all other animals – Brian was beginning to feel that the guy needed counselling – or maybe sacking. The only birds that were seen were those spotted by his charges, which Peter then generally misidentified – if one could understand what he was saying, that is. Because, as over dinner the previous evening, he favoured an indecipherable mumble as his means of communication and, against the noise of the Land Cruiser's engine, this amounted to no communication at all.

In short, Peter was proving to be the complete antithesis of Super back at Jack's, and the complete antithesis of super. He was a dead loss. (Although, having failed to find any lions, he did find an elephant carcass and an even smellier zebra carcass. So, with that earlier wasp demise, a bit of a dead specialist as well…)

Brian was happy when the drive was concluded and they were back across the river. Now he and his wife could have brunch and a verbal exchange of views about the inadequacies of their mad companion – to confirm what their exchange of glances had already revealed. Although first they would need to freshen up in their chalet. This was when they met Fred again. For he was standing at the entrance to their chalet with a mini cold-box in which there were two cold flannels. As he handed these to his returning guests he asked them how they had enjoyed their drive, and Brian and Sandra lied convincingly. For how could they do otherwise? It would have been just as discourteous as asking Fred whether his over-manager duties entailed anything other than his dispensing flannels (as this was the first time that Brian had seen him involved in any sort of activity whatsoever).

Well, brunch was a big improvement on the drive. Albeit, as Moss and Moleba had already left and Brian and Sandra were now the only lodge residents, it was a little over-generous. The buffet looked as though it had been prepared for a visiting football team, none of whose members had eaten for weeks.

However, that was just the way they did things here: their way and, as Peter had demonstrated beyond doubt, rather strangely.

A post-brunch beer brought some much-needed sanity and an opportunity to observe some of the wildlife around the lodge, which proved significantly more rewarding than on the drive. There were bushbucks about, hornbills, pied crows, chattering queleas and, directly across the river from the lodge, a huge herd of zebra. They were ambling down to the river bank, drinking there and then ambling off again, threading their way through the throng of other zebra who were still arriving. It was spellbinding, and it would soon prove even more spellbinding when observed from the river. Because, for their second wildlife excursion of the day, Brian and Sandra had opted for a boat-ride rather than a car-drive, on the basis that Peter would have less opportunity to screw things up, and there might also be fewer horseflies about. Anyway, getting close to the zebra as they drank was marvellous and, to Peter's credit, he did manage this in a professional and sensitive manner. He drove the boat gently and gingerly and he was circumspect in all his actions. But then, when he left the zebra to take his guests further downstream, he reverted to type. His credit was extinguished within minutes and soon after this it was in serious debit.

He startled birds with his incautious navigation, he stampeded some kudu on the bank of the river with the same careless progress, and then he saw a hippopotamus grazing on a little island in the river – and accelerated towards it to make it jump in the water! Not quite content with this degree of stupidity, he then approached an elephant crossing the river, and didn't stop approaching it until it turned and retraced its steps. He had interfered with it – and with all his other victims – in a way that Brian and Sandra had never seen before and never wanted to see again. And by now, it was becoming difficult not to let their feelings be known. Sandra, in particular, used the stage-whisper technique to convey her opinions on Peter's behaviour, and this seemed to have some effect. He certainly proceeded more slowly thereafter, and, by drifting down the river rather than charging down it, much more was seen. So onto the list went Senegal coucals, marabou storks, black crakes, white-crowned shrikes, brown-headed tchagras – and more kudu, more giraffe – and even two lions, who had presumably parked themselves at the side of the river to underline Peter's failure to find them earlier in the day.

The boat-ride culminated with a sundowner in the middle of the river (with the boat wedged into a raft of vegetation) and then a silent return to the lodge, where Fred was waiting for them again with his cold box and his flannels. (This really did seem to be the extent of his duties). And then it was soon time for another "interesting" dinner…

However, before this there was an aperitif and a chat with Nelson, Ollie and Fred (but not Peter). And Brian noticed something: that they were all quite relaxed and surprisingly talkative. He remembered that they were similarly "looser" the previous evening – before the eating had got underway. It was only when they had sat down that it had all got so laboured and awkward. So, Brian was now developing a theory as to why this might have happened, and it concerned the formality surrounding the eating process and, in particular, the way in which this formality was inaugurated. Because, last night, as soon as the diners had taken their places at the table and before even the wine had been poured, a silence had descended to allow introductions to be made. Not introductions around the table, but introductions close to the table – of the evening's catering staff. They were all lined up as if on parade, and then one by one they had been presented to the diners. First there was the chef, then the bread-maker(!) and then the waitress. And when this protocol had been concluded, the chef had then embarked on an explanation of the evening's menu. It was all quite charming in a way, but at the same time its somewhat earnest character and its solemn delivery had set the mood for the meal. It appeared to have imbued it with a blend of stiffness and reserve from which it would never recover. Spontaneity and humour would never get a look in.

Well, was his theory valid and, if so, would it happen again tonight?

The answer seemed to be yes. More introductions of the catering staff and more pre-announcements of the menu were followed by another stodgy experience at the table. And for the next hour and a half, the only relief for Brian and Sandra came in the form of the tantalisingly evocative names of their two table companions (Captain and Nelson) and in their own contributions to the proceedings, some of which may have rather confused these companions. Such as Brian's discourse on the use of technology…

It had started with an observation made by Sandra that one could divide the use of computers between their good use and their bad use, and that their good use was characterised by the saving of time whereas their bad use was characterised by the wasting of time. So, for example, booking holiday accommodation over the internet was easy, efficient – and good, whereas surfing the net for six hours just to see what came up was pointless, mindless – and distinctly bad. It was the difference, she explained, between using a computer as a tool and as a toy. And she was, of course, quite right, albeit somewhat careless. Because, by introducing this topic to the table, she had unwittingly provided her husband with a platform for a lecture. And whilst it started innocently enough, with an observation about British dockers, it then went on – and on...

'Did you know,' he announced out of the blue, 'that during the war, dockers in Britain were a bit of a problem?'

From the expression on their faces, Brian quickly gauged that Captain and Nelson did not. And he was also pretty confident that they might be unclear as to which war he was referring. So he tried again.

'You see, during the Second World War, Britain was dependant on lots of imports. Food and armaments and all sorts of stuff. And, of course, as fast as we were bringing it in, Germany was trying to stop us – by sinking our ships. It was all very tricky. Ships had to be gathered into convoys – for safety – and even then some of them would still be sunk by U-boats.'

Captain and Nelson now seemed engaged, but that U-boat reference may well have confused them. Nevertheless, Brian pressed on quickly.

'So you'd think, wouldn't you, that the dockers in Britain would do their damndest to unload the ships as soon and as efficiently as they could... '

At this point, Nelson nodded encouragingly.

'... well, not a bit of it. They were more often lethargic in their work or just downright obstructive. And apparently, dockers in Glasgow, who loaded ships for the Arctic convoys to Russia, were so bloomin' careless in their work that lots of stuff that arrived there was damaged, if indeed it hadn't shifted around in high seas and sunk the ships that were carrying it.'

Well, despite that nod, Nelson was now clearly bemused – as was Captain. But Sandra had experience of her husband and must have gauged that it was now time to make an intervention.

'Brian,' she announced in her favourite intervening tone, 'you're confusing our hosts. But, as I'm sure you have a point, why don't you make it – now?'

Brian knew that tone and responded immediately and, for him, rather succinctly.

'My point is that dockers have always been a problem. If they weren't disrupting things they were stealing things or just striking. Which is why technology was introduced so successfully, essentially to eliminate them as a feature of dockyards.'

'You mean containerisation?' confirmed Sandra.

'Yes. If you have an element in society that has become insufferable, you try to get rid of it. And with technology – whether of the IT variety or otherwise – you now often can.'

'Really,' observed an apparently underwhelmed Sandra. 'And is that it? Or is there more?'

'Well yes. You see, I'm picking up your point about the good use of technology – as against the bad use.'

'As in containerisation?'

'No, not just containerisation. I mean… '

'Well, drug dealers are pretty insufferable,' interrupted Sandra. 'How would you use technology to eliminate them?'

Brian recognised the challenge being made here, as well as the bewilderment of the Botswanan audience at the table. And he chose to ignore the bewilderment and rise to the challenge.

'Easy,' he responded firmly. 'As with the dockers, you remove their function.'

'How?'

'Well, drugs are all about getting good vibes, aren't they? So you'd develop electronic helmets that deliver these good vibes to the brain directly – and eliminate the need for drugs and therefore the need for drug-dealers. And before you say that's just too fanciful, think where they've already got to with *Strictly Come Dancing* and the *X Factor*. And that's even without helmets...'

'Lawyers?'

'Same approach. You just put together a sophisticated litigation programme, then you feed in all the facts of a case, and the programme delivers the verdict and an appropriate sentence – without all that perverting advocacy stuff. And it'd be similar for all the non-litigation stuff as well. Coz that's mostly how they do it already. You know, standard contracts printed off a computer with names slotted in. It would be a doddle.'

'Terrorists?'

'Ah well... that's more an educational solution than a technological one. You know, teaching them that it's quite in order for people to hold views that don't necessarily accord with your own, and that humility is not an affliction, but that rampant, ill-informed bigotry generally is. That sort of thing. Although, there again, I suppose you could develop a technologically sophisticated virus – which just went after degenerate morons...'

And it was at this point in the proceedings that Brian became aware that he had entirely dispelled the mood of solemnity around the table and replaced it with one of acute perplexity for its Botswanan contingent and a sort of resigned weariness for his wife. So some sort of progress there, even if he hadn't reached the sunlit uplands of amusement and hilarity. And the meal was nearly over. He could now get by with just a few observations on wine-diving moths and the continued heat-wave for what little of it remained. And then he could retire with Sandra to their chalet and contemplate how to deal with tomorrow. And, in particular, how to deal with Peter. Could they eliminate him by making him redundant – even in the absence of some appropriate new technology?

Brian already thought that they could. He thought that they could remove the biggest imperfection in this paradise really quite easily, and all it would take was not a computer or a container but just a bit of resolve. And Brian was good at resolve. Probably even better than he was at bewildering the locals.

Sandra had resolve as well. So when finally they had secured the refuge of their chalet and Brian had explained his formula for eradicating Peter, she concurred immediately.

If only, he thought (as he stubbed his toe for the fourth time), he could now come up with a similarly brilliant strategy for the removal of that bloody door-stop…

18.

The Peter-elimination strategy was to eschew any further drives and the resolve required for its implementation was simply to confirm this intention in the morning – to reiterate what Brian had already imparted to Nelson the previous evening: that he and Sandra wanted to spend the day at their chalet. So not a strategic masterpiece and not the ultimate in a test of resolution. But it worked. And, after a latish breakfast, Brian and his wife had the prospect of a whole "day at leisure" – and a whole lodge to themselves.

Well actually, Ollie and Nelson were still around and there was the odd gardener and cleaner as well. So when Brian accompanied Sandra to the lodge pool for a post-breakfast, pre-chalet dip, he did so in his conventional swimming shorts and not in his Speedos. He now knew a little more about Botswanan culture, but he was still unclear as to where it drew its lines in respect of public decency. And in no way would anybody who was asked to select the word that best described the appearance of his lanky frame in just a pair of Speedos choose the word "decent". Nor for that matter "proper", "modest" or "seemly". And furthermore, his Speedos didn't have a pocket in them for his hankie…

So anyway… after a relaxing swim (and after wringing out

the hankie which he'd forgotten to remove from the pocket in his shorts), Brian was able to lie back on a lounger by the pool and savour the moment. For here he was, under the shade of a tree, with his wife, with uninterrupted blue sky all around, and with that much-discussed paradise pressing in from all sides. And some of this paradise was very close. Just yards away, on a large acacia tree, were two hornbills, and below them, a young cardinal woodpecker being fed by its mum. A little further away were red-billed francolins and a pied kingfisher. And across the river was the spectacle of hundreds of zebra, a dozen or so elephants, a small group of kudu and a pair of giraffes. This, thought Brian, is what the Garden of Eden must have been like. Albeit the loungers struck a slightly discordant note, and he knew that neither his shorts nor his Speedos would have featured in that original version (just as he knew that the whole proposition that such a place ever existed was based on some pretty shaky ground). But these were just (manageable) imperfections in the tableau, and the fact remained that Brian was experiencing a rare pleasure in a rare environment – and there was even the imminent prospect, not of a measly apple, but of a delightful, mouth-watering brunch. (And, of course, no casting-out stuff thereafter.)

It was done. A sufficiency of delectable calories had been ingested, a post-brunch lager had helped them to settle into the stomach, and Brian and Sandra were ready to slope off to a more private slice of nirvana. At which point Nelson appeared and suggested that nirvana might be enhanced by another lager, and would they like some at their chalet. This was an illustration of the real hospitality that lurked below the surface of all that Botswanan reserve, and his offer was accepted with the sort of alacrity that Brian rarely displayed. And then, with the sort of generosity rarely displayed at any commercial hostelry, Nelson soon reappeared not with a couple of glasses of the stuff but with a consignment of it. He had with him a giant cold box, which he then carried to their chalet and which, when opened there, proved to contain a dozen cans of the amber liquor nestling in a cushion of ice. Nirvana would certainly be enhanced, even if it could not be brought to mind after the event.

However, now that Brian and Sandra were alone in their chalet, there were still decisions to make. First, how to arrange the loungers on the deck of their chalet, how to dress themselves on this deck – or whether to dress themselves on this deck – and then with what to intersperse their deck-time and quite when this interspersal should be made. Well, in the event, decisiveness arrived promptly and... decisively. Soon Adam and Eve were established on their suitably arranged loungers, appropriately dressed, and with their planned interspersal deferred for the present. For now they would simply divide their time between wildlife studies and some mugging up on their knowledge of lager, neither of which pastimes involved apples or serpents.

The lager cramming proved very agreeable, but not quite as sensational as the schooling in animal behaviour that was on offer as well. It was everywhere: elephants eating reeds in the channel directly below them, giraffes ambling along on the opposite bank – and one suckling its young – and now, not just hundreds of zebra visiting the river, but thousands of them. Because at this time of the year, just before the rainy season was about to arrive, the zebra were gathering to move eastwards deeper into the Makgadikgadi National Park, where soon there would be new vegetation to feed on, and occasional water to be found. But just now, before that rain had arrived, they were tied to this river, and they were making just short expeditions into the park, only to return every two or three days to fill up on water. And today appeared to be some sort of zebra happy hour, where every zebra from miles around was intent on drinking as much as he or she could, and these chaps not only lined the bank of the river but they also carpeted the approach to the river across from the lodge. Nelson had already told Brian and Sandra that (since the mid 1990s) this channel used to be a dry channel, and that the only water available was that which the lodge pumped to the surface – to attract wildlife for its guests. (And more on the phenomenon that transforms rivers into dry channels and back again into full-blown rivers later.) But now there was so much more of the wet stuff around, the zebra – and all the other animals – still remembered where the pumped waterholes used to be. And this is why they returned to this spot, and when happy hour was in full swing, in such gigantic numbers.

Brian and Sandra could have stayed here watching this pageant of nature all afternoon. And, but for a mid-afternoon intermission and a few visits to the cold box, they did. They were still watching it as the sun began to sink and the browns and beiges of the scene before them became infused with pink and then with purple. It had been a memorable experience, and so memorable that, despite its lager component, it would be remembered very clearly. As would one of the discussions Brian had imposed on his wife, which had been engendered by the abundance of so many animals. And this concerned "threats to the world"…

Brian had recently read about some symposium on the world's future, where the attendees had been asked to determine the greatest threats that now faced our planet. And this is where Brian kicked off.

'You know,' he explained, 'that they decided that the biggest threat of the lot was the accumulation of all that government debt. You know, the stuff they're still pretending we can somehow pay off. And after that it was income inequality, and presumably what this will mean for social cohesion – as in the likelihood that people will start kicking the shit out of each other. And then connectivity…'

'What?' interrupted Sandra.

'Connectivity. You know, all the computer stuff and how it's all interlinked…'

'That's a threat?'

'It is when you look at the incidence of cyber attacks these days – and the likelihood that they could screw everything up.'

'Ah, I see.'

'And then,' continued Brian, 'it's failure of regulation…'

'Yeah…'

'And then global warming – and just squeezed in at the bottom, "population growth"'

'Below all those others?' shrieked Sandra (who was not given to shrieking). 'They must be mad. And why "population growth"? Why not just plain "population"? Don't they know this place is pretty over-stuffed as it is?'

'My thoughts exactly,' responded Brian. 'But this list tells you something even more disconcerting about those who compiled it…'

'Which is…?' encouraged a genuinely engaged Sandra.

'Which is that "threats to the world" are synonymous in the minds of these idiots with threats to us – us humans. As always, there seems to be a depressing inability for people to see anything in this world other than from their own perspective. I mean, ask those zebra over there what they think might be the greatest threat to the world, and I can guarantee it won't be government debt or the failure of regulation. It will be one thing and one thing only: population – as in the bloated population of humans on this planet. And I'll tell you something else as well. And that's that most of those threats, if they ever come about, could well be seen as their salvation. The more dystopia they engender – with all the wars, carnage and population shrinkage that would inevitably follow – the more the zebra would be happy.'

'You're crediting these zebra with an awful lot of intellect. I'm not sure they're really that clever.'

Brian frowned.

'I'm just using the zebra as an illustration. You know, as a representative of all life in this world, of which we are only a small but highly disruptive part. So I'm trying to explain what the greatest threats to the world are if you regard the world as the sum of all its inhabitants and not just as the sum of all those who think that the world belongs to them. Like all those tossers at that symposium.'

'So what are you going to do about it? How will you teach them to see it from a zebra's perspective?'

Brian regarded his wife with a look of despair and resignation. Why did she always douse his futile reflections with a deluge of inescapable and pertinent pragmatism? Why was he so often left regarding his intellectual musings with a feeling of impotence or even paralysis? And that's certainly how he felt now: powerless to pursue his point any further and more than ever in sympathy with all those zebra – who weren't even given the opportunity to make a point in the first place. So he responded in the only way he could. With an indeterminate noise and a practised withdrawal.

'Uhmmm... well you're right, of course. I can't. I don't even know how I'd get myself invited to a symposium. And we're all doomed anyway. Might as well have another lager.'

This seemed to satisfy his wife and it even elicited a consolation. For Sandra presented him with an enormous smile and assured him that: 'You're quite right, Brian. It's just that, as you say, we're all doomed, and the quicker we are, the better for the zebra. And my money's on that cyber stuff. Or maybe a virus...'

So, in the middle of the Garden of Eden, Adam and Eve had reinforced their bond of gloom and the world seemed a better place than ever, despite the existence of all those threats. And despite the prospect of another meal with the folks at Leroo...

It couldn't be ignored. They had to eat. So, a little after seven, Brian and Sandra left their chalet and, with their pre-arranged escort, arrived at the lodge's main building for a pre-dinner drink. Their companions there were Fred and an apparently un-resentful Peter – and Fred had some news. It concerned their dinner. For it appeared that the lodge had received a late booking, and Brian and his wife would, this evening, be sharing a table not with any of the lodge's staff but with a minister and his driver. Brian almost choked on his drink. How could he manage a whole meal with a man of the cloth without putting his foot in his mouth all the way down to his stomach? He was bound to say something inappropriate or just plain insulting. And who knew what the laws concerning blasphemy and heresy were in Botswana? He could end up spending the rest of his holiday reciting repeated Hail Marys. However, Fred then amplified his piece of news. It appeared that Brian would have to cope not with a minister but with a Minister, as in a member of the Botswanan cabinet, who was using the lodge as an overnight stop on his way to open a new library in a nearby village. So Brian would not have to concern himself with blasphemy or heresy, but instead, with any number of crimes against the state. He would have to be careful what he said.

Fred went on to inform his guests that the Minister and his driver would be here for an eight o'clock start to dinner. And he also informed them that the Minister in question was the Botswanan Minister for Youth and Culture. This meant that Brian had almost three quarters of an hour to formulate a few polite enquiries in readiness for the meal. For he reckoned the more he could think of, the fewer real contributions he'd have to make at the time, and the fewer chances he'd have of saying something out of order. So while Fred droned on about the role of men in Botswanan society (which, in his opinion, appeared to be that of domestic monarchs) and Peter ate the canapés, Brian set about his task.

It was more difficult than he thought, and by five to eight all he'd come up with was a question about how the Minister divided his time between his two responsibilities (which was no more than: 'Do you do Youth in the mornings and Culture in the afternoons?'), an enquiry as to whether the Minister was aware that in England, Youth and Culture are often mutually exclusive – and a third, a reserve question, as to whether he knew that by appending the word "club" to both his portfolios, he could end up with a popular British venue for listening to music in the Eighties and the name of one of the bands that might have been listened to in such a venue. (Although he thought it would be unwise to extend this one to a discussion about the New Romantics…)

So, it was just as well that when eight arrived, it arrived without the arrival of the Minister and his driver, and it was therefore decided that Fred and Peter would play their parts instead. Which meant that rather than Brian having to dice with the perils of infractions against the state, he would now have to contemplate another journey into the realms of conversational dyspepsia – as in a disorder of the vocal chords leading to a weakness of speech, a loss of the ability to communicate and a depression in the will to make even the slightest contribution to any active debate. And no way would this trial by silence be made better by the fact that one of its participants was the shunned-for-the-day Peter, who by now must have been harbouring quite a sizable grudge.

However, it was by no means a trial. Maybe it was to do with the choral singing by the assembled lodge staff before the event (and before the normal-formal introductions) or the frisson engendered by the delayed arrival of a Minister of State. But whatever it was, the meal was conducted at more a canter than a plod, and it even saw Fred admitting to a few lodge home-truths. Like, for example, that quite a few people found it very difficult to locate the lodge (!) and that many more, when confronted with that big park fence, turned around and gave up (!) and that maybe the lodge should make it a little easier for people to find it (!). All of which was reinforced in the most sensational way possible when Nelson approached the table to inform Fred that the Minister and his driver were lost. They were in a village by a river (the same village Brian and Sandra had unavoidably visited two days previously) and they could not find their way to the lodge.

Brilliant! But it got even better. Because Nelson and Captain were immediately dispatched to bring in their stranded cabinet member but, in the process, they themselves got lost! A tree had fallen across the regular sand-track, and in taking an alternative track to the village, Nelson and Captain had lost it – the track, that is. And it wasn't until nearly nine thirty that they made it back to the lodge with a very peeved-looking Minister and the Minister's (marginally less obese) driver, who just looked as though he wasn't expecting to keep his job. The trouble was that it wasn't his fault. This lodge really was amongst the most well-secreted lodges in the whole of Africa, and it would have taken an official driver with a GPS implant to find it, and even then he would probably have hesitated at that fence. Even with a minister in the back seat – and even with his GPS throbbing almost painfully – he would have had his doubts. Just as Brian and Sandra had just two days before.

But anyway, everybody who should have been at the lodge was now at the lodge, and Brian and Sandra were even treated to a greeting and a handshake by the Minister for Youth and Culture as he took his seat for his dinner. It would be with his glum-looking driver, and Brian would be denied the opportunity to ask him about his daily diary and to enlighten him on the contribution of Culture Club to the UK's culture. But he'd get over it. Especially as he discovered, when he and Sandra were back in their chalet, that the lodge had installed in their room, an ice bucket, two champagne glasses and a bottle of bubbly – to thank them for their stay!

Brian felt about six feet short of his normal six feet two inches. It seemed that the more horrible he was, the more he'd be proved to be wrong. Knock the conversational abilities of the local staff, impugn their facility to be other than solemn, conduct a hatchet job on their principal guide – despite none of these people having done other than everything for you – and you get your completely unjustified rewards. In this instance, in the form of an expensive bottle of effervescent joy, complete with an almost humble expression of their gratitude for your stay. (The attached card did seem to suggest that they were very relieved indeed that the lodge hadn't been entirely empty, especially when the regional manager was in attendance.)

Ah well... Brian and Sandra couldn't manage bubbly at this time of night, not after what they'd already imbibed and with the prospect of a fairly early start in the morning. So Brian packed the bottle in his holdall while Sandra did some last-minute "sorting out", and then he got into bed. There, he took a few minutes to assess their stay at this place and to remind himself that whatever shortcomings he'd identified in its performance, they were either a product of his own character defects, or, if in any way real, they paled into insignificance when compared with its paradise situation. And furthermore, they were predominantly in that first category; they were predominantly a function of his own personality. Yes, he had to admit it, the only real shortcomings presently in residence at Leroo La Tau were all his own. That's to say, his jaundiced views (on anything and everything), his sourness, his propensity to see the worst of all worlds, and his tendency not to give people the benefit of the doubt. In fact, the more he thought about it, the more he thought that he should get himself along to one of those stupid symposiums. And then all he'd have to do was to be himself. That way, he'd be so at odds with the enthusiasm, optimism and general "can do" attitude that infest such events, that he'd soon stand out from the other delegates. And when, by standing out so much, he had their attention, he could then use the moment to give them a view of the world from the perspective of a zebra – and thereby maybe change their conclusions. (Oh… and if his poisoned character didn't succeed in securing their attention, then there were always his Speedos.)

19.

It was nine o'clock in the morning and time for Brian to rekindle his regrets of the previous evening – time for him to remind himself of what a bastard he'd been. And this was achieved with consummate ease by his receiving a send-off from the assembled staff of Leroo La Tau that was not only effusive but also genuinely moving. It was quite hard to bear. And after this, Peter boarded one of the lodge's vehicles and kindly led Brian and Sandra along a sand-track that brought them directly to the main road without their passing through that famous village. And Brian checked; where the track met the road, there really was no signpost or any other indication of the lodge's existence. Even a couple of tethered balloons would have helped…

But no. He'd heaped far too much criticism on Leroo La Tau already, and hadn't he just learned his lesson all over again? And furthermore, he now had more immediate matters to deal with, like finding his way to Maun – and avoiding all those donkeys.

There were more of them than ever, and far more of them than there were cattle and goats. And not only were they a continual concern – if not an actual hazard – but they were also something of a mystery. Because Brian had now established that the Botswanans rarely, if ever, ate them, rarely used them for other "animal products", and only infrequently used them as beasts of burden. They just seemed to own them, and simply left them to graze at their leisure and generally live out their donkey lives with the minimum of human intervention. It was all very odd, and Sandra's suggestion that they were in high demand during the nativity play season didn't convince him at all. Nor her suggestion that there'd been a mix up on a massive order for "monkeys", and these ubiquitous "donkeys" were the result of a massive returns programme. Perhaps it was just a desire on the part of Botswanans to retain a reminder of the past – when they would have used their donkeys extensively. A bit like the way Brits hang on to old red phone boxes back home, even when they've been stripped of their phones. Anyway, he would never discover for sure, just as he would never establish whether there were more donkeys in Botswana than there were people. (Even though he was sure that he'd now seen about twice as many four-footed nibblers as he had two-footed citizens.)

However, despite the uninterrupted succession of Eeyores along the road, the journey to Maun was pretty straightforward. After only a couple of hours of driving, the emptiness of Botswana, broken only by the occasional settlement of traditional roundels, was giving way to the signs of something rather more packed with people. There were some larger houses, some workshops and warehouses, and then, at the bottom of a shallow incline, the unmistakable view of a veritable metropolis. Only, of course, this was a Botswanan metropolis, so, although it was the largest town that Brian and Sandra would encounter on their entire trip around this country, it was no bigger than somewhere like Daventry. Although, unlike Daventry, it was renowned for being the "Gateway to the Okavango". And its gateway status was why Brian and Sandra had come here, and why they'd flown here three times before (from Windhoek). It really was the only place where one could gain access to the Okavango Delta, which, without wishing to exaggerate, is probably one of the most desirable places in the world to which one would want to gain access. And this is because the Okavango Delta is simply magnificent – and unique.

Around two million years ago, the Kavango River, which flows south-eastwards from the highlands of central Angola, probably joined with the waters of the mighty Limpopo and made it to the sea. But at some point those pesky tectonic plate movements stuck their oar in and the Kavango got itself diverted into the Kalahari Basin. Right up to a few thousand years ago, this meant that it ended up in a huge lake that covered the (recently visited) Makgadikgadi Pans. But silting, together with a little more uplifting of the land to the east, caused this lake to disappear and a new basin to form that now traps the majority of the river's flow. Indeed, only a tiny percentage of it finds its way out of this basin and into the Thamalakane River (which runs through Maun) and an even smaller percentage of it makes it even further to the Boteti River (the river which runs past Leroo La Tau and towards those Makgadikgadi Pans). And this basin is, of course, the "container" for the Okavango Delta, a huge fan-shaped area in the north-west of Botswana where every year nearly nineteen billion cubic metres of water arrive from Angola across the Caprivi Strip – for the majority of it to be absorbed by the sand or by the dry thirsty air.

Of course, that much water brings a lot of other stuff with it as well, stuff like sand, topsoil and leached nutrients. Which means that, rather than being just a big patch of damp in Botswana, the delta is a maze of lagoons, channels and islands – and an ideal environment for a huge assortment of wildlife, and especially for some of its bigger representatives, such as elephants, buffaloes, wildebeests, giraffes and hippos. It is also, of course, the sort of pristine landscape that is beautiful in its own right, and is considered by many (and by Brian and Sandra) to be amongst the most scenic in all Africa. On top of all this, it is one of the few places in the world where humans take the back seat. It is such a precious part of Botswana's natural resources (and contains 95% of all its surface water) that it is highly protected, and is essentially run as a giant 16,000 square-kilometre wildlife haven, and, for those fortunate enough to be able to visit it, as one of the most sensational wildlife destinations on the planet (and one that, for Brian and Sandra, will never lose its appeal).

Well, with that sort of build up, it is easy to understand why these two travellers were quite prepared to invest a night in Maun at a pretty ordinary hotel in readiness for a flight into the delta the next day, where they would then spend the following five nights. And the first part of this investment process was to find this establishment, the rather misleadingly named "Maun Lodge".

It proved quite easy. Maun really is a very small place. And it was equally easy to find the airport and the offices of "Wilderness Safaris", the mammoth company that would be transporting Brian and Sandra into the delta and housing them in two of its lodges there. Sandra had thought it would be a good idea to spend time finding this office today rather than failing to find it in time tomorrow and thus missing their flight. Brian agreed. And anyway, he was beginning to resent the fact that he would be abandoning his trusty Land Cruiser for a whole five days and he welcomed any opportunity to drive it while he still could. (And to flaunt its "exotic" Namibian plates around the streets of Maun — albeit he wasn't going to admit to that.)

So, the reccy job done, it was time to return to the Maun Lodge and to check in. It really was a simple place. Unlike the receptionist who just gave the appearance of being simple. It was her mix of indifference and ineptitude, which, judging by the behaviour and demeanour of her hotel colleagues, was not unique here. Brian quickly decided that the Maun Lodge was the sort of place where winning the employee of the month award wouldn't be too much of a problem…

And there he was — at it again. And he'd only got as far as reception. So he slapped himself on the wrist, reminded himself that he'd already been warned that this hotel was "unsophisticated but comfortable", and made every effort to be as nice as possible to the receptionist, even smiling at her as she dithered.

So, ten minutes later, Brian and Sandra were ensconced in their room and contemplating its ambience. It could be best summed up, thought Brian, as… unsophisticated but comfortable — although it was at least sophisticated enough to have a telly. It also had an air-con system, which, given that the heat-wave had abated only a little, was very welcome indeed. In fact, almost as welcome as an early lunchtime drink in the hotel's boma. For Brian and his wife had now forsaken their room and its air-conditioning for a bite to eat — and a drink — in the hotel's newly constructed "eating corral". It was essentially an outdoor restaurant and bar, modelled on a traditional Botswanan boma, but much larger and in an urban rather than a rural setting. But no matter. It was very well done, and so too were the cheese toasties it served. It provided Brian and Sandra with just what they wanted and set them up perfectly for an afternoon of in-room entertainment…

Some of this involved the telly and, in particular, the catching up with world events. After all, what could be more entertaining than discovering what had been going on around the globe through the eyes of CNN? This lot didn't just present the news; they moulded it into a performance – with the principal performers made to look like either aliens or mannequins. And one couldn't get away from it: real plastic never looks as plastic as those complexions, and Widow Twanky would just die for that hair. However, if one tried, one could ignore the theatrics of it all and just focus on the news, which was fairly entertaining in its own right.

For example, there was first the news that some Pakistani cricketers had been found guilty of cheating, which was a good curtain raiser. Then there was the news that a Polish aircraft had successfully landed without an undercarriage (through a mechanical failure and not through a memory lapse on the part of the crew), which was a real crowd pleaser. And then the news that the Greeks were busy screwing up their latest euro bailout, which was a fitting finale to a genuine variety performance. It appeared – on this last item – that the bailout deal was going to be put to a referendum sometime in the future, in the full knowledge that a majority of Greeks were against the austerity involved and would vote against it, albeit that a bigger majority wanted to stay in the euro. Which sounded to Brian like a clear case of having your baklava and wanting to eat it.

But now it was time for dinner, and dinner was back in the boma. What appeared on the plates there wasn't very exciting, but what appeared in the centre of the boma was distinctly more enthralling. This was a local dance troupe in local minimalistic garb, made up of a number of energetic males and a smaller number of rather less energetic females, most of whom would have been well advised to be more energetic. These female dancers were all young, but the majority of them were already well on their way to acquiring a local "traditional" shape and the sort of Body Mass Index which accompanies this shape. But at least they weren't looking for a bailout from Europe.

Yes, that Greek news item was still playing on Brian's mind, and soon he was imparting his latest thoughts on the matter to his long-suffering wife. He had a solution, he announced. A novel, imaginative solution. Why don't the Greeks, he argued, simply sell Crete to the Chinese? They could easily get enough for it to pay off their debts, and they'd even be getting rid of that dreadful airport at Heraklion as well. Then, when they'd been sorted, Brussels could invite China into the European Union (because part of it would now be part of Europe), and they would then be able not only to sting the Chinese for a massive EU contribution and so solve the whole of the euro problem, but they would also be able to saddle them with all those EU regulations, which would inevitably bring China's economy to a shuddering (and probably permanent) halt. Job done – and, as a bonus, no more of those interminable images of platform shoes and trouser suits, because Sarkozy and Merkel would have no further reason to keep meeting every week – and smiling at each other.

Sandra conceded that this was a novel idea, but argued that it was probably more a demented idea than an imaginative one. And anyway, wasn't it about time that they both went to bed? They had a flight to catch tomorrow, and if they stayed in this boma any longer, there was also the risk that Brian might dream up another novel and imaginative solution to a world problem, and she wasn't quite sure she was up to that.

Brian got the message and, with Sandra, he returned to their room. On the way there, he noticed that the automatic shoe-polisher near reception had no English instructions on it but was instead covered in Chinese hieroglyphics. For a moment he thought he'd been whisked off to Crete. But then he remembered where he was: in Botswana – and in Maun, the gateway to the Okavango. And tomorrow he'd be in the Okavango itself – at one of its lodges, where even he might have difficulty in finding any faults…

20.

Breakfast was from a buffet in the boma. Unfortunately, due to the restrictive practices concerning toast making and a byzantine system surrounding butter procurement, it was more a meal to be negotiated than one to be enjoyed. But it did remind Brian of where he was going – and how matters would soon improve. The first sign of this improvement was at the offices of Wilderness Safaris. This was where Brian and Sandra dropped off their vehicle, and where they got their first taste of that same Wilderness hospitality they'd so enjoyed in the past. And that meant a welcoming chat with the office staff and then an escort to the nearby airport by the office manager and the office dog. Here, when the office manager had sorted out the check-in stuff and wished them a good trip, Brian and Sandra made their way to the departure lounge to await their flight – and discovered that it was to be a virtually full one. There were already two other people in the lounge.

Maun Airport does have a conventional commercial airline activity – with planes with lots of seats taking off for places like Johannesburg and Windhoek. But the vast majority of its business is facilitating the ferrying of foreigners – and local lodge staff – into the Okavango Delta, for which purpose it handles somewhat smaller planes. These are either Cessna

"Caravans", which take about a dozen people, or Cessna 172s, which, including the pilot, take only six. Brian and Sandra were in a 172 this morning, with two local girls who were returning to their lodge after a scheduled break. This was good news. Not only because both Brian and Sandra preferred these smaller craft, but also because they had learnt that just a couple of weeks earlier, one of the Caravans had lost power after taking off from Maun, had crash landed and burst into flames. Only two of its passengers had survived… Brian knew that lightning rarely struck in the same place twice, but lightning didn't come off the same aeroplane production line. So he was more than a little relieved, and far more than he was prepared to admit.

However, relief gave way to pleasure as soon as the diminutive Cessna left the ground. Because Brian's "Delta adventure" had already started. For the next hour or so he would be flying low over its endless flat landscape, and he would therefore be able to savour the delight of its ever changing form and its ever changing colours. It was an experience not to be missed.

To begin with, the land below was where the delta's waters "only just make it". Here, at the height of the wet season, the annual flood creeps towards the outer edges of the delta basin and, in doing so, determines the elevation of the land with absolute precision. Where, just inches higher than that surrounding it, it remains dry. Where, below this, it is inundated either partially or completely. And now, at the end of the dry season, when most of this water has gone, the ground bears the evidence of this hydrological resolution. Where the water never penetrated – and where there is no vegetation – there are islands of beige. Where the water made just an ephemeral visit, there is apricot – often as a ring around some beige. And threaded between these largely lifeless hues, and indicating where the water had run and stayed (and in some places is present even now), is green, the unmistakable green of life-loving life. Give it just a taste of that precious liquid and it springs from the earth. And here, just north of Maun, it decorates the dry sandy earth with this delicate lacework of green, a vivid illustration of both the vigour and the fragility of all living things.

Soon, however, the green becomes the predominant colour. This is where that delta basin is imperceptibly lower, but in hydrological terms, a bit of a push over. There are still patches of beige and apricot, some of them very large, but this is now more a water environment than a land one. There are trees down there – near the water, reeds – in the water, and even clear water, real crystal-clear ponds, deep enough to take a bathing hippo – and persistently irresistible to elephants… And one can see them from the plane! Troops of slow-moving pachyderms, looking impossibly small, processing across the vastness of the land below, and maintaining one of the millions of pathways which criss-cross its face. For here, in these wetter realms, and looking like veins on a giant leaf, elephant walkways have been scored into the surface of the land and, with the help of hippos, through the reed-beds as well. And without this invention called an aeroplane (and the resources needed to be on this one), Brian would never have seen them, or the totality of the splendour that the delta embraced. Shit, he told himself, he was such a lucky bastard…

Although maybe not quite so lucky as the girl beside him and the girl behind him who saw all this stuff on their way to work and, on top of that, had a job in the middle of Shangri-la. Or maybe they didn't see it quite that way. Maybe a job is a job wherever it is, and anyway, they probably got to see more of the inside of a lodge kitchen than they did of the marvels of the delta. And how could one use one's iSpud out here or even have a night out at Nando's (yes, there is one in Maun)? They'd probably be happier in somewhere like Newcastle, where not only could they be continuously connected but where they could also enjoy a good night out every night. However, he would never know for sure, just as he would never know to what degree his prejudices against the habits of the young were misplaced. And this was because of the noise in the plane. Cessna 172s are pretty nifty aircraft, offering the prospect of close-proximity accommodation with strangers on every trip, but not the ability to chat to them or conceivably to chat them up. So when the two workers on board had been deposited at an airstrip near their lodge and had been replaced by a young American couple, the curvier and more attractive of which had been squeezed next to Brian, he could no more converse with her than he could invite her to join him in the mile-high club, even, assuming for a moment, that he could ever harbour such a despicable ambition. And this despite her confession, as she boarded, that she might need to hold his hand. And anyway, the Cessnas never got anywhere near a mile high in their progress. It was more like a thousand feet, which for spiritual rather than sexual satisfaction was more than ideal. Because below the aircraft there was yet more of that magic green – which soon petered out into fawn, brown and bronze…

Yes, the Cessna had now reached the north-eastern side of the delta and was leaving it for the land just beyond. This land was technically not the Okavango, but instead the southern part of Chobe, where further north, Brian and Sandra had earlier spent such a wonderful time at Muchenje. But for Brian and many other visitors to this place, it was still a product of the

Okavango and therefore a real part of it – only considerably drier. In fact, the ground beneath the plane was so dry that the green had now entirely disappeared and the landscape, with its mosaic of all shades of brown, more resembled the stretched skin of a giant giraffe than it did of anything to do with the delta. This was Arid-land, but Arid-land with a green surprise at its centre.

First though, there was another airstrip, another "line in the sand" inscribed onto the surface of the wilderness and, like the airstrip where the Cessna had landed earlier, far too small for a Cessna landing. But it did land. Just as it had landed here probably a thousand times before – bumpily and disconcertingly, but still quite safely and with a dozen or so yards of airstrip to spare.

And now it was the Wilderness with a capital W experience in earnest. For there, waiting at the side of the strip, were four safari Land Rovers. Two had aboard them the Cessna's return contingent. One other was parked there for the two Americans – to transfer them to their lodge. And the last one was parked there to transfer Brian and Sandra to theirs – a place called Savuti Camp, a hostelry that they had visited twice before – albeit not in its present condition. Because when they had been there on two previous occasions, this camp had been one of the driest in Botswana. It sat on the side of the Savuti Channel, which had last seen any flowing water back in 1980. Since that date – due to the vagaries of rainfall in Angola and, more significantly, the shifting of those tectonic plates below the delta – it had been as dry as a dead dingo's donger (just as the Boteti River had been back at Leroo La Tau in the late 1990s), and the only water in it had been that which the lodge had pumped to the surface (as in Leroo La Tau, for the benefit of the local animals – and its guests). But in 2008, as a consequence of higher rainfall and more shifting of those tectonic plates, a Leroo/Boteti type "redemption" had been triggered and the water returned. Without notice and without any puny human intervention, it had crept back up the channel – from the delta – and within just one year had converted one of the driest lodges in Botswana into one of its dampest and most verdant.

On the way from the airstrip, this magical conversion was difficult to believe. The sand-track to the lodge ran through a parched landscape populated only by mopane trees, all of which, without exception, had been cropped by elephants to within eight feet of the ground and all of which had not a single leaf about their branches. It looked like a scene from a post-nuclear holocaust, and one where all the water had been boiled off into space. So when Brian and Sandra's driver (who answered to the name of Chaplain) began to explain to them how to deal with a hippo when one encounters one whilst swimming in the channel, it all sounded rather surreal. Not to say, completely irrelevant. There was as much chance of Brian having a meeting with a hippo whilst bathing in the Savuti River as there was of his having a meeting of minds with Piers Morgan whilst bathing in the reflected light of his über-smug smile.

But then they arrived at the lodge. And although it looked just the same at its approach, when they were taken to their tent, it was only too clear how it had changed out of all recognition. Where before, the tent had overlooked a long, wide indentation in the land (the Savuti Channel), with a small, almost indiscernible waterhole in its centre by the lodge, it now overlooked a long, wide and very wet river. The tent was no longer on a ridge of a dry channel; it was on a river bank. And this was a real river, with reeds, water plants, water-birds and fish, running through a landscape that now bordered on the luxuriant. And all of this had arrived here since 2008. Just three years to convert an area of intense desiccation into a veritable hotspot for moisture. It was completely stunning, not to say completely implausible. But it just had to be plaused. Because it was here for real: a new environment and a host of new possibilities. So that when, for example, Sandra was asked by her new guide, Goodman, whether there was anything she particularly wanted to see – and she replied 'wild dogs' – Goodman was able to assure her that she would have sight of them no more than twenty minutes after she'd finished her tea. 'Because the wildlife here is now more abundant than ever.'

He sounded confident. And very soon his assertion would be tested. Because Brian and Sandra, having settled into their sumptuous accommodation by the river (their tent was modelled on Cleopatra's bedroom, only it was slightly bigger), and having subsequently reported for afternoon tea, were now about to be taken out for their first drive – by the inscrutable Goodman. (This guy had the superficial demeanour of an employee of Leroo La Tau, but, as would soon become apparent, inside that austere shell there was something more austere still, as well as a daunting knowledge and a profound understanding of all the wildlife of Savuti.) Oh… and with them on this drive would be an American lady from South Carolina by the name of Iris.

As Goodman pulled away from the lodge (in another safari Land Rover), Brian soon decided that Iris was a very brave woman. Because it was revealed almost immediately that this was her first time in Africa, she was travelling on her own in Africa, and… well, she had probably bought her first pair of proper stockings before Brian had even been born. She was not a young woman, and even the term "middle-aged" might be considered to be something of a "terminological in-exactitude". But here she was – in the middle of a Botswanan wilderness – ready for anything and ready to learn all she could. And there was a lot to learn. Living in South Carolina had inevitably not equipped her for what she was about to see here.

The first new sight she encountered – and a sight that Brian and Sandra had only once seen before – was the promised pack of wild dogs. Goodman had found them within minutes of leaving the lodge. And what can one say of these creatures? Well, how about that they look irredeemably scruffy, seriously menacing and a little devious and, as their name suggests, just plain wild, but that they are in reality, very handsome (in a scruffy sort of way), incredibly sociable within their packs, clever, fearless, completely fascinating – and inevitably endangered. This part of Botswana is one of their last strongholds on this planet (or should that be one of their last footholds?). And to see nearly thirty of them in one pack, all looking healthy and well-fed, was a privilege and a comfort. It was genuinely reassuring that for those few who remain there are still havens like this area of Savuti. Even if it might not be quite so reassuring for their prey.

Some of these featured next. With Goodman's nose for wildlife, his trio of guests were soon treated to views of impala, kudu and warthog, and a few further species that might well be beyond the ability of even a thirty-strong pack of dogs – such as elephant, buffalo and hippos. There were also, of course, more than enough new birds about to keep Brian and Sandra on their ornithological toes, even if, with specimens such as ashy flycatchers, they needed Goodman's help with their balance.

And on a par with all these new marvels of nature was the prospect of their first Savuti sundowner…

This was taken shortly after a close encounter with a small herd of grazing elephants and what was probably Iris' first encounter with close-quarters elephant flatulence, which is indisputably a very rare occurrence within the confines of South Carolina. So too, one might imagine, are stunning purple sunsets of the African variety, which have the ability to promote the practice of taking a sundowner to an almost psychedelic experience, albeit one without real hallucinations and one where the colours aren't presented in swirling patterns but in a sky-wide wash towards the west. It was a fitting finale to a wonderful first drive – and the ideal preparation for some more of that Wilderness hospitality.

This was dinner in the main lodge building, which meant dinner in a handsome open-sided construction on the river's edge with a dozen or so other guests, most of whom were, like Iris, from the Land of the Free. Some of them, however, looked less than entirely liberated and more like prisoners of their own conscience – and, in particular, a foursome of two men and two women who were clearly trapped by a terrible secret. They were uncommunicative with their fellow guests to the point of rudeness, and they were just uncomfortable with other people and probably with themselves. Brian reckoned he knew what it was. The male members of this coy coterie were probably, he thought, New York investment bankers who, like many of their number, had confused "investment" with "divestment", and had therefore now self-exiled themselves to Botswana in an attempt to save their skins. Which is more than their female partners could ever do. Too much time in the Florida sun and too much time in a Florida clinic had seen their skin reduced to plastic, and their ability to express their emotions with just their face muscles almost completely removed. Or maybe, thought Brian, bankers' wives don't have any emotions. That's why they end up with bankers.

Anyway, this dodgy lot ended up at the other end of what was a long, narrow dining table, and Brian and Sandra had the company for the evening not of New York divestment bankers but of two New York lawyers. And these lawyers were both married – to each other. They were called David and Bonnie and, despite their being lawyers, they were extremely personable and chatty and, at the inception of the meal, managed to express their utter loathing for Sarah Palin. So essentially they were very good guys, and Brian would have no difficulty whatsoever with their company, and, if he avoided a debate about lawyers, they might not have too much of a problem with his.

He did. He kept his lip buttoned on both the law and lawyers and instead introduced topics of conversation such as the inefficiency of democracy. Here, he argued that if you regarded a government as essentially a business – which exists to provide a country with a product called "the administration of its affairs" – it is a fairly rum do that this business is run by one load of executives with another (theoretically) equally capable load of hotshots trying to frustrate their efforts at every turn. It is not a model of any business in the world that has been successful or that has lasted for more than a few weeks. But it is the model we use for our democratic governments across the western world, and the one we try to impose on the inevitably more efficient autocracies in the world, where, whatever other faults they might have, they don't have this inbuilt internecine drain on their strength.

David countered this proposition with the rather obvious argument that, whereas in a normal business it is the brightest and the best who run things, in most democracies in the west it is a bunch of plonkers. Although he didn't use this term. Brian seemed to recall that instead he referred to them as a group of self-seeking bastards whose selection for a jury he would challenge every time – on the grounds of both their intellectual incapacity and their moral turpitude. Therefore, the more that they could be frustrated in their delusional ambitions by another load of inadequates, the better, while normal people just got on with their lives. Brian didn't have a response to that one, but he did point out that autocratic regimes had problems of their own. North Korea, for example, had to make do with a series of jerks who had all been subjected to a vasectomy of the brain. So that whatever was still going on up there never made it into cogent behaviour, and the only proficiency they displayed was in the arena of terrible haircuts and vacant expressions – while their subjugated subjects continued to suffer and starve.

At this point in the proceedings, Sandra tried to lighten the mood at the table by suggesting that wild dog dynamics might provide a better basis for the conduct of human affairs. After all, she reasoned, the dogs all worked for the common good, none of the pack was ever neglected in its needs, efficiency was paramount in everything they did, and none of the dogs ever bored the pants off all the other dogs by engaging in an interminable round of primaries, which, as often as not, saw a top dog emerge whose only talent was a talent to disappoint and to underperform in about equal measure.

Well this, thought Brian, was an interesting idea, but he was concerned by the fact that she'd pinned the inadequacies of democracy so firmly onto the side of American politics, given the fact that she was in the company of two Americans. After all, she could have pointed not to the primaries system but instead to the ghastly electioneering of her own politicians, and all the PC nonsense that surrounds the selection of candidates (where now ethnicity and gender far too often trump ability or plain common sense). But David and Bonnie both took it well, and Bonnie even made the point that, as a lawyer, she was already well disposed to the habits of wild dogs – and especially their ruthlessness and their tendency to strip their victims to the bone…

It was something of a shame that David and Bonnie were moving on in the morning. Like their fellow countrymen in Muchenje, Rick and Cindy, they were oppressed by that American work ethic that frowned upon extensive vacations (or even turning off your BlackBerry for more than just a few hours) and were therefore in Africa for only nine days! Shit, that wasn't even long enough to shake off the effects of jet-lag, let alone immerse oneself in what Africa was all about. Or indeed, to learn how to avoid opinionated Brits and their opinionated wives. Or to learn how to go about the reform of democracy in the United States – starting with those friggin' primaries.

21.

When one particular blueberry muffin was placed on a plate with nine similar muffins, it had no idea that it would be stolen. If it had any idea of anything at all, it would have been when it was taken out on that plate to the outside dining deck of the lodge lapa, and the idea would have been that it was about to be consumed by one of the lodge's guests. For here, on this deck, was where early-morning breakfast was served, and it and its fellow muffins were one of the food items on offer. Even now these guests were appearing, and soon the muffin might be plucked from its plate. Well, in due course, it was. But not by a guest, but by a very cheeky vervet monkey who had swung down from a tree above the deck and before you could say 'Iowa State Caucus' had made off with his prize.

Brian just caught the action as he spooned some muesli into his mouth. He'd been standing at the edge of the deck watching the fish below him in the river, and just as he turned from the river he saw the simian villain make his play for the food. And, of course, he was delighted. Not just in catching the action, but in the knowledge that he was sharing his first meal of the day with a creature of the wild (even if the creature in question was probably more a lodge resident than a truly wild beast). It just emphasised where he and his wife were. Slap bang in the middle of an untrammelled natural world, the sort of natural world where during the night you were kept awake by the sounds of frogs, hippos and other assorted unidentified animals, but were not bothered that you were. Even if you had to rise at five in the morning to eat an indecently early breakfast – with a monkey.

But now it was late. It was five forty-five, and it was time for a drive. Time to join Iris and Goodman for another ride through the bush.

Their first encounter (just as Goodman had predicted) was with a group of sixteen lions – of the female persuasion. They were sprawled under two bushes near a hippo-filled lagoon – eight lionesses to each bush – and they were fairly inactive. A bit of half-hearted stretching and yawning was all they could manage; otherwise they were essentially inert, sleeping off what must have been a more than ample meal from the previous day. Indeed, they were so chilled out that Goodman was able to drive his open Land Rover between the two halves of the group and thereby bring his passengers to within a lion's length of their dozing forms. Any closer and, as their last act on this Earth, his passengers could have reached out of their vehicle and stroked them.

Brian studied them closely – and marvelled at the state of their teeth. It was remarkably good, and given that they didn't own a toothbrush between them and had no access to a dentist, incredibly good. This got him thinking about what else they had to cope with on their own, without devices or outside assistance and without even human hands and fingers. So, for example, how on Earth did they cope with an itch in an ear, and how did they get a bit of grit out of an eye? They could hardly resort to a cotton bud or the corner of a folded hankie.

And then he thought some more and thought about the choices they had or, more accurately, about the choices they didn't have.

Because what could one of these lionesses here do, if she woke up one morning and decided that she was pretty pissed off with the way she was living? Every day, a new hunt to conduct, a new animal to catch and dispatch, and even if you were successful in this endeavour (after expending a great deal of time and effort), all you got to eat for your troubles was meat! And meat every day… Well, it was so sameish, so stupefyingly boring, and often so terribly gristly. If only occasionally there was something else on offer and something that didn't take quite so much effort, something like a blueberry muffin for example. And all this hunting, eating and sleeping left you hardly any time to do anything else. How nice it would be to have just a little time to play with a big ball of knitting yarn, or to jump through a hoop, or maybe to learn how to count or even to divide. And yes, how often must you wish you could divide by sixteen every time you and your gang set about the carcass of a kudu, even if you found its flesh somewhat chewy? Or, there again, Brian reminded himself, this was a pride of lions he was in the middle of, and lions were highly unlikely to indulge in such senseless musings. That sort of stuff could be left safely to him.

Yes, he finally abandoned his ridiculous cogitations on lion life choices and returned to savouring their intimate presence for what it was: a privileged insight into their form and their nature at very close quarters – just before Goodman announced that he was moving off. It appeared he had an appointment with a leopard.

She was sitting in a patch of grass as if in a trance. But leopards are never in a trance; they are just in a constant state of readiness. What may look like a pair of glazed-over eyes are, in fact, the eyes of a creature in intense concentration, the steady stare of a superb hunting machine as it works out what's around it – and whether what's around it includes a meal. And, of course, this hunting machine comes in such a stunning package that Brian's first thought, when he saw this lady leopard, was not how focused she was on her environment, but how ugly he, Brian, was. And not especially ugly, but just human-ugly – as when compared with a leopard. For how can the angular, lumpy, indisciplined, knobbly-kneed shape of a naked ape possibly compare, other than very badly, with the smooth, sleek, streamlined and supple form of an exquisitely patterned cat? It was like comparing a Ford Anglia with an Aston Martin. And right now Brian felt like a Ford Anglia, looking on with envy at the ultimate in organic engineering; and not only with envy but also with admiration. This leopard was just such an incredibly beautiful animal.

She even moved beautifully. For now she had decided to stand and then to stroll – right past the Land Rover and without taking the slightest interest in its occupants. She moved as though she were in another dimension, a dimension that didn't require any effort to bring about movement, even when the movement entailed a twelve-foot leap into a tree. Yes, the cat had now decided that her life would be better conducted for the moment from the vantage point of a wide bough in a large tree, and she had effortlessly conveyed herself to that place as though gravity just didn't exist. She now lay along this bough just staring straight ahead and appearing almost to be ignoring the Land Rover and its occupants on purpose, as though she knew she was an Aston and that down there below were just some cheap and cheerful cars that weren't worth a second look – or even a first, come to that. And in a way she was right. Brian wouldn't go far to look at himself or any of his fellow humans. After all, apart from anything else, they were just so bloody common. They were everywhere. You simply couldn't avoid them.

It was just at this point, as Brian was dispensing with the human race as being of any real interest, that one of its representatives (the one with the steering wheel in his hands) announced that it was time to move on. He had, it appeared, a further appointment, this time with a lion (and not with another lioness). Within minutes, his passengers had seen this lion – and were able to continue to see him, again at close quarters, as he lay in the shade. As Goodman made clear, he was the "owner" of the sixteen lionesses they'd observed earlier, and was obviously having a bit of "me time" before he resumed his ownership duties. And they were ownership duties. Because in the first place, one cannot pretend that any creature who has sole rights in the carnal department to sixteen other creatures, and also requires these same creatures to feed him, isn't their owner. And in the second place, one cannot dispute that fulfilling the obligations that come with those rights-to-passage don't at least sometimes feel more like a duty than they do a joy. No less than one can pretend that lions like this chap aren't the ultimate in full-on, undiluted, no-doubts-about-it masculinity. Brian looked at him and saw that he was not only enormous but also that he had a wonderful male-lion face, muscles aplenty, a most impressive shaggy mane – and a pair of testicles under his tail, which, if he'd been rendered in bronze by a talented sculptor, would have together weighed more than a shot-put. Maybe with sixteen wives, all this was no more than inevitable, but it did get Brian thinking again, not this time about the Ford Anglia nature of the human race, but about its male members and their ambivalent status…

Most men are not like this lion. And those that are would soon be accused of a variety of crimes. Polygamy would probably arise first, but ignoring the law per se and any cultural conventions, there would also be accusations of exploitation, coercion, confinement and restraint, plain sexual abuse, irresponsibility and insensitivity, to say nothing of selfishness, self-regard and the sort of self-admiration that is normally only ever found in the ranks of body-builders. No, men these days have to walk a very different path, one which plays down their function as inseminators and instead emphasises their role as "partners" and as the equals of women. No posing, no flaunting of purely masculine traits, no lording it over the weaker sex (or references to the weaker sex) and definitely no multiple couplings as one's principal occupation. And Brian, for one, thought that this was all very proper. Indeed, he found it really offensive that overt displays of testosterone-fuelled machismo were still all too common. But… at the same time he was concerned that maybe things had gone a little too far, and that we'd now ended up with the male in our modern society who was so lacking in a confidence in his maleness that he was often even unsure whether he should stand up when he peed or sit down on the seat. And this lion here would never have such a problem – and not just because he didn't use a lavatory, but also because he was certain of his role and of his whole identity as a male, and of his relationship with all his wives. And why, with such clarity in his life, he didn't look a little happier than he did, Brian was at a loss to understand…

That said, Goodman never had a smile on *his* face, and he had a clarity of purpose that was quite exceptional. For here was a man who was dedicated to the natural world and even more dedicated to showing all its wonders to those in his charge. His almost methodical detection of the lions and the leopard (to a rigid timetable) was just one illustration of this "desire to reveal". But there were others. Within a space of just a couple of minutes, at a little pond near the river, he found not just an obvious crocodile, but also a brown snake eagle, a hammerkop, and two almost impossible to see painted snipes as well as a couple of essentially invisible fan-tailed cisticolas. And there was no choice. If you were in his vehicle, you were obliged to see them. He wasn't going to move off until you had.

Nothing was other than an opportunity to inform and reveal, and in no better way was this illustrated than by his "reading the signs". So, for example, the sight of ground-living helmeted guineafowl sitting in trees meant that there were sizable predators around – as did impala just standing and looking rather than feeding. And he was right. Even the increased incidence of flies was of significance, because this indicated that there were lots of big animals around (offering moisture around their eyes and their mouths and in their droppings!). And he was right again. He was spot on as well when he saw some impala running at speed. He immediately announced in his rather robotic voice that they were being chased, probably by a pack of wild dogs or by a dog on its own. And there it was, a big male dog snapping at the feet of the hindmost impala – and the cue for Goodman to put his foot on the accelerator and give chase as well. Hell, there might be a kill to see – in real time – and his passengers just had to see that...

Well, he tried. As much as the dog did. But as the dog was unsuccessful, so too was Goodman, and all he could show his guests was a bunch of exhausted but still-alive impala, for which all his guests were clearly mightily relieved. Brian, in particular, would have had a problem with the sight of the Technicolor disembowelment of one animal by another, accompanied, no doubt, by a bone-crunching soundtrack that would have made him crave the music of even somebody like Beyoncé in its place. Only Goodman appeared disappointed.

Nevertheless, he soon got over it. For there was still stuff to find and stuff to show, and he still had Iris beside him. As has already been noted, Iris, unlike the two know-all Brits seated behind her, was a first-timer in Africa and, for Goodman, was therefore a virgin canvas onto which he could paint his insights and knowledge. And she'd even sat next to him – in the un-elevated front seat – to be on hand for his brushes. Goodman really was doing his best, not least because Iris was unused to wielding either a pair of binoculars or a camera, and often found it difficult to locate what Goodman had already found.

But his perseverance paid off. Primarily because Iris was a good canvas and a good learner. She began to see things with her binoculars, she began to spot things herself, and she even took on board Goodman's instructions not to include any part of the Land Rover in her photos of animals 'as this detracted from their natural presentation'. Brian thought that, given just a little more time, Iris would become a natural herself. That she would easily embrace every aspect of a safari drive, see more and more of everything as she was driven around – and she might even accept that, out in the middle of nowhere, it was no more than common sense to regard the far side of a termite mound as a suitable substitute for a regular bathroom…

So… in five glorious hours, Brian had seen all sorts of marvellous creatures – and had learnt a little more about their behaviour and their form, but also a little more about how these twin features of other animals can stimulate a consideration of our own behaviour and form. And on top of this he had learnt a little more about their enigmatic guide and about the learning capacity of a brave adventurer who was just past her first flush of youth. But now it was time to learn what was for brunch.

It was rather more than just blueberry muffins, and it was all-round delicious. So too was the bed back in the tent, where both Sandra and Brian "gathered their strength" (at the cost of only a few snores) in readiness for an extravagant mid-afternoon tea, which was immediately followed by a "trip down the river".

Iris went out with Goodman again. But Brian and Sandra, having visited this camp before when there was more gin here than water, desperately wanted a ride in a boat. Chaplain, who the previous day had picked them up from the airstrip, was on hand to provide it. So, very soon, they were in a small aluminium craft, creeping slowly down the flooded channel with Chaplain at the helm. And they were seeing things. Not many big things, but lots of feathered things – like woodland kingfishers, purple gallinules and little bitterns. And this suited them perfectly, as did the whole unhurried feel of the excursion, together with Chaplain's consideration for all the wildlife around – from hippos to jacanas (and which was in sharp contrast to Peter's behaviour at Leroo). Ultimately, what suited them equally well was an idyllic, slowly-on-the-move sundowner. It was nothing less than an insight into the inner circles of heaven: a placid waterway lit by a dramatic setting sun, birds flying in to roost, two very comfortable seats on the boat, liberal helpings of juniper juice, and even a generous selection of nibbles. Hell, *Three Men in a Boat* never got as good as this, and Brian heretically doubted that even the very centre of paradise could really be better. But he kept that last thought to himself. For all he knew, Chaplain was a real one, and he wanted to get back to dinner.

This was held on the outside deck – as the only guests remaining in the camp were Brian, Sandra and Iris. This trio, together with Goodman and another guide called Harry, made up the dinner party, surrounded on all sides by beautiful oil lamps to provide illumination. Heaven had just got extended.

The food was excellent but interesting. The starter was a lentil and cabbage-leaf roulade, which whilst exceptionally tasty was hardly a harbinger of a windless night. And then there was the main course – for the three vegetarian guests (of varying resolution) – which was a dish of springbok… Well, at least this seemed to please the two guides, and it also led to a discussion about the provenance of meat products in general and the manner in which animals were dispatched in the meat production process – which was when Brian put his foot in it.

Basically, one does not criticise the practice of producing halal meat when one is sitting across the table from a fellow diner whose religion calls for meat which is (literally) kosher! Iris was Jewish. Fortunately, she was also intelligent and open-minded and could clearly recognise a wally when she saw one. So the issue was quickly brushed aside to be replaced by a discussion about her grown-up sons, one of whom was a "liberal" Jew and an astronaut(!) and the other of whom was a strict, observant Jew and a physicist(!). Brian was bemused. He had no problem with the astronaut revelation, but he could not reconcile in his mind how somebody who held presumably rigid and certainly proscriptive religious beliefs could also be a physicist, or indeed any sort of scientist. In his mind, a believer/scientist was no less than an oxymoron – or, if the believer in question were an Orthodox Jew, presumably an orthodoxymoron. (Although, thankfully for all concerned, he didn't put this last thought into words. He had no wish to offend Iris for a second time.) And, in any event, she was keen to tell her British and Botswanan companions about her other son, the astronaut, Scott. And why not? There are so few mums in the world who can claim to have given birth to someone who has gone into space. There are fewer still who can claim to have worked as a PA to the director, Peter Bogdanovich, for much of their life, or who have met not just Brian's Sandra but also the Sandra with "Bullock" as her surname. Yes, Iris was proving to be quite a fascinating woman – as well as a brave one – and the more Brian learnt about her the less he was surprised that she'd taken off on her own for Botswana. And he was glad she had. Because how often did he get the chance to talk to the parent of an astronaut who also knew the female lead in *Speed*? Answer: once. And this once was now – in the middle of nirvana.

Well, eventually it was time to leave the dining table and for Brian and Sandra (not the Bullock one) to return to their tent. Here, sleep came easily to them both. However, almost inevitably for Brian, there was a need to arise in the night. The effects of lentils and cabbage could not be contained. And interestingly, his mid-night relief coincided with a similar nocturnal gas-evacuation by a nearby elephant – against which his own effort was no more than incidental. And what a fitting conclusion, he thought, to this visit to Savuti: a final confirmation that whether it was wild dogs, lions, leopards or ellies – or any other animal one cares to mention – humans fall short of their performance, their physique and their behaviour in any number of ways. And he also thought, as he climbed back into bed, that Goodman could only agree with this conclusion. Even if he might never agree to cracking his stern-looking face...

22.

Well, just to prove Brian wrong yet again, when he and Sandra joined Goodman and Iris for a late breakfast, Goodman was sitting there smiling from ear to ear. And this despite these wayward guests eschewing a short early-morning drive and wasting valuable game-viewing time by remaining in bed. In Goodman's eyes, this was surely a sin. But he said nothing about it and continued to smile, even after Brian had slipped him his tip. Indeed, there was just a very nice feel about this breakfast, made nicer still by Sandra giving Iris some much-needed batteries for her camera – and Iris giving Sandra and Brian an "astronaut pin". This wasn't a device for fastening astronauts to their spacecraft but a commemorative brooch commemorating a trip into space and, in this instance, a Shuttle flight to the International Space Station, when Iris' astronaut son had been charged with taking some Russians there. So it was a rather more generous gift than a couple of AA batteries (and they weren't even rechargeable). But Iris insisted her gift be accepted, and there was no way it wouldn't be. Because, as far as Brian was concerned, not only was this a really nice gesture on the part of Iris, but… well, what might be amongst the most unlikely articles that a visitor to a camp on the edge of the Okavango Delta could acquire when he was there? Answer: an astronaut pin, and not any old astronaut pin either, but a Shuttle astronaut pin – and from the hands of the mother of the astronaut himself. Put that in a book and nobody would believe it. But it was true. Just as it was true that Brian and Sandra's time at Savuti was approaching its end.

There just remained a final gaze at the Savuti River and a round of fond farewells from the camp's staff, and then it was off to the airstrip. Goodman drove and Iris was there too. So even fonder farewells were conducted at the airstrip as the guide and his guests all went their different ways, which, for Brian and Sandra, involved their boarding one of those twelve-seater Caravans…

It was fine. Not least because there were only two other passengers aboard it. These were a couple of middle-aged South Africans who answered to the names of Tim and Ingrid, and who were on their way to a lodge called "Vumbura Plains". This was also Brian and Sandra's destination. It was in the delta itself, and it was a forty minute ride from the airstrip at which the Caravan had finally landed – and it was splendid.

It sits in an area of the delta that in the wet season is flooded to a depth of some feet. Accordingly, it is raised above the ground – which sounds relatively simple. But given that the main lodge building is an extravagant exercise in the stylish use of wood, and between its library at one end and its dining area at the other, there is a walk of over eighty metres, and that beyond the dining area, the walkway that leads to all the elevated chalets (and to a mirror-image sister lodge to the south) stretches for a further 1.5 *kilo*metres, it can be appreciated what a huge undertaking this retreat in the bush represents. And that's even before one is introduced to one's chalet.

It is one of just eight chalets set to one side of the seemingly endless walkway and it is thirty metres or more from its nearest neighbour. (Hence the endless nature of the walkway.) It is approached by its own walkway "spur", and this leads to a large wooden door set in a large wooden wall. Through this door is the chalet's deck, which whilst not quite as large as the foredeck of the Royal Yacht Britannia, isn't far short of it. And Britannia's deck hasn't got a large covered lounging area, a sparkling plunge pool at its edge and a splendid view of a huge, reed-filled lagoon. But this is only the deck. And one inserts that "only" qualifier when one steps through a large sliding door into the chalet itself. For this is truly stupendous. Below a cathedral-sized roof, almost disappearing into darkness at its towering apex, there is a chamber in which one could stage Aida and still have a little room to spare. One would, of course, first have to move the oligarch-sized bed, clear the sunken lounge area of its bed-sized settees and make safe the squash-court-sized shower. But when one had done all this, one would have at one's disposal a very serviceable venue for any number of grand operas.

Now, this assessment of their new accommodation went through Brian's mind as he led his wife into its interior. Inevitably, in the process of negotiating its way through the twists and turns of his grey stuff, it may have got itself a little distorted, not to say somewhat exaggerated. But the fact remained that Brian and his wife had at their disposal, for the next three nights, one of the most spacious and most well-appointed chalets in which they had ever stayed. And better still, this was an upgrade! Yes, they had booked to stay at Little Vumbura, another nearby Wilderness lodge where they had stayed three times before. But there'd been a cock-up or a mix-up and this had resulted in a leg-up – to this rather grander accommodation (and Little Vumbura was hardly "simple"). So Brian intended not only to cope with this promotion but also to relish it as much as he could. Although just tearing himself away from the chalet to participate in a drive might be a bit of a problem. And for Sandra as well.

But they managed it. At 3.30, after staring at the lagoon for two hours – whilst listening to the calls of long-tailed starlings and, intermittently, to the sound of lager being poured – Brian and Sandra moved from their crib. Ten minutes later, after a hot hike along the walkway, they were in the lounge by the library, having afternoon tea and meeting, for the first time, Raymond and Gertrude.

This couple were to be Brian and Sandra's companions for their forthcoming drives. They were Swiss and half the age of the two Brits. They were also shorter and stouter than Brian and Sandra, and Raymond had a terrible handicap; he was a Swiss banker. Fortunately, he was clearly not of the shark variety but more of the back-room nerd persuasion. So Brian barely bristled and, much to his own surprise, took to him very quickly, and similarly to his wife. And, as she worked for Swiss National Railways, Brian was more than reassured that she and her husband would never be late for a drive.

Their guide was a chap called Ban. He was even stouter than Raymond, with a thick neck, a bald pate and a facility to find wildlife which matched that of Goodman. Soon after leaving the lodge, he had located a hyena and a sable (by no means together) and a clutch of tsessebe with their very young young. And soon after this he had tracked down four sleeping lions. They were all male and apparently siblings, yet to acquire for themselves a cluster of wives. Which is probably why they were sleeping. There was nothing else to do.

There again, they could have savoured the scenery. Because in this patch of delta it was particularly fine. It was mostly mopane woodland and grass. But within this somewhat desiccated terrain there were stands of larger trees, where the ground was marginally higher and where they had thrived to form groves. These bigger examples of the local flora were predominantly jackalberry trees and sausage trees, which, despite their rather inelegant names, were some of the most elegant trees one could wish to see. And no, sausage trees are not a source of sausages; they just have enormous sausage-shaped fruits that are apparently awful with mashed potatoes.

Anyway, after more sightings and more photos (Raymond had a giant lens device that made Brian's Canon look like a pistol), it was time for a sundowner. Ban picked a perfect spot next to a small lagoon with a perfect view of the setting sun. But, in fact, it wasn't quite perfect. There was a problem. Indeed, there were four problems: four nearby hyenas who were indifferent to the presence of the Land Rover, but who would probably have taken an intense interest in anybody who left the Land Rover to pour the gin and tonics or who (if the pourer had got that far) left the vehicle to drink them. The occupants of the Land Rover were stuck, but, as a great consolation for the absence of spirits, they had an excellent view of hyenas at rest. And what a sight they were.

They did very little to start with, other than sprawl and stretch on the edge of the lagoon. One of them did no more than lie on his back in a muddy depression – with his legs in the air (an obvious sign, thought Brian, of a highly contented critter). But then they began to socialise a bit, jumping on each other and rolling around in mock fights. And then they began to laugh! Yes, they really do, or at least they make a sound that can easily be mistaken for a laugh, and they seem to make it when they're happy. So, as far as Brian was concerned, it was a laugh. Although he still doubted that hyenas had much of a sense of humour, and he suspected that alternative comedy would leave them cold; as it did many humans who did have a sense of humour.

The hyenas left as it was becoming gloomy, and then Ban left. He drove his vehicle back to the lodge to arrive there in the dark and to deposit his quartet of guests into the traditional Vumbura Plains welcome, which involved a small party of greeters, a tray of refreshing wet flannels – and an escort to one's chalet. For even though the walkways were more than six feet above the ground, they were still within reach of chaps such as leopards and, of course, elephants. In the dark, this might not always be apparent until it was too perilously late. And the lodge preferred its guests still to be alive for their dinner.

So, after a series of escorted walks *back* from their chalets, all the guests of the lodge were assembled for their evening meal, which began only after they'd also been escorted from the bar. There were about a dozen in total, and Brian and Sandra ended up with Gertrude and Raymond and a young English guy called Oliver, who worked for a travel firm in Britain. He was racing around a whole string of lodges in Botswana, researching their facilities for his firm and clearly having the time of his life. How was it, thought Brian, that a similar career choice hadn't been brought to his attention before he went off and invested three years of his life in a degree in chemistry? He was pretty sure that if he'd been able to master the meanings of entropy and enthalpy, he would have had no trouble whatsoever in sussing out the quality of lodge grub and the state of the loos. But that possibility had passed, and instead he could now look forward to an haute cuisine meal. (For the lodge had its own English chef – from Oxford

(!) – and from what Brian had already heard, the food here would be rather better than good.)

As it turned out, it was excellent. And the company proved not too bad either (at least from Brian's perspective). Raymond was quite chatty – although not about banks – and Gertrude gave Brian a whole new insight into the running of railways. Things did get a little sticky on occasions, when, for example, Brian asked Gertrude whether she owned any lederhosen. But the moment soon passed and Brian appeared to survive it. She was very forgiving and, with her husband, very forbearing – as when, later on, Brian started to drivel on about the mystery of shaving…

Shaving, he explained (as in shaving one's chin), is a very strange thing to do. Just like the idea of placing between one's lips, a tube of burning vegetation and sucking on it, the whole concept of, each morning, dragging across one's face, a sharp slice of metal, just doesn't make sense. It's time consuming and it's dangerous and, what's more, its effects only last twenty-four hours and, for some men, even less than this. And if only modern society wasn't quite so enthralled by the need to be hairless – and not just on the chin – then this fatuous daily routine could be abandoned forthwith. Or, even better, if only modern science could come up with a permanent beard-suppressing solution. Because, as Brian was forced to concede, the inevitable consequence of a more enlightened attitude to facial hair would be a world full of mullah and Gimli lookalikes. And even he didn't want to look like one of those. So yes, scrap this stupid shaving nonsense, but replace it with an enduring hair-annihilation technique, something involving anti-matter maybe, like they were playing about with in that Hadron Collider thing at CERN. In fact, maybe this could be the next

Swiss thing. Clockwork watches and secret banking were both on the slide. So, if the Swiss could create a beard-beating technology, based on something that was going on in their very own back yard, they'd be set up for years.

Now, it has to be understood that when on holiday, Brian was less reserved in his drinking habits than he was at home. He also knew that he had a wife who was very diligent in her monitoring of his ramblings and was always there to pick up the pieces. Always ready with some soothing words for anyone who had been offended during the course of his discourse – and always ready to suggest that it was probably now time for bed.

So Raymond and Gertrude had learnt no more about shaving and beard growth than they'd known when they'd first sat down, but they had probably learnt a great deal more about the English race and about the tolerance to alcohol of one of its members. But, as far as Brian could remember, they were still smiling when he left the table, so they may in some way have been entertained as well. And they must at least have discovered that Brian was pretty harmless – even if lacking in tact.

Not that Brian was still thinking about them as he flopped into bed. No, now he was thinking about hyenas and lions – and also about staging a production of Tosca in the chalet. And he decided that he wouldn't let this thought slip his grasp until the fat lady sings. Only, of course, he did – just as soon as he dropped off to sleep.

23.

It was five o'clock in the morning and Brian was thinking about Carmen instead of Tosca. After all, it had all the best tunes, and the sunken lounge would make a fine arena for the bull-fighting bits. But soon he was thinking about how awake he was and how infrequently he was awake at all at such a preposterously early hour. It must, he thought, be something to do with where he was and the fact that there was another drive in the offing – and that this drive was to commence at just after six.

Breakfast concluded, it began. And again it was with Raymond and Gertrude – and with Ban. Yes, poor old Ban had pulled himself out of bed – as he pulled himself out of bed day after day – to take his latest crop of guests around an area which was heaven for them, but which, for him, must now have begun to lose its charm. Because there wasn't only this literally matinée performance; there was an afternoon event as well, which ran right into the evening and then into entertaining the guests over dinner. And then it started all over again the next day, until sometime in the distant future, a furlough arrived, and Ban would be free to go home and see his family. It was a tough and demanding life, and Brian began to appreciate why Goodman never smiled much. Getting up at five in the morning in anticipation of a date with nature was one thing; doing this for the nth time with the prospect of a long day ahead and more driving and yet more driving was clearly something else.

So when Ban was as chatty and cheery as ever, Brian felt not only grateful but also humble. And when Ban then found two giant eagle owls perching within the gloom of a tree, he felt not only grateful but now also amazed. The birds, although enormous, were extremely well concealed, and for Ban to have spotted them was quite incredible. And then even better. Because he was also able to bring his Land Rover to within observing distance without disturbing them, from which vantage point it was clear that giant eagle owls have taken to wearing pink eye-shadow on their eyelids… Well no. It is just their natural colouring. But it is a colouring that is so incongruous and so incompatible with their role as beefy predators that one immediately thinks that they've been watching too many episodes of *The Only Way is Essex* – even if one has had the very good sense not to have watched any oneself.

However, there were no such make-up associations with the next crop of birds. Because all fifteen varieties of them, including spoonbills, pelicans and assorted storks, gathered around a crowded waterhole, were of the fresh-faced persuasion. There wasn't so much as a touch of mascara or a dab of rouge between them – albeit some of the storks could have done with at least a bit of help around their fizzogs. They are not the most beautiful of birds. Nor for that matter are warthogs the most handsome of animals (although Brian and Sandra both loved them) and, whilst there were a number of them around this morning, none of them looked very jolly – as if they'd all overheard that phrase about 'well, I'm sure his mother loves him'. And one had to confess, they weren't quite in the same league as lions. And there they were: the four lions Ban's little group had seen the previous day – at rest. But now they were walking – and interacting.

That may not sound that exciting. Walking isn't in itself a particularly startling activity, even for a lion, and none of their interacting involved anything as demanding as combined trapeze work or as challenging as synchronised swimming. But it was engrossing all the same. Ban constantly edged the Land Rover ahead of their path, without upsetting their progress. And this allowed its occupants a perfect head-on view of these four extravagantly maned cats, constantly marching towards them whilst sometimes nudging each other or almost leaning on each other, and occasionally exchanging furtive glances (as if they knew that they were putting on some sort of performance). Then they stopped to drink at a pool. Then they stopped again, having sensed the presence of a baby reedbuck that was hiding itself in some long grass – and hiding itself successfully. And although they never found this potential meal, they did then find the side of a grassy mound, where they all flopped down together to consider the state of the world, until it was time to flop again, still all together, under the shade of a tree – and then to fall asleep. The whole "interactive" performance was something that Brian would never forget. And even if he did ever forget, he now had about a hundred photos of this feline transit through the scrub with which he could remind himself at any time. (And quite a few of them were rather good.)

Back at the lodge, brunch featured beer. (Why hadn't it before?) And then the afternoon featured a lot of indolence, as Brian and Sandra had chosen to decline the second drive of the day in favour of an extended session of very little of anything back at their chalet. The reasoning was that the chalet was surrounded by birds, it had a view of animals across the lagoon (and of a number of epauletted fruit bats under its eves), a supply of fortified refreshment in the fridge and a plunge pool, and it was generally far too wonderful to be abandoned for the seat of a Land Rover for any more than just once a day. And furthermore, Brian had, nestling in his head, a very important issue that desperately needed discussing with his wife. It concerned the supremacy of cupidity or stupidity – in the defining of man...

So, in between the application of binoculars to passing black-collared barbets, paradise flycatchers and scarlet-chested sunbirds, Brian regaled his wife with his latest thinking on his fellow brethren and, in particular, how he had not been able to resolve in his mind whether what defined them as a species was their cupidity, in terms of their instinctive desire to acquire wealth and possessions, or their stupidity, in terms of their blindness to the impact of their avaricious nature. And to start with he veered towards cupidity. For how could one ignore, he argued, the fact that our modern societies were not only built on an unending rapacious desire to "have more stuff", but that's how these modern societies had come about in the first place? Man had soon become fed up with living in a cave with no iPhone and no broadband, and he was never going to be satisfied with just a bigger cave. So he invented societies based on agriculture, which would enable the development of societies based on industry and then science and technology – with the explicit purpose of, one day, being able to acquire a fridge and a microwave – and then anything else he could get his hands on. The sky would be the limit. He would be able to build up enormous wealth (or credit card debt) and in the process fulfil all his cupiditous ambitions and fill up his cave – which would by now be a very nice house – with all manner of very nice stuff.

And we are all at it, claimed Brian. It's what our lives are all about. Getting stuff and getting more stuff. And for many of us that stuff can include power as one of our possessions. Indeed, for some, power beats even a Porsche 911 and a flat screen, HD, internet-enabled TV taken together! Just look at all those so-called leaders strutting around Brussels and Strasbourg, every one of them a victim of unrestrained cupidity, where, in their mind, the ultimate possession is the wielding of power. And they'll do anything to acquire it, retain it and, if possible, even add to it. After all, cupidity doesn't have a cut off. And in the same way that an oligarch with one ocean-going yacht will want a second ocean-going yacht, so a power-wielding megalomaniac (even if he's just the EU commissioner for cheese straws and yogurt) will want further and ultimately unlimited power. And, of course, suggested Brian, it is this out-of-control desire to have more of everything, this cupidity gone wild – which either defines mankind or is the pointer to what really defines him – which is the unthinking, reckless stupidity that his cupidity involves.

For who could argue that mankind, in making that long journey from an empty cave to a chattel-crammed edifice in London or Lisbon, hasn't made a bit of a mess of things. He's been so stupid that he's come very close to cocking up everything: the climate, the land, the seas, every other species on the planet – and even his ability to continue his resilient habit of acquiring more and more stuff. And boy, this habit really is resilient – even in the face of growing evidence that it can't be continued; that we can't have more and more of our species acquiring more and more stuff. Heck, only a fool wouldn't see that. From which one must conclude that we are all fools, and cannot grasp our predicament or indeed the predicament into which we've plunged the whole of our world. Which must mean, concluded Brian, that what defines us as a species is our stupidity. Unless, of course, it is our cupidity. Because, as Brian readily conceded, there were holes in his argument. For example, cupidity can clearly be placed before stupidity, as it is the cupidity that causes the stupidity. Unless, of course, it is our inherent stupidity that is at the root of our cupidity… At which point Sandra told him to put a sock in it. Had he lost sight again of where he was – and of what he should be savouring – rather than pointlessly ruminating all the time? Was he really that stupid?

And this remonstration by Sandra did it. Not only did it shut him up, but it also allowed him to come to a conclusion; it was stupidity and not cupidity that defined him and therefore, by extrapolation, the whole of mankind. He was finally satisfied, and now happily resigned to some genuine indolence – without rumination – but with the real possibility of seeing the occasional passing bird. Like that wattled crane in the distance, a bird that was not only rare but one that, unlike virtually all un-wattled humans, was noted for its non-avaricious nature and its plain common sense. A little like Helen was…

Brian and Sandra had now relocated to the bar for a pre-dinner drink, and had discovered there a new guest at the lodge who answered to the name of Helen. She was tall, attractive, clearly of unsullied English ancestry, and she was engaged in an Oliver-like exercise. That is to say, she was researching lodges in Botswana (and Namibia) for her travel company back in Britain, albeit at a more relaxed pace than that of the now departed Oliver and therefore rather more thoroughly. She was at Vumbura Plains for a whole two-night stay. A conversation ensued, in which, early on, Helen admitted that her travel company was not a well known one, and employed only a handful of people – and was tucked away in Totnes. At which point Brian asked her whether its name was "Reef and Rainforest Tours".

Amazement erupted. First from Helen and then, when she'd confirmed that it was this company, from Brian and Sandra as well. For this was the travel business that had, over the past fifteen or more years, arranged eight holidays for Brian and Sandra, involving expeditions to places such as Papua New Guinea, Guyana, Borneo and Costa Rica. It was what it did: organise tailor-made itineraries to places with… well, with reefs and rainforests. But what it didn't do was meet its clients. Its business was conducted over the phone and with emails, not by requiring its clientele to make trips to Totnes. So Helen, like all her colleagues, never met her customers, and clearly never expected to meet them in the Okavango Delta, just as Brian and Sandra never expected to meet a Reef and Rainforest person here. Not least because Botswana wasn't one of its offered destinations. However, according to Helen, it soon would be – along with Namibia and South Africa. It seemed that many of its clients who had chosen to visit Madagascar were now expressing a desire to complete their holidays in one of these mainland African countries. And Brian could well understand why. He and Sandra had been to that remarkable island nation, which, for all its magic and wonder, could still leave one desperate for a period of recuperation – in somewhere as idyllic and undemanding as Botswana or Namibia. Hence Helen's excursion to southern Africa and her residing at Vumbura Plains. Brian was sure that her mission would be successful, but wondered how, by extending its offerings to countries so deficient in reefs and rainforests, her company could retain its name. Maybe they could rename it "Desert and Rainforest Tours", and have a reef subsidiary. Or maybe it might be simpler to go with something like "Tropical Trips", "Faraway Forays" or "Thomas Cook". Although, come to think of it, that last one might already be taken…

Indeed, Helen confirmed this at the dining table. For now Brian and Sandra had retired there with all the other guests (which, incidentally, is a word that some time ago Brian had recognised as being an anagram of "gusset"). Anyway, there were now only ten gussets… erhh ten guests left in the lodge, and these were all accommodated around a single table. Next to Brian and Sandra was Helen, and across the table were Tim and Ingrid, the South African pair with whom they'd arrived at the lodge. And so the conversation this evening was within this faction of five and, through Sandra's "guidance", more upbeat than usual. For she had insisted that Brian, just for once, abandon his doomsday prophecies and his misanthropic musings and instead only make contributions to any debate which were incontestably "uplifting". This worked (but only after Sandra had remembered to remind Brian what the word "uplifting" meant) and it saw her husband initiating a discussion on the greatest achievements of man! Yes, he invited his fellow guests to suggest what were the top attainments of the human race – and made not even a passing reference to their cupidity or their stupidity…

Ingrid responded first, and for her, the most impressive accomplishments of mankind had to be its artistic endeavours: its works of art, its works of literature – and its enormous catalogue of music. Nothing, she contended, came near these fruits of its combined genius, and nothing ever would. Well, of course, this wasn't a unanimous opinion – as her husband soon made clear. Tim owned a Volkswagen dealership back in South Africa, which, just for a moment, made Brian believe that he was going to put forward the Volkswagen Golf as man's greatest achievement. But no, it wasn't this, or even the way that mankind has devised a way of making more money out of the financing of a vehicle purchase than out of its sale. It was something on a larger scale and a little less controversial. It was man's achievements in the arena of science. How, he argued, could you look at the advances in genetics, quantum mechanics (not workshop mechanics) and astrophysics, without concluding that where man really excelled was in his ability to "do science" – and to do it bloody well?

Uhmm… two good contributions, and maybe difficult to top. But nevertheless, Helen had a go, and her suggestion was "human society". OK, she conceded, the arts and the sciences were all very impressive, and both had enriched the wellbeing of humans beyond imagination. But, to be blunt, they were largely the product not of mankind per se but of a tiny minority of its exceptional members. Most people, she argued, weren't Rembrandts, Bernsteins or Einsteins. Indeed, most people would probably find it difficult even to spell Rembrandt, Bernstein or Einstein. They were carved out of rather baser rock and, as a consequence, their abilities were limited in every sphere of human endeavour. However, despite their paucity of talents, they had contributed in full measure to the creation and maintenance of human societies, and it was only through the existence of these stable communities of man that their more gifted members had been able to produce their great works of art and their advances in science. So there you had it. In Helen's view, the greatest achievement of mankind – and not just of its elite – was the conception, development and preservation of societies. Oh, and some human societies were possible greater achievements than others.

Well, it was Sandra's turn now, and she had a novel contribution and one that could well have come from Brian – in that it was just a tiny bit jaundiced. Because she proposed that mankind's greatest accomplishment to date was its survival. Her argument was that the human species was so dysfunctional – and so prone to waging wars, destroying its environment and generally buggering things up – that it was amazing that it still existed and, for the moment, that it was thriving so well. Forget the arts and science and society, and consider instead the staying power of humans, their unsurpassed ability to "hold it all together" and not to disappear into a vortex of their own destructive and foolish behaviour. Although she did admit to the fact that this paramount achievement of the human species might not be sustainable indefinitely, and could well fail if it didn't soon change its ways.

Ouch! And it was she who had instructed Brian to be uplifting. So… in an attempt to comply with this instruction – and to redeem the situation at the dining table – Brian presented his own suggestion for the greatest achievement of man, and this was his facility to make cheese…

Just consider, he declared, the variety of cheeses that man has created – out of such an ordinary substance as milk – and how different they all are and how absolutely splendid they all are. Whether it's a Stilton or a Brie or an understated Manchego – or any one of a thousand other types – cheese is the ultimate testament to man's ingenuity. For not only is it a function of science, practised as a vernacular occupation in settled societies, but it is also an art form. And yes, if Brian had to choose between a Damien Hurst original and half a pound of mature

Cheddar, it would be the Cheddar every time. Oh, and cheese has probably played a significant part in mankind's survival, not least because it's really quite difficult to wage war when you're making or eating this wonderful food.

Brian wasn't quite sure whether Helen or Ingrid looked the more bewildered by his proposal. (Tim and Sandra simply looked amused.) But what he was sure of was that he had met his wife's requirement to be uplifting – whilst not necessarily remaining rational or convincing. In fact, he was probably the only person at the table who agreed with his cheese argument or thought it in any way a valid contender for the "greatest achievement" title. But what did it matter? After all, he knew he was right, and the others might well come around to his way of thinking as soon as the cheese board arrived. It was a very good one here at Vumbura Plains, and it would be very persuasive.

Although, there again, Brian thought, maybe he should have argued instead for wine. Now there was a real achievement and a half; all those different grape varieties, all those luscious tastes and subtle colours – and very often wine was a great deal more uplifting than a tasting of cheese…

24.

Wine, however, leaves a deeper mark than cheese usually does, and this may have been the reason for the fuzziness that accompanied Brian's wakening on this new delta day. Nevertheless, such was the anticipation of yet another bite of paradise that soon the fuzziness had burnt away like an early morning mist and Brian was ready for anything. He was definitely ready for a boating trip. So too was Sandra and, directly after breakfast, so too were Pro and ST.

These two chaps were the guides who had been assigned to take Brian and his wife on their aqueous adventure, ST to drive them to the boat station, and Pro to drive the boat when they got there. This was a long way away, and much closer to Little Vumbura than it was to Vumbura Plains. Indeed, when they arrived there, both Brian and Sandra recognised it immediately as the place they'd used to get to Little Vumbura when they'd stayed at that lodge in the past. Little Vumbura stands on an island and is surrounded by an extensive area of watery delta, and it was on this spread of both open and reed-filled water that they were now about to embark in a small just open and not reed-filled boat.

Not that it wouldn't have been very easy to fill it with reeds, or with papyrus for that matter. Because very often their course through the water-world around them took them through narrow

229

channels where the reeds and papyrus pressed in and made forward navigation very difficult. So much so that much reversing and revving of the outboard was required to free it of weed in readiness for another push forward. And in these situations, in particular, the vegetation was there for the picking, and for the boat-filling if required. However, Pro ignored this available bounty, but for a couple of stems of papyrus, one of which he stripped of its outer covering – to enable him to eat its tasteless centre – and the other one of which he robbed of its extravagant top to wear as a hat. Both demonstrations of the many uses of papyrus were probably, thought Brian, meant to act as a distraction and as a compensation for there being very little of anything around.

It was true. There were a few water-birds about, but not that many. And this trip was little more than a slow water-borne meander through what was one of the permanent wetlands of the delta, just as Brian and Sandra had known it would be. Yes, it was no more and no less than they had expected: a relaxing excursion through another facet of delta beauty (and over unimaginably clear water) and a welcome reminder of their earlier sojourns at "Little Vum".

Pro finally "got" this, but he still felt the need to provide further distractions, which eventually took the form of a discussion about Premier League football back in England, at which point Brian was obliged to search for a distraction for Pro. And having failed in this task and having noticed that the sun's intensity was increasing at an exponential rate (and he didn't have a papyrus hat on his head), he readily agreed with Pro's suggestion that they call it a day – or at least a morning – and return to the lodge.

So soon, all four boaters were bouncing back to Vumbura Plains in ST's Land Rover, and Pro was still attempting to distract his guests. He pointed out every animal he saw and, where possible, passed a comment on them as well. Such as on the three newly-born wildebeest he spotted, which he claimed were made out of all the parts that were not used in making other animals, and that this unconventional assembly process would become even more apparent as these young 'uns grew up into adults. Brian understood what he meant, but for him, wildebeest were amongst the most handsome animals there were, even if something of an acquired taste (albeit not as bush meat, of course).

Anyway, an arrival back at the lodge was followed rapidly by a brunch with lager, and the information that whilst two activities were offered every day here in Vumbura Plains, the lodge was so attractive as a place to reside that many of its guests made do with just one a day (normally a morning drive) and that they then chilled out around the lodge or, more usually, back at their chalets until it was time for dinner. So Brian and Sandra felt far less guilty than they might otherwise have done – in choosing (again) just such a plan for their day. Yes, for both of them, it was finish brunch, hike back to their chalet, settle down with another lager, and then, as soon as possible, act like a sponge, which is to say, act like a creature that can soak up anything around it, and, in this instance, the luxury of its accommodation and the splendour of the surroundings. Albeit, unlike a real sponge, other (non-lodge-provided) activities might also intervene…

And so it came to pass, and eventually it came to an end and it was feeding time again. Or, more accurately, time again for a pre-feeding drink at the bar.

Raymond and Gertrude had left earlier in the day. So Brian and Sandra found themselves with Helen, Tim and Ingrid again – and with Wayne, the lodge chef. Helen kicked off the conversation with an account of her afternoon drive – with Ban (as she had not capitulated to the attractions of her chalet). Her account was of a confrontation between a wildebeest and a pack of wild dogs, who were apparently intent on some of those left-over parts of other animals. It appeared that they very nearly got some. But then the wildebeest retreated into a lagoon, which was just deep enough to keep the dogs at bay. And whilst they spent a great deal of time "snapping at its heels", the wildebeest didn't panic and just stayed there 'til dark, at which point the dogs remembered that their ASBOs involved a curfew and withdrew. The wildebeest had survived and the dogs went away hungry, and Brian was more pleased than ever that he had remained in his chalet. Because had he and Sandra gone out for an afternoon drive they would have been with Helen and, no matter how exciting the wildebeest assault might have been, he was not at all sure that he could have coped with a gang of one of his favourite animals trying to tear apart one of his other favourite animals, even if they'd failed. Wildlife was one thing; wild-death – in close-up Technicolor – was quite something else. (A fact that was reinforced in spades when Wayne mentioned the ability of a single wild dog to bring down a full-grown kudu – by biting its balls off so that it bled to death...)

The chef then had the sense to move on from genital eradication to Land Rovers, which proved a less appetite-suppressing topic as well as a very interesting one. Because it appeared that Wilderness Safaris, in all its lodges, used Land Rovers in preference to Toyota Land Cruisers, for the simple reason that the Land Cruisers were not up to the job! They were OK, apparently – as Brian could readily confirm – but they just couldn't cope with really deep sand, especially when this sand was flooded – as it was here and at other Wilderness lodges during the wet season. They had tried them, Wayne explained, but they had all failed.

This was very heart-warming news, as it would be for any Brit who has seen the pre-eminence of British manufacturing shrivel in the face of foreign competition over his long lifetime. And for this pre-eminence to have been retained by such an old stalwart as the Land Rover Defender, when matched against the might of Toyota, was especially sweet. Although, inevitably, there was a sting in Wayne's tale. And this was that the Land Rover company, to the annoyance of all its safari-operator customers like Wilderness, had not been able to resist the temptation to introduce sophisticated technology into its products. It hadn't been content to continue with plain old tried and tested technology – and technology that works. So, for example, they had supplied Wilderness with a batch of safari Land Rovers with their new "computer-driven" improvements, and had housed the computer under the driving seat. This meant that, although these vehicles were also fitted with snorkels to allow them to drive through deep water, the computer (which did not have the facility to shift itself from under the seat to, say, the top of the windscreen when deep water was encountered) was comprehensively drowned and thereby disabled. And so too were the Land Rovers themselves – as their computers were critical to their functioning as machines that could move.

The guys back in Solihull had eventually accepted the error of their ways and had then made the necessary vital modifications. But apparently they were still keen to upgrade the technology of the Defenders – when it didn't need upgrading. Indeed, when it was far more important to retain the simplicity of their product and a simplicity that has seen it outpace even a Land Cruiser in performance and made it the first choice for really challenging environments. Wilderness had even had to join the chorus of Land Rover customers (including overseas military forces) who have petitioned that company to retain its Defender model at all! Incredible really. Only in Britain would you find a concerted effort going on to exterminate a world-beating product that enjoys such an established reputation around the globe. For it really wasn't just Wilderness who held its Land Rovers in such high esteem. Back at Nunda Lodge on the Kavango River, there had been that sign, hadn't there? The sign that advised all its readers that they were in Land Rover country, and that at night they could lie and listen to the Toyotas rusting. And then there was Richard at Muchenje; as a Land Rover technician (amongst other things) he wouldn't have a Land Cruiser near him (and he was certainly less than impressed at the sight of Brian and Sandra turning up in theirs). Oh… and Brian had driven a Land Rover in England once – over an off-road trail – and its ability on all sorts of surfaces and all sorts of gradients had scared the shit out of him. So, he thought, why isn't all this good news about a good British product being shouted from the rooftops? As long, of course, as it wasn't within earshot of that Land Cruiser waiting for them back in Maun. (Or, for that matter, a particular Touareg waiting for them back at Heathrow.)

Tim, the Volkswagen dealer, didn't, to his credit, attempt to assert the supremacy of this aforementioned machine in the 4x4 debate, either at the bar, or when he was safely out of earshot of Wayne at the dining table. Instead he commented on the shifting population of safari lodges, and how the population of this one was now reduced to just five. He was right. The discussion group at the bar was now the full complement of guests, and these five were now seated around the sole dining table for this evening – with Ban and with one of the lodge's managers, a petite and finely featured woman by the name of Lorato. And with everybody in earshot of everyone else, Brian's challenge this evening was not only to sustain an uplifting tone to the conversation, but also (although he was unaware of it) not to plant in the minds of the two locals, or reinforce in the minds of his fellow guests, the suspicion that he might not be rational. Which meant Sandra suggesting to him that he steered clear of any subjects involving cheese. And whilst he didn't quite understand the reasoning behind her request, he abided by it and instead talked about the points of a compass…

He'd had this thought, he explained, about the unwieldy nature of all those compass points that weren't just plain north, south, east and west, all those points like south-east, north-west, and even worse, north by north-west and east by south-east and so on and so on. And wouldn't it be better, he proposed, if there was a bit of obvious abbreviation introduced into this cumbersome terminology?

At this stage of the proceedings, Sandra made a valiant but doomed attempt to turn the conversation towards lodge life for staff and how much they loved it or loathed it. But Brian was not to be dissuaded from his course, no matter along which newly defined compass point it was heading. And so it was time to present his new terminology.

'OK,' he began. 'Well, I reckon it's pretty straightforward. And you start by dealing with the principal intermediate points, the north-wests and the south-easts – which become, going clockwise around the compass, neast, seast, sest and nest… '

Here, he stopped and looked around the table for reactions. Strangely, there didn't seem to be any outside incomprehension and blank stares. But he wasn't to be deterred. He would carry on – to the bitter end.

'So,' he continued, 'with those in place, you can then sort out the… well, the intermediate, intermediate points as it were, which come out as neaster, easter… no, eneaster… errh, seaster… no, eseaster and then errh… s… ss… '

'So, Lorato,' interjected Sandra, 'How long have you been here? And, more importantly, how are you enjoying it?'

Brian felt a little deflated, although he could understand his wife's intervention – which ran its full course and precluded any further discussion of compass points or cheese. But in a way, he thought, it was all her fault anyway, because it was her instruction to stick to the uplifting that was at the root of the problem. If she'd given him free rein and allowed him to be as depressing, disheartening and discouraging as normal – by talking to his normal portfolio of subjects such as over-population, failing political systems and failing everything – he wouldn't now be concerned about how his fellow diners thought of him, and whether they thought he was sane. For yes, it had now registered that relabeling the compass – ineptly – was hardly an outward sign of complete normality within. And what, for that matter, had they thought about his cheese proposition of the previous evening?

Well, he was quite relieved when the dinner was at an end, and already eager to get back into a Land Rover in the morning for what would be his and Sandra's last drive in the Okavango Delta. And tomorrow, apparently, Ban was going to drive them to an area they'd not been to before, an area that from the lodge lay a little way off to the seast…

25.

If Brian were to be reincarnated, he had decided that he would like to come back as a latter-day David Attenborough or maybe as Richard E Grant (it was just his voice and the persona he'd created in *Withnail and I*, the perfect degenerate with a taste for good wine). But he knew that he'd not get a choice, and he'd probably end up as something like a football agent or an MEP. And what's more (at least from Brian's perspective), this whole reincarnation thing was all rather daunting. For no matter whom you came back as, there was still the prospect of a whole new life, just after you'd finished your old one. And how scary was that? Christ, one life was quite exhausting enough. But the prospect of multiple lives, each one following on from the other as part of some infinite series, was simply horrifying, and literally enervating just to think about. And then, of course, there was always the possibility of not coming back as even a football agent but as something other than human – like an antelope or an anteater or an ant. Well, for some reason, Brian had woken up with these thoughts in his head, and would have cause to revisit them just a few hours later. Just as his last drive through the delta was reaching its end…

It had started very well. Ban had set out (seast) in his Land Rover, with Helen in the seat behind him and Brian and Sandra behind her. Immediately, they had stumbled upon a hyena and, soon after this, upon a pair of enormous elephants with suitably enormous tusks, busy reducing a tree into mouthfuls of elephant breakfast. The spectacle was breathtaking and, at the same time, not a little intimidating. There was just so much power on display. And then… there were more of those giant water-birds on show, a whole cluster of them around the remains of a lagoon, including literally hundreds of great white and pink-backed pelicans. It was a really ostentatious display of wildlife, and one that wasn't eclipsed even by the arrival of a flock of carmine bee-eaters and a solitary but extremely rare "Souza's shrike". Yes, this drive was proving to be as rewarding and as engrossing as it possibly could be – right up to the point where Brian became aware of his back…

Something had bitten him, he was sure. There was a real itch there, just where his back became his right side. And he just had to scratch it. But then he had to scratch further to the left – and then further left still – while at the same time still needing to scratch to the right. And now it wasn't so much an itching – in a wide swathe across his back – as a burning. It was as though somebody had poured an irritant chemical all over the rear of his torso and it was now inflaming every nerve ending it encountered. As much as he scratched and as much as he wriggled in his seat, scraping his back across the seat-back, he could get no relief. And it was all becoming too much to bear.

It wasn't, however, becoming too much to bare, and soon he was exposing himself to his wife – and to Helen – in an attempt to get either some relief or just an amateur diagnosis. Was there something obvious there, and could it be dealt with? Well, yes, there was something there. According to Sandra, a huge red rash which stretched all across his back, and which was decorated with the sort of tiny, livid blisters one experiences with shingles… But no, she had no idea of how to deal with it. How could she? All she could do was sympathise with Brian's condition, and then point out the small, unexceptional ant on his shirt. It was currently traversing the left shoulder area of his shirt – until Sandra flicked it off – and it was clearly the culprit. Just as clearly as it was a reincarnation. Yes, thought Brian, it was probably the reincarnation of some grossly over-rewarded captain of industry who had been knocked off his gilded perch and had returned as the real insect he was and with an all too clear recollection of his former pampered life. And how he resented his fall, his demotion from being a very important parasite to being a very insignificant ant amongst millions, but an ant who could bite and an ant who could vent his bitter resentment on any passing fool. And that fool just happened to be poor old Brian.

The burning and the general discomfort didn't get any better when Ban stopped for their coffee break – and for a renewed inspection of the afflicted area. Nor were matters much improved by Ban's admission that he'd not seen anything like it before and that he doubted that it could be the work of a single ant. Shit, thought Brian, maybe the whole board had been knocked off and what he'd experienced was a concerted attack by a mass of the little blighters. Or worse. It wasn't an ant attack, but some new menace unknown in the naturalist world and possibly lethal within hours.

Well, whatever it was, it hadn't dispatched Brian by the time he'd finished his brunch back at the lodge, but its impact wasn't transitory. His back still hurt like hell. Fortunate then that Brian was such a stalwart in the face of pain, and was still able to attend to the niceties of a departure from a Wilderness lodge. He and Sandra had been presented with gifts from Vumbura Plains: a handsome book on the local wildlife and a print of a wildlife scene, and to reciprocate, he and his wife had showered Ban, Lorato and a squad of their colleagues with their unreserved thanks and then some generous tips. And now the bitten traveller and his unbitten spouse were on their way to the airstrip.

By the time they'd arrived there, the burning sensation had abated, but not very much. So that when two Cessna 172s arrived to pick up first Helen and then Tim and Ingrid (who were all on their way to other lodges), Brian was still preoccupied with his back and had to make a conscious effort to attend to the attendant farewells. Even when another three of these aircraft appeared – delivering a new contingent of Germans to Vumbura Plains – he wasn't entirely engaged, either by their close-formation flying or by their close, one-after-another landing. Although he did wonder whether a third aircraft landing while the two in front of it were still tearing down the runway was completely normal or completely safe.

He also wondered whether the first Cessna that took off again would ever leave the ground. It didn't even have a full load, but it was now almost midday, the air was thin and there just didn't appear to be enough of it to provide the necessary lift. But it made it. Just. And then it was Brian and Sandra's turn…

All was well. Their own Cessna seemed to have less of a problem, although it was piloted by a South African lady who was so brusque in her manner that Sandra made a whispered reference to her behaviour and to something else concerning dates, something, Brian thought, about the time of the month…

Anyway, she delivered them intact and unharmed to Maun Airport. And within half an hour, Brian was again at the wheel of his trusty Land Cruiser (which had happily received no reports of the supremacy of Land Rovers) and he was pointing it towards a place called Ghanzi. This was a town three hundred kilometres to the south and the nearest town to their next destination, another lodge in the middle of another stretch of nowhere. Indeed, by looking at his map, Brian was able to confirm that Ghanzi itself was at the epicentre of a real void, a large, empty area of western Botswana that was bordered by just more empty land. It looked like a great place to head for.

The journey there was quite uneventful. There were a few bends in the road to start with – and some less than ideal road surface – but soon the highway had resolved itself into the normal Botswanan thoroughfare: a long stretch of tarmac running through endless scrub, with more donkeys on it than vehicles and with no turn-offs. And there were no turn-offs because there was nothing to turn off to – for three hundred kilometres. No towns, no villages, no Little Chefs and not even any Ikeas. Indeed, the only "features" on the way to Ghanzi were some hills. They weren't very high and they soon fizzled out, but they were the first mounds of any sort that Brian and Sandra had seen in the whole of Botswana. The country must be one of the flattest in the world – as well as one of the emptiest.

So, arriving in Ghanzi was something of a relief. Even though it was little more than a giant lay-by next to the main highway – a single road with a few shops and a filling station – there were people here, people in the middle of nowhere and people who might be able to direct two travellers to their next destination. And so they could. Apparently, the lodge they were looking for was further along the single road and then about forty kilometres along a gravel road where the tarmac ran out.

Great! It was still light, Brian had secured a fill-up of diesel, and he had a firm fix on where he was going – with every chance of their not getting lost again. No, the only probability now was of getting a flat tyre. The gravel road was littered with rocks and looked as though it should have been littered with stranded vehicles, and was not, only because there were no other vehicles on it. However, the Land Cruiser made it – to the gate of the lodge – where there was then a ten-kilometre drive up a track that seemed to be paved with the sort of rocks you could use as razors. Brian proceeded carefully and eventually arrived at a game-fence – with all his tyres still intact. In this fence there was a gate – with a sign. And the sign informed you that you were now only 1.6 kilometres from Motswiri Lodge, and that if you passed through the gate you would soon be in possession of a cool welcoming drink. Result! And it was still light – just.

Well, there was a welcoming drink, but it was deficient in alcohol and it was presented to the new arrivals by the "lodge steward", a thin black man who rejoiced in the cheery name of "Morlin" and clearly regarded the practice of conversation as an unnecessary extravagance. Indeed, the only information he imparted, as Brian and Sandra quaffed their drink in the lodge's small lounge, was that they had been expected to arrive for the afternoon game drive, which kicked off at four o'clock – with the implication that they must have dawdled on their way from Maun. Brian was tempted to respond to this mild rebuke by sharing with their new host the fact that their Land Cruiser, not having been fitted with a Merlin engine or a set of afterburners, could not manage a speed of two hundred kilometres per hour, and that really they'd done very well to get here when they did. But he decided against it. He preferred a miserable Morlin to an irate Morlin, and anyway another guy had now arrived, a young black guy who was called KB and who smiled and who then asked whether anyone wanted a beer. This seemed to depress Morlin even more and he withdrew, and Brian and Sandra were left with their new companion and two Windhoek Lagers. Result again!

KB wasn't loquacious, but he had a lot more to say than Morlin, and started by informing Brian and his wife that they could have dinner whenever they liked, because they were the only guests in the lodge (again). He also told them that dinner was served ten feet from where they were sitting in the lounge – on the small table that occupied the other half of the lodge building. Yes, this Motswiri place was really tiny and, as would soon be discovered, it had just four "luxury tents" for the use of its clients. What would also be discovered, when KB escorted them to theirs, was that these "luxury tents" weren't quite in the Vumbura Plains league. Indeed, they were far from it, and were the sort of tents in which one might expect to find a discarded scout leader lying in a corner. That said, they were more than fine and quite roomy enough for two. And all four of them were set well apart from each other and faced a truly beautiful stretch of arid blonde "parkland", bounded by thorn trees and in the middle of which was a small waterhole. Brian was going to like it here – even if he still had a back which was as itchy as hell and tender to the touch.

He did, however, have a bit of a problem with dinner. It was "hearty". And when there are only two of you, and neither of you can cope with the sort of heartiness that covers the entire surface of a plate and has a measurable height – and there is a smiling but almost deferential waiter (KB) in attendance – it can all get a bit awkward. There is nowhere to hide, and certainly nowhere to hide all the uneaten food. Nevertheless, KB didn't appear to take offence, and was happy, after the meal, to provide his guests with a couple of digestif lagers and to leave them to take in the twilight. For they had now relocated themselves to a pair of comfortable armchairs that gave them a view of the lodge's parkland – and of its waterhole. It was spellbinding: a moon-lit view of a tranquil slice of Botswana, hardly bothered by the presence of what was a very insubstantial lodge, and, in the foreground, at the edge of that waterhole, a small gathering of springbok and waterbuck. And whilst neither of these species was rare or indeed special, they were "just right", just the perfect unexceptional animals to complement a scene that was itself not in the least bit unexceptional – and entirely sublime. The springbok and waterbuck also stirred a thought in Brian's mind, and this thought concerned their circumstances, their sipping at that waterhole while Brian was here on this comfy chair sipping lager with his wife. And as he'd never been known to keep a thought to himself, he commenced to air this one, and opened his broadcast with the following words: 'I wonder whether they'll ever get a turn.'

'Come again,' said his wife.

'These springbok and waterbuck here. Do you think they'll ever rule the roost? You know, when we're long gone… '

'As in extinct?'

'Yes.'

'No.'

'No? No what?'

'You asked me whether they'd ever "rule the roost",' explained Sandra. 'And, well, I don't think they will – ever. They're just not equipped to do that. Not only physically and mentally, but they also lack the necessary "cupidity and stupidity". Remember?'

Brian did remember, and he knew Sandra was right. Even if, one day, meerkats inherited the world (which he strongly suspected they would), these ill-equipped antelopes would never get a turn.

'It's so unfair, isn't it? It's been our turn for so long now, and we just don't give any other animal a chance. And that's the real problem. We know that no matter how badly we behave, it's always going to be our turn, and we'll never get our just desserts. Whereas if we knew it was, say, the donkeys' turn next – you know, to be in charge – it wouldn't half change the way they were treated. They wouldn't all be left to nibble nothing at the side of the road. And in other parts of the world they wouldn't be treated like shit… '

'I don't think donkeys are much better placed than springbok or waterbuck,' observed Sandra.

'I know,' responded Brian. 'I was just using them as an example. And in fact, it would be better if we didn't know whose turn it was next, but just that some other creature was going to take over. That way we'd have to treat them all as though one day they might be our masters. Which would just about put paid to intensive farming and battery chickens overnight. I know I wouldn't fancy being a battery human in a chicken world. No way.'

Sandra shook her head slowly and regarded her husband.

'Great sentiments, Brian, but a crap hypothesis. Chickens and cattle – and waterbuck… none of them is going to end up dislodging us. And we're never going to give up our turn. Not until we do ourselves in. In which case we'll probably take all the chickens and cows with us, having already got rid of all the waterbuck and springbok. So forget it, and just enjoy the view.'

'Well OK,' retorted a newly enthused Brian. 'But if we won't give up our turn, maybe we can just apply this same principle to our own condition.'

'What?'

'Well, you see, I accept that those guys by the waterhole are never going to get a go with the bat, but just think about how many people there are who are left equally batless because some other bugger hogs their turn… '

'Uhh…?'

'Politicians, Lords, top bankers – the usual suspects – the whole range of bat-hoggers who are collectively known as the Establishment. And they're all cemented into their positions so firmly and so *permanently* that they get away with murder. Whereas… if they knew that they had just a temporary slot at the top – and that soon they'd be on the receiving end of power rather than on its wielding end – they'd probably behave themselves a helluva lot better.'

'Brian, you're back into crap hypothesis territory again… '

'Ah, but bear with me. I mean, why couldn't it be done with politicians? You'd hardly need to change any of the existing arrangements – other than limiting their time as MPs to just one term. Three or maybe five years, and then you were out, and you could never get back in. And then you'd have to look for another job – a real job – in the environment you'd been responsible for creating. Might, if nothing else, encourage you to get rid of a bit of red tape. And think of all the MPs back home now – and how many of those you'd like to see working in a shoe shop or on a bin-round. If, of course, they could manage it… '

'What about their political experience? Wouldn't you just be throwing that away?'

'Political experience is the parliamentary and administrative equivalent of biofouling.'

'Biofouling!'

'Yes, biofouling – as when barnacles attach themselves to the bottom of a boat. They become more and more tenacious in their grip the longer they are there, and they do more and more damage. Just like MPs. Because, let's face it, real political experience means learning how to play the system, how to bend to the prevailing imperatives and how to secure a stronger hold on power and influence. And consequently, political experience is only ever a benefit to the politicians themselves; for everybody else, just like barnacles, it's a problem.'

'I suppose the Lords will be on a meter as well.'

'Yes,' confirmed Brian. 'And the whole of the rest of the Establishment, all those non-executive directors, all those members of remuneration committees, all those bosses of quangos… '

'Which is all very laudable – and very aspirational,' interrupted Sandra. 'Erhh… but how does one do it?'

'Well, Big Bang possibly. You know, a revolution. Or, more likely, some sort of Somali slicing… '

'Do you mean "salami slicing"?'

'Yeah. You know, a few minor changes here and there – that nobody will really notice – until this "having your turn and clearing off" mentality becomes embedded in the psyche; so that everybody, including the Establishment, accepts it as the norm.'

'And the first changes… ?'

'Oh, I don't know. Maybe newsreaders. I mean, who wouldn't like to see the back of that Huw guy? And then maybe TV chefs. And I can think of any number of them who shouldn't have had a turn in the first place. And I'll tell you another one: siblings. Just think what moving them on could do for improving Christmas. And you could still send them a card.'

'Right,' announced Sandra, 'that's quite enough. I think you've had more than your fair turn with the bat and you now ought to give it a rest. And me a rest. I don't know whether I've ever said this before, but you do go on. And sometimes on and on and on… '

'Well, you were encouraging me… '

'Not to arrive at recycling my brothers… '

'Well, that was just to dramatise my point.'

'Or to illustrate its total non-viability. It depends on one's perspective. Talking of which, you really couldn't ask for a better outlook, could you? I mean from where we are now.'

Sandra was peering at the waterhole again – and Brian got the message. It was essentially: 'Savour the moment, and don't crowd it out with more of your ramblings. Yes, please, please, no more of your ramblings.'

So the rest of the evening was devoted to a quiet contemplation of the scene outside the lodge, a surreptitious bit of back-scratching on the part of Brian, and a mental turning-over by Brian of his mildly flawed hypothesis. Because… if he could only introduce some motivation into the equation – or even some blatant duress or a threat of naked violence. After all, one should never become squeamish when one was pursuing a great idea…

Just as one should never become reserved about admitting how tired one was, even though it was only eight-thirty. So Brian did and discovered that Sandra was weary as well. It had been a very long day with a drive and a flight and then another drive (albeit not at 200 kph), and they had every right to feel knackered. So, very soon they were back in their tent, Brian was having another clandestine scratch, and Sandra was probably worrying about the early symptoms of intellectual impairment. Or... she might even have been worrying about the possibility of intellectual impairment brought on by ant-bite. But not for long. Because, within just a few minutes, both she and Brian were fast asleep, and Brian was dreaming about Ed Miliband – at Asda. He was stacking shelves there – with packets of chocolate digestives. And behind him, serving at the meat counter, was Gordon himself – looking surprisingly neat...

26.

The good news was that his front, his face and all his limbs were perfect – at least from a therapeutic if not an aesthetic perspective. But the bad news was that Brian's back was far from perfect. In fact, it was worse than it had been the previous day, and he had become aware of this deterioration in its condition during the night. He had not been able to ignore it: a stinging, prickling sensation over the whole of his reverse, right down to his waist, and acute, blazing discomfort whenever he moved. And now, in this first morning at Motswiri, it was clear that he had something that was potentially serious – and a serious threat to his enjoyment of the lodge.

But he tried. He tried to ignore the pain and the burning at breakfast and again while he and Sandra took in the view from their tent (it having been decided that in his present condition, anything more than sitting and staring might be unwise). But even here it was difficult. It was increasingly hot as the morning proceeded and a wind had blown up, not a cooling wind but a roasting wind. It was as though somebody had switched on a giant hairdryer, and was intent on adding to Brian's distress by first overheating him and then by agitating his shirt against his back, and so causing him a further escalation in his suffering.

Well, it was time to ignore it, time to focus instead on those groundscraper thrushes and those golden-breasted buntings – and then on the prospect of lunch. For lunch would be preceded by a drink and, judging by the restraint that was evident in the breakfast offering, it might even be manageable…

It wasn't. It was, for both Brian and Sandra, a pair of lavishly packed baps. And that is lavishly with boiled egg and tomato sauce. So now Brian, back on his bed (with a soothing wet towel beneath him), could focus only on the promise of the next distraction – which, of course, was the afternoon drive.

It commenced at four o'clock, just as it would have done the previous day if Brian had managed to fit that Merlin engine into his Land Cruiser, and it was a drive into the managed game-farm that surrounded the lodge.

Brian and Sandra's guide for this excursion was Jacob, and Jacob was a young South African of rugby-player build who was here in Botswana learning game-farm management. This learning process was part of his university studies which, when completed, would allow him to take up a position in his chosen profession back in his home country – where game-farms abound. He was therefore enthusiastic, modest in his level of achievement (he was still sorting out his birdcalls and the birds themselves) and he was eager to make the drive as interesting as possible for his guests.

He managed this task pretty well, considering that it was largely a drive through Kalahari thornveld in which there were very few animals. There were some kudu and waterbuck about and even the odd oryx and steenbok, but not a great deal else, and in the end Jacob was reduced to finding aardvark holes at the side of the track – with flies at their entrance (as flies hovering around indicated that there was an aardvark in residence even if one couldn't see it). And then there were the rhinos…

There were twelve on the farm (which apparently extended over sixty thousand hectares of Botswana and was owned by a guy from Sunderland(!)), and five of these twelve had been born on the farm. Unfortunately, they all had an intimate knowledge of the farm – and where to go to avoid the prying eyes of visiting guests – and none of them was seen. However, the consequent hiatus in game-viewing did provide Brian with an opportunity – and this opportunity was triggered by a fly.

It was on Jacob's head – at the centre of his scalp. Brian could see it because he was seated directly behind Jacob in his safari Land Cruiser (!), and he could also see that Jacob was unaware of its presence as he was driving. This was not good – as the fly, from a creationist's perspective, did not have the appearance of something put together in that great production plant known to them all as "God Enterprises Inc", but instead something that must have come from that unlicensed set-up down the road, which traded under the name of "Surprises from Hell". Or, more prosaically, it was a red and black, ominously-squat fly that looked as though it was trying to decide whether it wanted to bite Jacob or bore into his brain. Brian advised Jacob of its presence – and Jacob brushed it off. He then expressed his gratitude, because the threat to his person had been a real one. What Brian had just removed from his head was a scarily named "cattle louse fly". And these flies are apparently impossible to kill – even with a hammer – and even if they don't bore into you, they often bite you to leave a painful bump that can last for up to three days.

Well, that was it. Here was the perfect opening for a discussion on the subject of ant-bites, and maybe on their appropriate treatment. Brian leapt in, and within just seconds was revealing his red and pimply back to a concerned and solicitous guide. Jacob was fascinated by what he saw and concluded that, whatever had bitten Brian, what was apparent now was a very nasty allergic reaction and probably one that should be looked at. This was good. Brian now had an opinion, not from a doctor, but from somebody who knew a great deal more about the potential dangers of Africa than he did. But it was also bad. Because really he needed an opinion – and possibly some treatment – from a doctor. And based on the number of people within a hundred-mile radius of where he sat on this Land Cruiser, there might statistically be just 0.005 of a doctor in the same area – which equated to effectively no doctor at all. He was in a fix.

But no. He wasn't. There was a doctor in Ghanzi! In fact, according to Jacob, there were two doctors there. And if, tomorrow morning, Brian and Sandra stopped off at that less-than-metropolitan settlement, they could easily seek out one of these physicians and secure whatever advice and treatment was required. This was great news and, on the scale of really welcome good news, was only just eclipsed by Jacob's subsequent announcement that it was time for a drink. It was sundowner o'clock once again.

So, very soon, the Land Cruiser had been brought to a halt and the gin and tonics poured, and Jacob had embarked on an earnest conversation. He wasn't a "British" South African but a Boer South African, but that didn't seem to stop him regarding two Britons from another hemisphere as two people in whom he could confide and with whom he could share some intimate thoughts. Maybe it was Brian's compassionate eyes or Sandra's angel-like features, or maybe it was just that he was stuck out here in the middle of sixty thousand hectares of nothingness, meeting only a trickle of visitors and with only Morlin and a man from Sunderland to talk to. But, for whatever reason, he was very chatty and very forthcoming in his views.

Essentially, they concerned his fears for the future of his country and what might happen to it in its post-Mandela phase, a time when resentment towards the ANC could only increase – as all those to whom it had made promises became more and more disappointed and more and more disillusioned. And certainly disappointed and disillusioned enough to give a hearing to people like Julius Malema (who, it may be recalled, is the former ANC youth leader whose behaviour has been compared to that of Hitler's – albeit not his taste in cars and accommodation, which is a great deal more extravagant than that of the Fuehrer). Anyway, Jacob was convinced that matters would only get worse and, whether justified or not, that there was now a siege mentality developing in certain parts of the country, which was not always just mental. In some instances it was accompanied by the creation of stand-by redoubts stocked with food and ammunition.

Brian wasn't sure how to react to these revelations, and he could see that Sandra was equally uncertain as to how to respond. It all sounded rather implausible. Maybe it was just a gross exaggeration of the actions of a few seen through the lens of a distant and out-of-touch farm in Botswana. But there again, Jacob appeared completely rational, and very clearly, for him, this potential Armageddon was all very real. And then, he told them, there were all the problems with immigrants in South Africa, all the impoverished refugees from Zimbabwe and Mozambique, not to mention those from the somewhat less than stable Congo… Which is when Brian decided to attempt to reroute the conversation – to deflect it towards an area that was a little less "intimidating" and a little more in tune with their immediate surroundings. To somewhere like the husbandry of rhinos…

This was an inspired intervention. Jacob immediately shifted from the end of South Africa as we know it to the challenges imposed in keeping and breeding rhinoceroses. However… he soon slipped into the challenges imposed by the poaching of rhinos, and it therefore became intimidating all over again. Because even though rhino-poaching in Botswana was still rare – and hadn't yet happened at Motswiri – Jacob was in possession of all the bad news concerning such poaching in South Africa and was eager to share this stuff with his two captive guests.

So, to begin with, they learnt that there had been over three hundred incidents of rhino poaching in that country over the last year, and that one of the contributors to the continued rise in these incidents was none other than the South African Special Air Services! Yes, it appeared that when one was dismissed from this service, one was rather neglected by the government and one could easily be seduced into using one's special skills to assist in the harvesting of horn. One could, for example, be helicoptered into a protected game farm under the cover of darkness, locate a rhino with one's night-operating skills (and presumably some retired SAS kit), do the necessary and be out again before the game guards had got out of bed. And there were, Jacob assured his audience, enough of these retirees to make a terrible impact on the poaching statistics, not least because the deterrents in terms of sentences and fines were weak – and there was a huge amount of money to be made. And this is where the conversation became not so much intimidating as downright defamatory. Because this is where he focused on the identity of those who supplied these huge amounts of money – and on their behaviour in general.

Well, their identity can be guessed pretty easily. But just to confirm it, there was, as one of the points in Jacob's presentation, a review of the counter-measures one could adopt against poaching. And for rhinos, these include the periodic removal of the horn (because, as it is simply a form of hair, its cutting causes the rhino less distress than it would suffer at the hands of a poacher – and it grows back) or, alternatively, the poisoning of the horn! This is best done with an arsenic compound and does no harm to the rhino as the arsenic does not enter its system. It just stays within the hairs of the horn. However, it can, of course, do a lot of harm to anybody who is stupid and irresponsible enough to ingest any products made from the horn into which the poison has been injected. Which might go some way to explain why, a few months after a particular poaching attack in South Africa, there had been a crop of arsenic-induced deaths in that place known as China… Yes, one game farmer had been liberal with his use of arsenic, and when one of his animals disappeared, so too did the life prospects for a number of Orientals. And so enthused was he by this result that he now proclaims on signs set around his farm that all its rhino horns come not with a promise of lither limbs, longer lives or stiffer willies – but with a promise only of a painful demise. Great! And why aren't all rhinos given this same toxic treatment? Cheap, effective, protective, and the worst possible news for every rhino poacher in Africa and every one of their odious paymasters. And well… somebody has to do something…

Jacob also told his guests that the problem had got significantly worse since some demented Vietnamese cabinet minister had claimed that a rhino-horn concoction had cured him of cancer – but clearly not of his imbecility. Since that time rhinos had come under increasing attack, especially in areas where there were Chinese workers about – and not many elephants left. So, all in all, he was a bit despondent, and in the absence of mass horn-poisoning or mass horn-removing (before the poachers got to them), he could see matters only getting worse.

This is when Sandra tried a bit of conversation rerouting – by talking about test cricket. She'd been clever enough to notice a passing reference to a cricketer that Jacob had made earlier. And she was spot on. Jacob was a cricket enthusiast of the highest order, and even admitted that one of his greatest ambitions was to watch Australia playing England at Lords (yes, not South Africa, but Australia). It proved a much less contentious topic for discussion than either the future of South Africa or the murdering of rhinos, right up to when Jacob made a comment about spot-betting in cricket. It was something along the lines that we now had to look to the east for most of our problems – to the Far East for the problems caused by nonsense superstitions and to the nearer East, the Indian sub-continent, for the problems caused by widespread corruption.

Well, for Brian, this hadn't been the most uplifting of sundowners (Sandra please note) but it had been rather stimulating – and memorable. How many times in the future would he watch the sun go down with a G&T in his hand, a rash on his back and his head full of thoughts about arsenic and Boers? Not very often, if at all. And probably never with a dinner with strangers to follow…

Brian and Sandra had been deposited back to the lodge by Jacob, had freshened up, and were now expecting another dinner for two. But instead there were four. After they had set out on their drive, a young German couple called Lena and Wolfgang had arrived – to use a tiny camping site beyond the lodge – and had decided not to make do with a camp fire but to sample the food on offer at the lodge. And so they would also have to sample Brian and Sandra's company, as all four of the visitors to Motswiri were seated around a single table (principally, of course, because the lodge only had this single table).

It all seemed to go quite well (and inevitably all in English). And this despite Wolfgang being a worker in IT (another practitioner in that most recent branch of the dark arts) and Lena being a German lawyer! Maybe it was something to do with Wolfgang insisting that he wouldn't inflict even a mention of computers on his fellow table companions and Lena confirming that in Germany there were far too many lawyers –'just like in Britain'. She even suggested that their numbers ought to be slimmed down – to a level that society could afford and one that didn't generate a raft of dodgy practices – which was now the only thing that was keeping all those bloody lawyers afloat. Wow! At this rate, Lena would soon be on Brian's Christmas card list, or he might have to lean across the table and kiss her. But no. Not recommended. Instead, he'd ask her how they'd got here. What route had she and Wolfgang taken to end up at Motswiri?

Well, a similar route to Brian and Sandra. That is to say, they had started in Windhoek, had driven into Botswana (below the Caprivi Strip), then to the Okavango Delta, and were now on their way back to Namibia with this stop at Motswiri. So a smaller loop than that performed by the official loopaholic, but one that, in at least one respect, was even more challenging. And this was that their lower entrance point into Botswana had meant that they'd had to tackle a very long demanding sand-track – in a 4x4 that wasn't either a Land Cruiser or a Land

Rover – and, in fact, they'd got stuck. It had taken them four hours to dig their way out.

So bloody good for them. And even better for them when they disclosed their views on the "European Experiment", the Euro, the Greeks and Mr Berlusconi. Because these views could have been scripted by Brian. And this made him think. And what he thought was that of all the nations in the world we could choose to pick a fight with, Germany should be almost at the bottom (with the likes of Denmark and Sweden). And the reason for this is that Germany is full of people just like ourselves (only they generally have more manageable hair and we have more irony in our make-up). But somehow, despite this intense affinity (and a borrowed royal family), we have managed to have a serious go at each other – and not just on one but on two occasions – and when we have on our doorstep a far more obvious candidate for our pugnacious nature – and one that's generally a great deal easier to beat. It must, thought Brian, be their leaders – like that Fuehrer chap – who was clearly far too persuasive in all the wrong ways. Just like Julius Malema…

So that was South Africa, China, India, Pakistan, Germany and France sorted out, and all within the matter of a few hours. Brian sometimes amazed himself. However, at other times he was a little more pedestrian in his achievements, such as when he was attempting to put his suffering into some sort of perspective. It wasn't, he kept telling himself, like drawn-out childbirth (surely?). Neither was it like the proverbial red-hot pokers or even anywhere close to the mental agony one can undergo at the hands of someone like Russell Brand. But even so, it was pretty awful. For he was now back in his bed again, squirming and wriggling in an attempt to relieve his discomfort

– and mostly failing. This back was not getting any better, and now he just couldn't wait to get to Ghanzi in the morning – and then onto a doctor's couch. As long, of course, as the doctor wasn't a practitioner of traditional Chinese medicine…

27.

Brian's boots had come to the end of the road. More precisely, they were both losing their soles, and therefore, in homophone terms, they would soon be meeting the fate of Vladimir Putin – and in practical terms, they would soon be unusable as footwear. Brian therefore decided not to abandon them as such but to leave them in the tent and to tell KB that he'd done so. That way he was pretty confident that they would be granted a new lease of life. The locals, he was sure, would be far more resourceful than he was, and would quickly find another road for the boots to walk, probably with the aid of some super-glue and some stitches. KB certainly looked pleased, and subsequently gave Brian and Sandra a very effusive send-off from the lodge, which more than made up for the lack of any sort of send-off from Morlin.

Fifty rock-and-gravel kilometres later (and with Brian in his sandals(!)) they were back in Ghanzi – and looking for a doctor. It didn't take them long to find one. In fact, they found two: the two locally-renowned physicians whom Jacob had told them they would find, and in the exact location that he'd promised. This was a little cul de sac in the settlement with a row of one-storey buildings to one side, one of which housed a pharmacy, and two of which, to either side of the pharmacy, housed a doctor's surgery. This trio of enterprises represented one of the most convenient concentrations of consulting and concomitant concoctions that Brian had ever encountered. He was immediately consoled albeit a little confused. Which of the doctors in these two surgeries should he choose?

Well, having left Sandra with the Land Cruiser – under a thorn tree to provide shade – he wandered past the open doors of both surgeries and inspected the contents of their waiting rooms. The first contained three waiting patients; the second none. This could have indicated that the doctor in the first surgery was better than the one in the second – or cheaper. But, as far as Brian was concerned, the primary criterion in choosing between the two was their availability. So, no contest. He walked into the second of the medical emporia.

Good decision. Details taken by medical secretary, details passed on to doctor in his consulting room, consultation conducted (thoroughly and amiably by a middle-aged sun-stained South African guy), prognosis made (allergic reaction), prescription delivered – and out and into the next-door pharmacy – all within fifteen minutes and at a cost of only 150 South African rand (say £15). Similar speed and economy within the pharmacy (five minutes and 70 rand) – and then back to the Land Cruiser and ready to go. Crikey. If only it was this immediate and this simple in Brian's regular surgery back home. There, one generally spent far more time waiting to be seen by a member of the medical profession than one did being seen, and often even longer than the surgery's own dispensary took to dispense any necessary medications. (What *do* those dispensing chemists do that takes them all that time? And if it's all about multiple record keeping – of what they've dispensed – why hasn't the record keeping been simplified? It would save the NHS billions every year…)

However, this was Botswana, where you can choose private medical treatment that is both efficient and affordable (at least for travelling lower-end plutocrats) and where it is a straightforward matter to administer antihistamine cream at the side of the road. One simply pulls off the main drag out of town, pulls off one's shirt, and one's wife smoothes it on one's back, confident in the knowledge that humanity is so thin on the ground around here that no one will observe what is happening. And so Brian at last had a little relief from his suffering, as well as the reassurance that there was nothing seriously wrong with him. It was *just* an allergic reaction, and it wouldn't kill him. Furthermore, he could now look forward to some further relief when he was finally able to take the antihistamine tablets that he had also been prescribed. These apparently made one drowsy and were not to be taken when one had a drive ahead of one. Especially a drive along another long straight road that went on for two hundred kilometres and that passed from one county into another (Botswana into Namibia) and rejoiced in the name of the Trans-Kalahari Highway.

Yes, Brian and Sandra were now on the A2, a road that runs west to the border of Namibia and that, as well as forming part of that lyrically-named highway, constitutes an important section of a route linking far away Johannesburg with Windhoek in Namibia. It also provides a home to quite a few donkeys – and to what is nothing less than a despicable trap…

Now, here it is necessary to recapitulate the nature of Botswanan roads – and to comment on their speed limits. So, to start with, it can be stated, without fear of challenge, that most of the roads, at least in the northern half of Botswana, are long tarmac strips, with no bends and very little traffic, running through a countryside that is empty of everything other than donkeys (and a few other domestic and not so domestic animals). Towns are as rare as a rational jihadist, junctions are as exceptional as an exemplary executive, and even small settlements are an unusual event. There are no more than a handful of these rural "hamlets" actually "on" any of the roads, and even this handful is only "on" them in the sense that one can glimpse a few roundels in the distance. Nowhere do these tiny villages come close to the thoroughfares that skirt them. However... their existence is acknowledged and it is acknowledged through the imposition of a lower speed limit. The normal limit of 120 kph is cut to 80 as one approaches a settlement and then to 60 when one is in it (that is, when one has sight of the roundels set back from the road).

Brian had found no problem with this arrangement. With so many animals on and about the roads, 120 kph was often difficult to maintain anyway, and even if one had reached this speed, slowing for a village was such a rare event that one could hardly resent it. Accordingly, Brian had been a paragon in his adherence to the speed limits in a way he could never claim to have been in the UK. So, when he was nearing the Namibian border and approaching the last village in Botswana, a place called Charles Hill (!), the last thing on his mind was a speeding infringement. He was much more focused on finding maybe a service station in the place – and any signs of a border post. So much so that, although he noticed the 80 kph sign and took his foot off the accelerator, he did not notice the tripod-mounted camera half a mile down the road. No, he only noticed that when he was waved down by a lady policeman and instructed to pull in to the side of the road.

Bizarrely, on this virtually empty road, there was soon another vehicle with him, a minibus driven by a Namibian guide and, like the Land Cruiser, with a Namibian number plate. Well, it transpired that by letting the Land Cruiser's engine slow him down rather than using its brakes, Brian was still rocketing along at 92 kph when he passed the 80 kph sign, and although thereafter (as shown by the recording on the camera) he was below the speed limit, he was still technically guilty of speeding. The Namibian guide was in precisely the same situation. But whereas Brian just fumed and sulked like a teenager, this Namibian chap went ballistic and even used his mobile phone to speak to his lawyer in Windhoek. But it was to no avail. He, like Brian, was stuffed with a fine, equivalent to over forty pounds and payable on the spot. And what was not a piece of genuine law enforcement but a mean, spiteful scam, designed to relieve visitors to Botswana of a few more pula just before they left the country, had worked yet again. Brian wondered how often they did this and whether the police here ever did anything else. He also thought that it was a terrible act to perpetrate on a couple of visitors to one's country, particularly when those same visitors had spent a friggin' fortune here already. It would have been better to have added it to all the bills in the first place: VAT X%, Botswanan Police Force Levy Y%. That way, they could even sting the visitors to Botswana who didn't arrive here by car.

So, as may have been sensed already, Brian was now in a less than sunny mood. He wanted only to be back in Namibia and beyond the clutches of Botswana's suspect constabulary. He did not want any delay in that country's border post, no unscheduled events there, and certainly not an instruction to move down the counter to talk to another individual after his normal cross-border business was done…

Yes, he and Sandra had arrived at their last Botswanan border post for this trip, had completed all the usual forms and registers, and had now been instructed to move further along the counter to do something else. Brian's initial thought was that sulking in police custody might be a crime in Botswana, and that he might now be facing another fine or something even worse. But then the chap who was waiting for them at the end of the counter smiled, pushed a questionnaire in their direction and announced that he was a representative of Botswana's Ministry of Tourism – 'and would you mind taking a few minutes to fill out this questionnaire on your visit to our country?'!

Now, it wasn't this chap's fault, but Brian could not prevent himself from acquainting him with the knowledge that he was now addressing a visitor to his country who was more than just a little pissed off. And that this said visitor was in this state because he had just been robbed by his state – and by, in particular, its less than honourable police force – and accordingly he was not in any mood to fill out any questionnaires. Furthermore… if the Ministry of Tourism wanted to enhance Botswana's reputation as a holiday destination, then it would be well advised to station its operatives not in this border post but half a mile down the road, where they could observe the egregious behaviour of their uniformed colleagues and possibly take some steps towards stopping it!

Brian should have made his point more deliberately and more clearly. He tended to become incomprehensible, even to Sandra, when he worked himself up. And, as he left the border post, he wasn't really sure that the man from the Ministry had actually got his point. But so what? Just one more set of border formalities to deal with – on the Namibian side – and he, his wife and their Land Cruiser would be back on "home soil", back to Namibia and approaching the end of his loop.

It was done. A simple transition into Namibian real estate and just a little more of that Trans-Kalahari Highway until they were at their last lodge of their trip – and Brian could pop down his throat a couple of those doze-inducing antihistamine pills.

It was called "Kalahari Bush Breaks", and it did exactly what it said on the tin. It was set in a huge expanse of the Kalahari bordering Botswana, it was surrounded by genuine Kalahari bush, and it offered breaks to anyone who was attracted to this sort of environment. Which, on this day, comprised Brian and Sandra and two Germans who were sunbathing by the lodge's pool – and were initially less than communicative. Not an accusation one could make of the lodge's matriarch, however. This was Elesebe, who was a Namibian German, and a middle-aged and self-assured woman – and a good greeter: chatty and affable, but very aware of her guests' desire to get to their rooms without further ado.

These were in three semi-detached chalets set around the edge of an enormous main building, which housed the normal eating and drinking facilities and, like the chalets themselves, was gloriously thatched. Brian and Sandra entered their room and discovered that, although it was spacious and quite attractive, there was an unnerving amount of leather on display. It was all supple to the touch – and stained burgundy red – and it was draped across the bed, across the bed's headboard and across the top of the windows as a sort of pelmet. It was mildly creepy, but did provide a flavour of the rest of the lodge. (Which was a flavour of meat, meat farming and meat "products".)

Brian would discover this later, just as he would discover that antihistamine tablets do make one drowsy. Heck, it was all he could do to drag himself outside for a restorative lager (after all those police perturbations) and take in the view from the lodge and the abundance of birds in its grounds. These included those groundscraper thrushes again, a few violet-eared waxbills and some marico flycatchers, all of which were committed to Brian's memory just before he retired to the room again and there fell asleep. Sandra let him doze on, until his automatic pre-dinner drink alarm went off in his head and he rose with a start – and with a resolve not to take any more of those bloody pills until he was back in Blighty. He wanted to enjoy what was left of his holiday, not sleep it away entirely. And that enjoyment could commence again soon – on a seat in the bar.

Here, Brian and Sandra were thrown into the company of the sunbathing Germans, who now had their clothes on and had deserted the sun. Indeed, the sun had deserted them. It was now cloudy outside and a wind had blown up that threatened a storm. Consequently, Elesebe had informed all four of her guests that their dinner would be served inside – where they could all revel in the "meaty" atmosphere of the lodge. It really was like this. Leather and skins everywhere, hunting and farming paraphernalia scattered around – and a disconcerting collection of dead animal parts. Yes, this was taxidermy capital, with a range of stuffed animal heads on the walls of the bar – and of the dining room – ranging from baboons and springbok right up to a giant eland and a ruddy great giraffe! And to be clear about this last chap, we are talking here about a giraffe head that was still connected to the whole seven feet of its supporting giraffe neck. The taxidermist responsible must have needed a stepladder to do it.

However, the diners, when they'd been seated at the dining table, were soon able to ignore this gallery of the grisly and to set about their food and a little exploratory conversation. This revealed that Helga and Gunter (for those were their names) were well-travelled Germans who, whilst a little younger than Brian and Sandra, had been to a number of places around the world that their English companions had yet to visit. Furthermore, on this trip they had driven around Namibia – and had picked up three punctures on the way – and had actually got stuck driving around this lodge! For earlier in the day they had decided to take the 4x4 trail that ran off into the distance from the lodge and only returned to it after a twenty-kilometre loop of demanding driving – to find it too demanding for their own (Nissan) 4x4. They had to be rescued. (And Brian and Sandra would have to try it tomorrow. It was a loop!)

But this was still today, and it was still time to engage with these two Germans at the table – which Brian did by bringing up the subject of Angela Merkel.

He congratulated them on their choice of leader. She was 'good material', he observed, and was doing an amazing job under impossible conditions. And if only she'd embrace the unavoidable truth that an artificial currency cannot be sustained indefinitely and realise that her desire for "more Europe" actually equated to a "more dysfunctional Europe", she would also be able to demonstrate how "good material" can be woven into something outstanding. In her case, into a truly inspired Chancellor who would be remembered for her foresight, her bravery and her plain common sense.

Helga and Gunter agreed, but then made the mistake of asking Brian about British politicians and, in particular, about those two gentlemen who occupied Downing Street for the opening years of the Twenty-first Century. What, they enquired, would they be remembered for? Well, inevitably, Brian answered this question dispassionately and objectively, putting aside any of his personal political inclinations – and starting with a description of the two leaders in question.

The first, he explained, was an odious, shallow, narcissistic, reckless, deluded, self-important seller of snake oil, who had no more idea of how to run a country than Popeye did. Whereas the second was an embarrassing, shambolic, rude, equally deluded, muddle-headed bully whose "towering intellect" was no more than the combination of megalomania and arrested development, and whose communication skills were right up there with those of a tin of pineapple chunks at the back of the larder. And then, having painted this impartial picture of each of the protagonists, Brian then invited his audience to place them in a drama, and this drama would centre on their role as the commanders of the ship of state…

Yes, just imagine, he encouraged them, a huge ocean-going vessel, called the SS Britain, sailing through the choppy waters of our modern world – when the command passes to the nautical equivalents of Laurel and Hardy. Only these new master-mariners aren't funny; they're just totally inept and totally ill-equipped to handle the task they've been given – first, because of all their devastating character traits as already described, and second, because of their complete lack of a sense of direction. Yes, they never knew where they were going, or, more importantly, where the ship of state was going. And so inevitably, after a long voyage through what they wrongly thought were ideal conditions, they managed to steer their mighty craft into a sea of debt – and, as it was now carrying far too many unwanted stowaways (and far too many crew) and it was listing heavily, due to an uneven burden of endemic indolence and rampant greed, it foundered on the rocks of reality – on which it still lies today. And the only good news is that those who took it there are gone, albeit, inexplicably, they haven't been made to walk the plank or even made to apologise for their actions. In fact, one has now been allowed to peddle his idea of what constitutes navigation skills all around the world – and to make a fortune in the process (which says everything there needs to be said about the world), whilst the other has become that strange combination of recluse and oracle, which emphasises elegantly that essential mix of arrested development and megalomania – and underlines how he is still at a loss to decide whether an "on the rocks" situation is a good or a bad thing for a ship…

The Germans nodded their heads. They may now have understood what these two British Prime Ministers would be remembered for, or they may simply have been at a loss themselves – in deciding whether Brian was being serious or whether what he'd presented them with was merely a typical example of that world-renowned "English sense of humour". But Brian would never know. Because Elesebe arrived at this juncture and, by asking her guests about their plans for the morrow, brought to an end the rather one-sided "political discussion". And then, after Helga and Gunter had confirmed that they would be leaving early in the morning and Brian and Sandra had confirmed that they would be doing the 4x4 trail in the morning, it was time for bed.

There, below the leather headboard and between the pair of leather pelmets, Brian considered the events of the day. There had been the boot-losing, the professional treatment of his ailment, the driving, the police entrapment and the return to

Namibia – and then the didactic engagement with two agreeable foreigners. And in his current afflicted condition, it was almost inevitable that it would be his encounter with the medical establishment of Botswana that stood out, not only for its relief-giving contribution, but also for how well it exemplified that country. Yes, for Brian, Botswana was a place, just like that doctor's surgery, where one could enjoy a civilised, restorative experience, confident in the knowledge that one would emerge from it feeling very much better and very much better prepared for whatever lay ahead. Even if what lay ahead was a mean-minded sting by the rozzers and, in due course, a return to a veritable wreck on the rocks…

28.

Brian was awoken by a groundscraper thrush pecking on one of the chalet windows. He wasn't very impressed, especially as it seemed that the thrush wasn't after any insects but just pecking at the glass for the pure hell of it.

'Bloody bird,' he pronounced. 'Why doesn't it go off and scrape some friggin' ground?'

'Maybe it's a new sub-species,' observed Sandra, who was already awake beside him. 'You know, something like a glasspecker thrush. Or maybe it's a masochist…'

'A masochist?' challenged Brian.

'Yes,' responded his grinning wife. 'It's not a glasspecker thrush but a paneseeker thrush. Get it? Pane as in window and pain as…'

'Yes, yes,' interrupted Brian. 'I'm not that dim.'

But he was rather shocked. After all, Sandra didn't often engage in wordplay in… well, in quite the infantile way that he did. And certainly not as her opening gambit for the day.

He regarded her with suspicion. But she didn't look other than her normal early-morning self, which was a mix of tousled charm and alarming alertness. Maybe, he thought, she was pining for a bout of concerted word gymnastics without actually realising it. In which case he knew it was his duty to rectify this without delay, or at least before the day was out. And he therefore made a proposal.

'How about a session tonight… ?'

'Pardon?'

'Words.'

'Ah, words.'

'Yes, words.'

'OK. Over dinner?'

'Yeah. Or after. Whatever you like.'

Sandra smiled at him.

'I haven't done any preparation, you know.'

'No, neither have I,' replied Brian. And then he smiled back at her. 'So should be a close contest, shouldn't it? If we're both telling the truth… '

This provoked an even bigger smile from Sandra, and then she flung back the sheet and leapt out of bed. And as she disappeared into the bathroom she added a final remark on the evening's arrangement, which was a stage-whispered 'Or if we're both telling fibs… '

And that was it. This cryptic exchange was at an end – for now – and Brian and Sandra set about readying themselves for a day in the Kalahari, which was due to kick off after breakfast with a car and a loop.

The car was their own, their wonderful sand-streaked Toyota, and the loop was that 4x4 trail that had defeated a Nissan only twenty-four hours earlier. It wouldn't, of course, defeat their Land Cruiser. But this didn't stop Brian collecting a two-way radio from Elesebe, just in case the impossible occurred – and Sandra couldn't manage to push the vehicle out…

Then they were off. It was initially quite tame, just a rough track through the bush. But then, as the landscape opened up, so too did the prospect of a vehicular mishap. The terrain had become undulating – and so had the trail. But not gently undulating, more "precipitously" undulating – with a mix of protruding rocks and yawning depressions that forced Brian to pay even more attention to his driving than a whole herd of donkeys had. Which was, of course, fantastic. As were the views all around. It was as though they were driving across a whole planet covered in Kalahari scrub. It just went on forever.

So too did the dry river bed that Brian found himself in without warning, and from which Helga and Gunter had been rescued the previous day. Yes, this was the trickiest part of the track, a long run through very fine, very deep sand – with a daunting sand slope at its only exit. Brian could see why there'd been a problem and he quickly engaged the diff-lock. And before he knew it, he was out of the sandy hazard and avoiding further rocks – before arriving at some rocks worth inspecting…

These were big flat rocks on which there were bushman paintings. Brian and Sandra had disembarked their vehicle to study them in detail, and to learn that for ancient bushmen, a spear was the graffiti image of choice. There were no representations of animals – or of themselves or aliens or pierced hearts with "Gary loves Sharon" beneath them (obviously) – and Brian was rather impressed by what this meant in terms of the bushmen's singularity of thought. Because it spoke of a simpler age, a time when attention spans could be measured not in seconds but in minutes or even hours, and where satisfaction could be gleaned from a simple concept or even a single object and didn't rely on a constant stream of miscellaneous and meaningless "stimulations". Hell, even he would have had a serious problem in engaging with just repeated pictures of spears all the time. But for those who are now super-glued to handheld electronic devices… Well, they'd be lost, swept away by a wave of utter incomprehension, never to be seen in the world of the sane ever again (where "sane" is used here as just a comparative term).

There again, they could always look at the animals. Real animals. Because around here there were quite a few. Brian and Sandra had already seen a number of kudu and zebra, and there were waterbuck and springbok around as well. There were even birds… like chestnut-vented tit babblers and scaly-feathered finches. But Brian didn't think many of the handheld device brigade would be too much interested in them. Even though they tweeted.

Well, the drive was resumed and then completed without incident, and Brian and Sandra found themselves back in the lodge and soon thereafter by the pool with a drink. There was then a short debate on the use of this pool for its intended purpose. But as Helga and Gunter had informed them over dinner the previous evening that a large venomous snake had been extracted from the pool while they'd been conducting their bathing in the sun, this idea was quickly abandoned. Instead, they would laze away the afternoon, cussing at the groundscraper thrush near their chalet, studying the other better behaved birds around the lodge – and surveying the bush-fire to the south…

It had, according to Elesebe, now been burning for five weeks, so it wasn't quite as bad as the other bush-fire to the west that had been consuming the bush – and livestock – for over two months. Nevertheless, even though a youngster, this conflagration was still a bit scary. It was huge, and whilst the flames were barely visible – because it was in the distance and the day was a bright one – the plume of smoke was only too evident. Indeed, it wasn't a plume; it was more like a cloud bank, a gigantic pall of greyish smoke climbing into an otherwise perfect blue sky. And it was still there when Brian and Sandra attended for dinner.

Tonight, this meal was to be held in the open veranda of the lodge – as the weather had reverted to settled and hot. And it was to be shared with a dozen new guests, albeit shared at a distance. Each of the two parties and the two couples dining here this evening would be dining at their own separate tables. This suited Brian and Sandra fine, as, in the first place, the parties were a little noisier than ideal and, in the second place, they and the other couple were all dining on oryx tonight… while the Brits had their anonymous fish. And in the third place, Brian and Sandra's isolation would enable them to embark on their word game as soon as they chose, which turned out to be over their after-dinner coffee.

Brian made the initial move.

'OK,' he said, 'how about "generalisation" – as in the mass promotion of a bevy of lieutenant generals… ?'

'Pretty awful,' responded Sandra, 'and not a patch on "gorgonzola".'

'Which is?' prompted Brian.

'One of the snake-headed sisters of Emile.'

'Terrible.'

'Well, give me something better.'

'I will. Like "alcofrolic" – as in an eruption of wine-induced merriment.'

'I thought you said better.'

'Well, can *you* do any better?'

'Yes. What do you think is the other name for acute transvestism?'

'Pass.'

'"Very cross dressing".'

'That really is terrible – and not anywhere as good as an "historical outburst" – which is an intemperate comment on past times.'

'You really haven't been preparing for this, have you?' observed Sandra. 'I mean, that's just about as bad as "latitude sickness".'

'Which is… ?' asked Brian again.

'The ailment that afflicts all societies that have tolerated too much liberalism and have granted too much leeway to their citizens as individuals.'

'Ooo… well, I don't intend to match that sort of stuff. Instead, I think I'll just suggest "crapricious" – as in the sort of unpredictability that will probably require some Imodium.'

'Brian, you're disgusting.'

'You're just jealous that you didn't think of it first. Or "canableism"… '

'Cannibalism?'

'No. "Canableism" – as in the facility to be put into tins.'

'Well, not only is that pathetic, but you've gone out of turn. So I'm going to have two now. And the first is "oiligarch" – which, before you ask, is a Qatari billionaire. And the second is an "awe-inspiring experience" – which is when a bloke first built a boat and found that he could only get it to move by using his hands as paddles… '

'Oh, I see… awe/oar. Well, I think I've heard better… '

'And, as you seem to have dried up completely, how about "a pair of tweeters"?'

'Yes… ?'

'That's a couple of mobile phone idiots fashioned into a device for plucking out brain cells… '

'I like it. And it reminds me of another. And that's "a pair of breeches" – which is… now let me get this right… errh, twins who were born buttock first. Although I suppose that doesn't happen anymore, does it? On account of the indignity of it all infringing their precious human rights… '

'Ah, talking of things that don't happen anymore, I've just thought of another one. How about "hedonism"?'

'Errh… '

'It's what Charles I wanted to practice with his own head – but wasn't allowed to because of this guy who turned up with an axe and a chopping block… '

This brought a guffaw from Brian and a few stares from the other tables. But the stares were ignored and Sandra joined her husband in his overt enjoyment of their nonsense. Every time they did these wordplays they got even worse, but they still found them entertaining and they still believed that they might even keep their grey cells on their toes for just a little while longer. And if they didn't, they probably wouldn't be aware of it anyway…

However, what they were fully aware of just now was a distinct glow of the bushfire to the south (it was really quite alarming) and of their need to get a reasonably early night. Tomorrow was another drive – and the return to Windhoek. Yes, Brian would be completing his loop and, in theory at least, his loopaholism would be sated for a while, if not his desire to interfere with all those defenceless words in the English language. Words such as… well, such as "macadam" – who was the very first man in the Garden of Oban. Or a "diphthong" – which is an item of underwear similar to a "full-beamhthong" but generally less blinding. And "colonnade", which is… well, one gets the general idea.

29.

It was becoming routine. A groundscraper thrush tapping at the window, overloud company at the other tables during breakfast and, in the distance, more smoke in the sky. The bush-fire was still going strong. As was Brian's itchy back, despite it having been anointed with more cream. However, he could just about manage that, and he certainly didn't want to resort to the antihistamine pills just yet. The drive to Windhoek was one of nearly three hundred kilometres, and drowsiness was not recommended.

By 9.30, he and his wife had commenced this drive, another jaunt along that Trans-Kalahari Highway, and one that was mostly uneventful. There was that other bush-fire to the west that seemed to be getting ever closer to the road but never actually arrived, and there was a speed trap… But Brian had learnt his lesson and sailed through this one unscathed. And then the only hurdle left was the mini-metropolis of Gobabis – which sounded like a word that deserved to be played with, as did the names of the two dry rivers they crossed: the Black Nossob and the White Nossob. But Brian was out of inspiration and, after four hours of driving, he was out of loop. He was back in the capital of Namibia and at the very spot where five weeks earlier he had set out with Sandra on their circular tour.

This spot was the home of the provider of their Land Cruiser and the booker of all their lodges, an ex-patriot from Britain who ran the leading safari company in the country – and who was not unknown to notify lodges of the dates of his clients' birthdays and not necessarily with his clients' prior knowledge. This was the already identified Robin Marsh-Taylor, who lived here with his attractive and indomitable partner, Jenny, and with their two dogs. And Robin and Jenny now regarded Brian and Sandra not just as clients but also as friends, which meant that the duo of returned travellers knew exactly what to expect. This would be two days of excellent home cooking (and home drinking) and a large helping of great company, before they were finally whisked off to Windhoek Airport for the start of their long journey home. Brian also knew that there would be ample time just to relax, and to gather together his thoughts on where he and his wife had just been, and ultimately to distil these thoughts into views – his views on Namibia and Botswana. And by the second day he had done this.

Now, of course, he and Sandra had been to Namibia and Botswana a number of times before, and therefore some of his views were not new, but as old ones they were reinforced. So, for example, his overriding view of Namibia remained that of a country that was stunningly beautiful and that provided its visitors with a genuine opportunity to revitalise their spirits. Here, they could soak up its scenic wonder, safe in the knowledge that there was little in the way of human "development" or even a human presence to get in their way. And they could also savour the delights of its wildlife, reassured by the fact that much of this wildlife was far less threatened than it is in many other parts of Africa. As Brian had already decided on his previous trips here, Namibia offered a "gourmet experience". It was a place where people who were lovers of fine fare could come and observe rare and beautiful creatures – in the tranquil splendour of an exceptionally spacious and ravishing landscape.

The Okavango Delta in Botswana had similar credentials. This last visit there had been Brian and Sandra's fourth, and what made them keep returning there was its unsurpassed combination of scenic grandeur and animal encounters, its "beauty and the beasts". It was difficult to think of any other spot on this planet that was so rich in natural magnificence and housed such a natural varied population of animals and birds. In terms of spiritual enrichment, five days spent in the Delta was equivalent to five months spent in most of the rest of the world. It really was that good.

So… top marks to both Namibia and the Okavango Delta – from Brian's rarefied perspective. Because he was also aware that his views of these destinations were just that: views of countries and parts of countries as destinations and not as somewhere to live, work and die. He wasn't stupid enough not to realise that the locals might look on their environment in a very different way. Not least because most of them wouldn't have seen the Crown Jewels of these places, unless they just happened to work in somewhere like the Etosha Park or the Delta. And one could not deny it; native Namibians and Botswanans only rarely featured as guests in these places, and Brian had observed none on this visit.

This might, of course, change. These two countries, which occupy a part of Africa that was regarded as "poor material" by both colonists and the locals for centuries – and a place where, because of the lack of water and good soil, the living would always be hard – are now two of the most stable and prosperous nations on the continent. Namibia has its diamonds, uranium and a number of other valuable commodities – as well as its farming and the prospect of oil – whilst Botswana has even more diamonds along with copper and nickel. And if… these riches can be shared out fairly between what are still encouragingly small populations, the day might arrive when a safari Land Rover in the Okavango Delta will be carrying not a couple from Windsor but instead a couple from Windhoek. However, he also knew that such a time was not that close, and this aspect of his thinking was probably more to assuage his guilt (of being in a position to enjoy the delights of these two countries) than it was a realistic prediction. But who could tell? And indeed, with what was going on in Europe, how long would it be before that couple from Windsor could no longer afford their seat in a Land Rover?

However, all this stuff was going over old ground. Brian had been here before. But, of course, there were parts of Namibia and Botswana to which he hadn't been before – and there was the odd new event as well. And these new elements of his African experience furnished him with the raw material for a number of new views – and three of them stood out from all the others. The first of these was the "Strip".

Yes, the Caprivi Strip, that cartographical oddity that starts at the top north-eastern corner of Namibia and squeezes itself between Angola and Botswana right up to a distant corner of Zambia. And it is literally a strip, a thin ribbon of land that forms part of an otherwise coherently shaped country only because of colonial wheeler-dealing in the Nineteenth Century. It is a construct and a very strangely configured construct at that. But it did set Brian's mind in motion, and what he arrived at as a result of this cerebral movement was a view on mankind's impermanence.

For here, he believed, were some lines drawn on a map, which, in mankind's terms and mankind's terms only, denote a distinction between one stretch of land and another. Just, of course, as many borders drawn on maps do, but to a preposterous and striking degree. Particularly when one appreciates the impossibility of distinguishing between an expanse of southern Angola, an expanse of the adjacent Caprivi Strip and an expanse of Botswana just to the south. And sure as hell, the elephants and many other wild animals make no distinction whatsoever. They haven't seen the map and instead see the land for what it is: a continuum – with only a stretch of river to denote any sort of difference at all.

This wasn't, however, to underestimate borders – or thin strips of land – as being important in human affairs. Brian was only too aware of how important they were – as evidenced by all those border posts that he and Sandra had been obliged to negotiate – and he accepted how real they were. Because people, he firmly believed, feel safe behind borders. Borders are like the walls of a house. They are essential to the wellbeing of those they protect, and they keep out all those who are not welcome (or at least they should…). But he also knew that they all share one feature: they are temporary and, in geological terms, transitory to the point of their being entirely ephemeral. Hell, even in their lifetime they have constantly changed, and they'll continue to change. And in the not too distant future they'll be forgotten. Because, although many of his fellow humans were not eager to admit it, Brian knew that, as a species, we are a flash in the pan, and that there was a very high probability that very soon (and not just in geological terms) we will be in the fire – and with us, our borders.

Whereas the next new element in his recent African experience would still be there, underlining mankind's transience on this planet and the absurdity of features such as the Caprivi Strip. Because this was a natural feature, one that has already been there for thousands of years and, in all probability, will still be there long after we've disappeared. And this feature is, of course, a "Pan". In fact it is *the* Pan within the complex of the Makgadikgadi Pans on which Brian and Sandra were driven after their sensational encounter with meerkats at Jack's, and which had stayed in Brian's mind as one of the most remarkable places he had ever visited. Not only was there nothing there, but the nothingness was part of a bigger nothingness the size of Portugal, which, at the time, had made him feel very insignificant and, in retrospect, very ephemeral – along with all those other humans and their lines drawn on maps.

So that was the heavy stuff: our impermanence versus the indifferent and enduring permanence of the world we occupy, along with many of its physical features. But there was a third element, remember. And this was the "Wrinkle"…

Yes, Brian was still, three days after the event, very aggrieved at his treatment at the hands of the Botswanan constabulary. OK, he'd been guilty of speeding. But that aside, he'd still been stung. And what made it all the more annoying was that this sting had been perpetrated at the very end of a stay in a country which, up to that point, had been consistently enjoyable. And more than enjoyable. It had been like a foretaste of heaven. But then, at the very last moment, the celestial firmament had developed this horrible wrinkle. It was not what he'd wanted and it had so much taken the shine off his visit. So much so that he could deal with it in the only way he knew how – by weaving it into a tag for the whole of the trip, a silly label by which he would remember this loop through Namibia and Botswana (and a bit of Zambia). And yes, that label would be "Strip Pan Wrinkle"…

Well, OK, it is just a little bit contrived. But this is Brian, remember. And what's more, who's to say that it's intolerably contrived, when it picks up so well the three unique features of the trip, and when it might just cause a recollection of a certain literary character who lived in the Catskills in America – and who was "an amiable if somewhat hermitic man who enjoyed un-crowded activities in the wilderness" – (and slept a lot)?

Although, as far as Brian knew, he didn't suffer from an itchy back that didn't settle down for over a week – and it was highly unlikely that he'd ever been a hopeless loopaholic…